THE
LYLE
OFFICIAL
ARTS
REVIEW 1985

While every care has been taken in the compiling of information contained in this volume the publishers cannot accept any liability for loss, financial or otherwise, incurred by reliance placed on the information herein.

All prices quoted in this book are obtained from a variety of auctions in various countries during the twelve months prior to publication and are converted to dollars at the rate of exchange prevalent at the time of sale.

British Library Cataloguing in Publication Data

The Lyle official arts review — (1985)
  1. Art auctions — Periodicals
  2. Painting — Prices — Periodicals
  338.4'375   N8670

ISBN 0-86248-045-0

S.B.N. 0-86248-045-0

Printed and bound by R.J. Acford, Chichester, Sussex.

THE
LYLE
OFFICIAL
ARTS
REVIEW 1985

COMPILED & EDITED BY
TONY CURTIS

Auction Acknowledgements

Anderson & Garland, *Anderson House, Market Street, Newcastle on Tyne*

Australian Art Auctions, *31 George Street, Sydney, Australia*

Australian Art Auctions, *25 Market Street, Sydney, Australia*

Bonhams, *Montpelier Galleries, Montpelier Street, London*

Bracketts, *27-29 High Street, Tunbridge Wells*

Butler & Hatch Waterman, *86 High Street, Hythe, Kent*

Butterfield's, *1244 Sutter Street, San Francisco, U.S.A.*

Capes, Dunn & Co., *38 Charles Street, Manchester*

Christie, Manson & Woods Int. Inc., *502 Park Avenue, New York*

Christie's, *8 King Street, St. James's, London*

Christie's & Edmiston's Ltd., *164-166 Bath Street, Glasgow*

Christie's (International) S.A., *114 Piazza Navona, 00186 Rome*

Christie's New York, *219 East 67th Street, New York*

Christie's South Kensington, *85 Old Brompton Road, London*

Chrystals Auctions, *St. James's Chambers, Athol Street, Douglas, I.O.M.*

Dacre, Son & Hartley, *1-5 The Grove, Ilkley*

Dee & Atkinson, *Exchange Salerooms, Driffield*

Dickinson, Davy & Markham, *10 Wrawby Street, Brigg, South Humberside*

Wm. Doyle Galleries Inc., *175 East 75th Street, New York 10028*

Dreweatt, Watson & Barton, *Donnington Priory, Donnington, Newbury*

Du Mouchelles, *409 E. Jefferson Ave., Detroit, Michigan, U.S.A.*

Hy. Duke & Son, *40 South Street, Dorchester*

Elliot & Green, *40 High Street, Lymington, Hants.*

R.H. Ellis & Sons, *44-46 High Street, Worthing*

Galerie Moderne, *Rue du Parnasse 3, 1040 Bruxelles, Belgium*

Geering & Colyer, *Highgate, Hawkhurst, Kent*

Germann Auktionshaus, *Zeltweg 67, CH-8032 Zurich, Switzerland*

Andrew Grant, *59-60 Foregate Street, Worcester*

Graves, Son & Pilcher, *38 Holland Park, Hove, Sussex*

Honiton Galleries, *205 High Street, Honiton*

Edgar Horn, *47 Cornfield Road, Eastbourne*

W.H. Lane & Sons, *Kinterbury House, St. Andrews Cross, Plymouth*

Lawrence of Crewkerne, *South Street, Crewkerne*

Thomas Love & Sons Ltd., *12 St. John's Place, Perth*

McCartney Morris & Barker, *25 Corve Street, Ludlow, Shrops.*

Morphets of Harrogate, *4 & 6 Albert Street, Harrogate*

Mortons Auction Exchange Inc., *643 Magazine Street, New Orleans, U.S.A.*

Neales of Nottingham, *192 Mansfield Road, Nottingham*

Osmond, Tricks & Son, *Regent Street Auctions, Clifton, Bristol*

Outhwaite & Litherland, *Kingsway Galleries, Fontenoy Street, Liverpool*

Phillips, *The Old House, Station Road, Knowle, Solihull, West Midlands*

Reeds Rains, *Trinity House, 114 North Enden Road, Sale, Cheshire*

Riddetts of Bournemouth, *Richmond Hill, The Square, Bournemouth*

Robt. W. Skinner Inc., *Bolton Gallery, Route 117, Bolton, Mass.*

Sotheby, King & Chasemore, *Station Road, Pulborough*

Sotheby Mak Van Waay, *Rokin 102, Amsterdam, Holland*

Sotheby, Parke Bernet & Co., *1 & 2 St. George Street, London*

Sotheby's, *34 & 35 New Bond Street, London*

Sotheby's, *980 Madison Avenue, New York, U.S.A.*

Henry Spencer & Sons Ltd., *20 The Square, Retford, Notts.*

Stalker & Boos, *280 North Woodward Ave., Birmingham, Michigan, U.S.A.*

Warren & Wignall, *The Mill, Earnshaw Bridge, Leyland, Lancs.*

Woolley & Wallis, *The Castle Auction Mart., Salisbury, Wilts.*

Worsfolds, *40 Station Road West, Canterbury*

The publishers wish to express their sincere thanks to the following for their involvement and assistance in the production of this volume:

NICHOLA FAIRBURN (Art Editor)
JANICE MONCRIEFF (Assistant Editor)
KAREN KILGOUR
JOSEPHINE McLAREN
TANYA FAIRBAIRN
FRANK BURRELL
ROBERT NISBET

Introduction

Here, in new format, is the eleventh edition of the Lyle Official Arts Review. Published annually and containing details of thousands of oil paintings, watercolours and prints, this is the most comprehensively illustrated reference work on the subject available at this time.

Every entry is listed alphabetically under the Artist's name for easy reference and includes a description of the picture, its size, medium, auctioneer and the price fetched at auction during the twelve months prior to publication.

As regards authenticity of the works listed, this is often a delicate matter and throughout this book the conventional system has been observed:

The full Christian name(s) and surname of the artist denote that, in the opinion of the auctioneer listed, the work is by that artist.

The initials of the Christian name(s) and the surname denote that, in the opinion of the auctioneer listed, the work is of the period of the artist and may be wholly or partly his work.

The surname only of the artist denotes that, in the opinion of the auctioneer listed, the work is of the school or by one of the followers of the artist or painted in his style.

The word 'after' associated with the surname of the artist denotes that, in the opinion of the auctioneer listed, the picture is a copy of the work of the artist. The word 'signed' associated with the name of the artist denotes that, in the opinion of the auctioneer listed, the work bears a signature which is the signature of the artist.

The words 'bears signature' or 'traces of signature' denote that, in the opinion of the auctioneer listed, the work bears a signature or traces of a signature which may be that of the artist.

The word 'dated' denotes that the work is dated and, in the opinion of the auctioneeer listed, was executed at that date.

The words 'bears date' or 'inscribed' (with date) denotes that, in the opinion of the auctioneer listed, the work is so dated and may have been executed at about that date.

All pictures are oil on canvas unless otherwise specified. In the dimensions (sight size) given, the height precedes the breadth.

Although the greatest possible care has been taken to ensure that any statement as to authorship, attribution, origin, date, age, provenance and condition is reliable, all such statements can only be statement of opinion and are not to be taken as statements or representations of fact.

The Lyle Official Arts Review offers a unique opportunity for identification and valuation of paintings by an extremely broad cross section of artists of all periods and schools.

Unless otherwise stated descriptions are placed immediately underneath the relevant illustrations.

We firmly believe that dealers, collectors and investors alike will treasure this and subsequent annual editions of the Lyle Official Arts Review (published in September each year) as changing trends in the fluctuating world of art values are revealed.

ARTS
REVIEW 1985

The first week of July 1984 was one that will be remembered by the art world forever. The most expensive drawing and the most valuable painting were sold within two days of each other at Christie's and Sotheby's respectively.

The drawing in question was Raphael's black chalk study of a 'Man's Head and Hand', which was one of seventy-one drawings from the Chatsworth Collection and it realised a record £3,564,000. However, this was just one of the million pound works by Holbein, Mantegna, Filippino Lippi, Raffaellino del Garbo and others which set the sale's total at a record £21,179,880, the highest sum ever taken by a single session sale.

Not to be outstripped Sotheby's then offered the collection of Lord Clark's paintings on July 5. Expectations were high for the late work by William Mallord Turner, the darling of the English collector, and his 'Seascape: Folkestone' did not disappoint when it sold for £7.4 million to Leggatt bidding on behalf of a private collector. It now holds the record as the most expensive painting sold at auction, beating the previous record of $5.3 million paid for Picasso's 'Self-Portrait' at Sotheby's New York in May 1981, it also lies in second place to the Henry the Lion manuscript, as the most expensive work of art ever sold at auction.

The sensational results of the season were not reserved for London only and purchasers at provincial auctions should note the success of Lawrence Fine Art of Crewkerne's sale in April which included Roelandt Savery's 'The Temptation of Saint Anthony', which came from a titled home and was inscribed 'R. Savery 1617'. It sold for £120,000, a record price for a painting sold in a provincial house.

You may think that these record results have little to do with your budget for purchasing pictures. However, you would be very wrong. There are lessons for all collectors and dealers to be learnt from these pictures. Whether the painting be worth only a few hundred pounds, the important points still remain its quality, the artist, its rarity, condition and provenance. It is not as easy as some think to buy at auction, the Getty Museum after all, used several London dealers of good repute to do their work for them at Christie's as did the private buyer of the Turner. If in doubt, take advice.

After all, although some might try and persuade you otherwise, the art market is not a roulette game and you can push the balance in your favour with just a little research. It is not difficult to see how the market has run in the last year or to guess at its trends this coming year.

One of the strongest areas this season has been the Middle Eastern market. There is no doubt that this market is continuing to pull in some extraordinary prices, even for Orientalists of very mediocre abilities. It is always a fair indication of the success of a certain field if a major exhibition is launched of their works. This was the case in 1984 and the Royal Academy of Arts mounted their successful exhibition of Orientalist works in the Spring of 1984. The crowds were drawn to this show just as the buyers were to Ludwig Deutsch's 'Middle Eastern Market Scene With Snake Charmers' (dated Paris 1888), which sold for a record £170,000 at Sotheby's in June. The top Orientalists, such as Deutsch, Benwell, Goodall and others are costly but going up in price due to the demand from Middle Eastern buyers. It is better to look out for some of the more minor but prolific artists, such as Tyndale and Lamplough. Even the amateur artists in this field sell well, which was demonstrated by Christie's South Kensington in May when John, 2nd Lord Wharncliffe's watercolour 'Views of Philae, Egypt and Syria', made £5,500.

Modern British works have also enjoyed a spectacular season, with most artists selling at prices well over the saleroom estimates. The easy appeal of this market and its relative availability makes them a good bet for this year. Sir William Russell Flint is one of the favourites and works like 'Olearia', a nude surrounded by frills, can collect £12,000, as she did at Christie's South Kensington; whereas a watercolour such as 'Nausica and the Handmaiden' was as little as £2,200.

All of the Newlyn School artists are in demand but they are difficult to find. The most popular names on the market at the moment being artists like Harold Harvey, Edward Frampton and William Kay Blacklock. Frank Wright Bourdillon's works are a good example of the upsurge in prices here: his two female figures walking 'Across a Beach', signed and dated 1887, sold in 1973 for £600, then sold in 1983 at Sotheby's Pulborough for £4,300 and was last seen in a gallery in 1984 at a cost of about £10,000.

The other Modern British artists to look out for are Dorothea Sharp, Christopher Wynne Nevinson, Bomberg, Burra, Dame Laura Knight, Gertler, Paul Nash and if you can find his works, John Singer Sargent; the latter being still in the opinion of many greatly undervalued.

The increasing wealth and interest from collectors in Australia, New Zealand and South Africa has meant that topographical subjects have enjoyed a good season too and are likely to do better in 1985. Let us not of course, forget the Americans themselves who will pay vast sums for views of their homeland too. Thomas Cole's 'Panoramic View of Boston', circa 1889, being one example, when it sold for $900,000 (£652,175) at Christie's New York in May. Frans Post's 'Brazilian Landscape with the Ruins of the Town of Olinda, 1664', also shot to $320,000 (£231,885) at Sotheby's New York in May.

Even here in London, Phillips found in March that Eugene von Guerard's view of 'Mount William as seen from Mount Dryden in the Grampians, Victoria, Australia', sold for

£22,000. Views of Perth and Sydney will certainly be snapped up and there are plenty still being turned out from country homes selling for a quarter of their potential price. If you cannot discover Australasian views, then fine views of London itself have a good steady market and a good middle range work like William Parrott's 'View of the Houses of Parliament', is a good guide and it sold for £3,200 at Phillips.

Previously illustrators art has not been classed as art in the truest sense. However, since salerooms will sell everything and anything the time was surely to come for the first sale of their works and it did at Christie's South Kensington on June 4. All the works sold exceptionally well and collectors with a smaller purse would do well to note the increasing growth of this market. It still has a long way to go, unlike others it has not yet peaked in price. The collectors are mainly private buyers but they seem happy to claim works by Walt Disney to those of Richard Doyle. The real master at the moment seems to be William Heath Robinson's works; his inimitable contraptions, such as 'The Eveready Bedside Bomb Extinguisher', made £1,400 at Christie's South Kensington.

Cats are always attractive subjects and it is worth watching the frenetic Louis Wain illustrations in the next year. Prices can rise as high as the £2,000 paid for his chorus of cats in a scene entitled 'Come Birdie Come Live With Me', which also sold at Christie's South Kensington in April.

Sporting subjects also held the attention of buyers and American and Continental buyers joined the charge for these subjects, especially those of Sir Alfred Munnings. Christie's held the cards for this artist and his 'Start At Newmarket' made £200,000 but a slighter sketch can make as little as the £2,800 bid for his portrait of 'Anarchist'. John Frederick Herring Senior's works also command high prices but although a scene at 'The Horse Fair On Southborough Common' sold at Christie's New York for $375,000 (£269,785), there are many coming up in country sales which are cheaper but are hotly pursued by London dealers. Henry Alken is another sporting artist whose prices run the whole range from £2,800 at Lawrence of Crewkerne in April for 'Full Cry', to the sale of four hunting scenes at Christie's New York for $70,000 (£48,950).

Animal subjects are also good sellers and none more so than Edgar Hunt, whose, farmyard scenes continue to rise in price and then there are Arthur Wardle's tigers which have had a good season. Archibald Thorburn's birds remain good bets and dog portraits also take some beating in the lower price range, which was demonstrated by the Bonhams' theme sale devoted to the four-footed creatures in February. The British love of sport is still keen and so hunting and shooting scenes in restorable condition are always wanted.

The sea is another feature of this country and as a result marine works invariably hold their value if not increase rapidly. More specialist marine sales have opened everyone's eyes to the many British marine and coastal painters. The steady sellers being artists like Thomas Bush Hardy, Montague Dawson and J. W. Carmichael. A Bush Hardy scene such as 'Shipping Off Dover' can collect from £600 up and a Dawson from the $70,000 (£48,950) bid at Sotheby's New York for 'The

Flying Clipper — The Cutty Sark', downwards.

The Pre-Raphaelite exhibition at the Tate Gallery this year proved as popular as the Dali show a few years back. It would be untrue to say that this was the reason for the continued success of the Victorian market which still runs up some heady figures. Nevertheless while major works such as Arthur Hughes 'The Knight of the Sun' sell at £160,000 at Christie's, lower down the scale there has been an upsurge. Buyers are looking for the 'right' image, rather than the artist. A fine mixture of sentimentality and glossiness seem to be the ingredients and so little known Victorians are worth watching. Edward Atkinson Grimshaw is known, but his works are worth a comment, since they, more than any other prolific artist of the period, are attracting buyers. If you have one tucked away in your attic or round the corner in a junk shop, now is the time to pull it out. A standard dockland scene might make as much as £15,000.

Scandinavian artists are also moving up the ladder at a steady pace and of Leonard Zorn, Peter Severin Kroyer and Fritz Thaulow it is the latter who has made the most leaps this season. At Christie's in February his 'Town on a River' sold for £5,800, in March his scene showing 'Haymaking at Stord' went to £31,000 and then in June 'Les Eaux Bleues' doubled its estimate at £75,000 at Christie's. Predictably the main buyers are Scandinavian but the Continental market is looking keenly at this field.

The feeling is still that the Impressionist and Modern market is in America, anyway most British buyers cannot close in on the $3,500,000 (£2,536,231) paid at Sotheby's New York in May for Gauguin's 'Mata Mua' or for a Degas pastel in the same sale entitled 'Au Musee du Louvre', $2,300,000 (£1,666,665); there are rewards to be reaped here but unless your capital outlay is large it is better to leave these to the richer collectors. Better by far if you must have an Impressionist to look at the lesser known ones, such as Paul Lucien Maze, whose works were exhibited in a Cork Street gallery last year and whose view 'On The Embankment' could be had for just £2,100 at Sotheby's Pulborough.

The same applies to the Contemporary Art market, the artists in demand are de Kooning, Rothko, Kline, Fontana and Dubuffet. Willem de Kooning's 'Bolton Landing, 1957', having taken some $770,000 in May at Sotheby's New York. It is also true of the Latin American painters' work. These are so prized by the Americans, that although the market goes up with sales of Diego Rivera's works — 'The Flower Vendor' sold in New York at Sotheby's for $390,000 (£282,700) — they are already too expensive for most.

Far better for the average buyer to look at the lower end of the market, it is often more exciting too. William Mellor's scenes continue to sell from a few hundred to a few thousand and so do Oliver and Vincent Clare's still lifes. Alfred de Breanski's standards were variable and so are his prices but a rough guide to the 1984 prices would be the sale of 'Burnham Beeches' at £800 and 'On the Banks of the Tay' and 'Near Dunkeld' at £8,500 at Henry Spencer & Son of Retford, Sidney Richard Percy and Thomas Sidney Cooper are two other good standbys.

Watercolours are always considered an English medium but of course watercolours in the high Victorian style, depicting Middle Eastern subjects or sporting ones are still steady. The genre scenes continue to surprise rooms; prices for Helen Allingham have calmed down and have settled in the mid thousands but the exceptional Myles Birket Foster still catches the odd sale-room by surprise; the record for the artist having been taken in May at Christie's with the sale of a scene outside a country inn at £21,000.

It is better to look out for artists like James Mackay whose watercolour of a young girl on a footbridge sold for £1,800 at Eldon E. Worrall of Liverpool in March; two years ago works by the same artist made around £900 and five years ago £40. The same story relates to artists like William Lee Hankey and Louise Rayner, whose watercolours have sold well in 1984.

Genre subjects by minor artists rely on the right 'image' too. Don't be put off by an unknown name, many artists produced one or two works that the market would snap up quickly today. Edward Wilson's bonneted girls, Edwin Harris's and Walter Langley's female figures enjoying mundane tasks, have all been well received. All rural interior cottage scenes, thatched cottages and garden subjects of good quality are worth looking at twice.

Lastly, a glance at the print market will show that all has not been smooth in this area. The best sellers tend to be those relating to the subjects selling well in the picture market. A set of four coloured aquatints of 'Views of Sydney' by Major Taylor 48th Regt., for example sold for £13,000 against an estimate of just £1,000 at Christie's South Kensington.

Rare prints do sell well and nowhere was this clearer than with the Odilon Redon prints of the 'Tenation de St. Antoine, Troisieme Serie', which sold for £79,000 at Sotheby's. The Swiss prints were doing well a year ago but 1984 saw no sensations in this market. Audubon prints were selling well and so were the works of Durer, Hopper, Bellows and Lautrec.

A slight upturn in the fortunes of British prints seems to bode well for the coming season. This has certainly not always been the case but works like Gerald Leslie Brockhurst's etching entitled 'Adolescence', which sold for £3,500 at Christie's in April, may mean better times are to come.

The season started shakily with the market moving well in January but sliding slightly by early Spring. However, by June the major sales showed no signs of a recession and the art market had little to complain about. As always buyers were selective, but that is an idiocyncrasy one would hope it never loses. The finest works are rare and dealers and collectors alike are quick to buy when they appear. However, do not despair the middle to lower range markets still provide many goodies for the astute buyer.

ANNA-MEI CHADWICK
(The Antiques Trade Gazette)

ALEXANDER ABDO – Crack Willow
Lane – signed with monogram, also
inscribed – oil on board – 10 x 14½in.
(Sotheby's)   **$825**   **£550**

JOHN ABSOLON – Travelling Players,
A Bright Spot – signed and inscribed –
pencil and watercolour heightened with
white – 6¾ x 9¼in.
(Christie's)   **$615**   **£410**

ABEL-TRUCHET – Fofolle Au Moulin
Rouge – signed – oil on canvas – 10½
x 8¼in.
(Christie's)   **$2,207**   **£1,512**

OSWALD ACHENBACH – Naples, On
The Beach – signed and dated 1882 –
28¾ x 39¾in.
(Sotheby's)   **$19,800 £13,200**

CHARLES JAMES ADAMS – Harvest Time, North Somerset – signed – watercolour over pencil – 10½ x 14¼in. *(Sotheby's)* **$627** **£418**

VALERIO ADAMI – La Doccia In Cucina – signed, inscribed and dated '69 on the reverse – oil on canvas – 95½ x 67in.
(Christie's) **$7,095** **£4,860**

JOHN CLAYTON ADAMS – A Quiet River – signed, indistinctly dated and inscribed on a label – 23¼ x 35½in.
(Sotheby's) **$1,686** **£1,155**

CHARLES JAMES ADAMS – Changing Pastures – signed – watercolour – 14¾ x 21¼in. *(Sotheby's)* **$1,262** **£880**

JOHN CLAYTON ADAMS – A River Landscape – signed and dated 1903 – oil on canvas – 14½ x 19½in.
(Sotheby's) **$1,183** £825

WILLIAM DACRES ADAMS – The Magic Circle – signed and inscribed – on canvas – 37 x 32in.
(Sotheby's) **$1,353** £902

MISS DOROTHY ADAMSON – Out To Pasture – signed – oil on canvas – 15½ x 24½in.
(Sotheby's) **$481** £330

JANKEL ADLER – The Dream – signed – oil and gesso on panel – 19½ x 23½in.
(Sotheby's) **$3,135** £2,090

LUCIEN ADRION – Le Port a St. Tropez – signed and dated '30 – oil on canvas – 23½ x 32½in.
(Christie's) **$7,775** £5,184

PIETER COECK VAN AELST, Circle of – The Nativity – oil on panel – 27½ x 20½in.
(Sotheby's) **$8,954** £6,050

17

PETER AERTSEN, Follower of – A
Kitchen Interior, With The Supper At
Emmaus – dated 1579 – oil on panel
– 38½ x 64¼in.
(Sotheby's) **$8,954 £6,050**

JAMES LAURENT AGASSE – View Of
The Thames At Southwark Looking To-
wards Blackfriars Bridge And St. Paul's
Cathedral, To The Far Right The Albion
Mill – oil on canvas – 13½ x 20½in.
(Sotheby's) **$17,325 £11,550**

WILLIAM AFFLECK – Feeding The
Ducks – signed – pencil and watercolour heightened with white – 20¾ x
16½in.
(Christie's) **$1,879 £1,296**

GEORGE AIKMAN – Hay Stooks –
signed and indistinctly inscribed – oil
on canvas – 7½ x 29½in.
(Sotheby's) **$578 £396**

JAMES AITKEN – A Loch Scene –
signed – watercolour – 12¾ x 19¼in.
(Sotheby's) **$295 £198**

JOHN ERNEST AITKEN – Bringing In
The Catch, Holland – signed and inscribed on a label on the reverse – watercolour – 13 x 19½in.
(Sotheby's) **$642 £440**

IVAN KONSTANTINOVICH
AIVAZOVSKY – A Welcome Sail –
signed, signed and dated 1865 on the
reverse – oil on board – 10¾ x 9½in.
(Sotheby's) **$5,104 £3,520**

MANUIL CHRISTOFOROVICH
ALADJALOV – Boats Moored Off The
Coast – signed – 13½ x 21¼in.
(Sotheby's) **$578 £385**

CECIL CHARLES WINDSOR ALDIN –
Trotting – signed and dated 1897 –
watercolour – 8½ x 20in.
(Sotheby's) **$412 £275**

IVAN KONSTANTINOVICH AIVAZOVSKY – And Moses Stretched Forth His
Hands Over The Sea (Exodus XIV: 27) – signed and dated 1891, also signed and
dated on the reverse – oil on canvas – 42¾ x 76½in. *(Sotheby's)*
$30,305 £20,900

CECIL ALDIN – 'Ar Never Gets Off',
Hunting Scene – signed – pen, ink and
watercolour – 11½ x 18¾in.
(Dreweatt Watson &
Barton)   **$1,146   £780**

EDWIN ALEXANDER – Study Of A
Mule – signed and dated 93/98 –
watercolour and bodycolour – 10 x
14in.
(Christie's &
Edmiston's)   **$1,275   £850**

EDWIN ALEXANDER – Two Collared
Doves In A Walnut Tree – signed and
dated 1902 – watercolour and gouache
– 20 x 18¼in.
(Christie's)   **$4,535   £3,025**

WILLIAM ALEXANDER – A Man At
Work Near A Farmhouse – pencil and
watercolour on laid paper – 8¼ x 7in.
(Sotheby's)   **$330   £220**

H. ALKEN – Two Racehorses And
Jockeys At The Gallop – oil on canvas –
10 x 14in.
(Dreweatt Watson &
Barton)   **$2,205   £1,500**

HENRY ALKEN, SNR. – On The Scent;
Putting Up A Pheasant; and Greyhounds
With A Hare; and a drawing of dogs,
ascribed to Crome – three, watercolour
over pencil – 9¼ x 13in. and smaller.
(Sotheby's)   **$1,155   £770 Four**

HENRY ALKEN – Full Cry – signed –
10 x 14in.
(Lawrence)   **$4,527**   **£3,080**

DAVID ALLAN – Portrait Of Lady
Elisa Hope, A View Of Hopetoun House
Beyond – 26 x 20½in.
(Sotheby's)   **$8,250**   **£5,500**

HELEN ALLINGHAM – Near Haslemere
– signed – watercolour – 10½ x 15¼in.
(Christie's)   **$9,720**   **£6,480**

HELEN ALLINGHAM – Cottage Near
Freshwater – watercolour – 7¼ x 5½in.
(Sotheby's)   **$2,145**   **£1,430**

HELEN ALLINGHAM – Hand In Hand
– signed and indistinctly dated – watercolour with touches of white heightening
– 4½ x 3½in.
(Christie's)   **$1,375**   **£918**

HELEN ALLINGHAM – A Gypsy Girl
– signed – watercolour – 4½ x 4½in.
(Sotheby's) **$297** **£198**

HELEN ALLINGHAM – The Butterfly
– signed – watercolour – 9 x 8in.
(Sotheby's) **$8,833** **£6,050**

HELEN ALLINGHAM – At Sandhills,
Witley, Sussex – signed – watercolour –
10 x 7¼in.
(Christie's) **$6,264** **£4,320**

SIR LAWRENCE ALMA-TADEMA –
A Difference Of Opinion – signed and
inscribed – on panel – 15 x 8¾in.
(Christie's) **$37,260** **£24,840**

D. VAN ALSLOOT – An Extensive Winter Landscape With A Ruined Abbey On A
Hill – 26¾ x 41¼in. *(Christie's)* **$11,340 £7,560**

HEINRICH ALTHERR – Weibliche
Halbfigur, 1921 – oil on canvas – 103
x 63cm.
*(Germann
    Auktionshaus)* **$3,004 £2,058**

CRISTOFANO DELL ALTISSIMO, After
– Portrait Of Cameria, Daughter Of The
Emperor Soliman – inscribed and dated
1841 – 37½ x 25¾in.
(Sotheby's) **$907 £605**

ABBEY ALTSON – Portrait Of A Young
Lady – signed – on canvas – 24 x 20in.
(Sotheby's)   **$1,485**   **£990**

AMERICAN SCHOOL, 19th century –
Seated Lady With Purple Violets –
signed on a label on the reverse – oil on
canvas – 18 x 14in.
(Christie's)   **$1,100**   **£797**

CUNO AMIET – Rosslispiel – signed with monogram and dated '31 – oil on canvas
– 81 x 100cm. *(Germann Auktionshaus)*   **$35,928**   **£23,952**

CUNO AMIET – Portrait Einer Jungen Frau Im Rosa Kleid – signed with monogram and dated '27 – oil on canvas – 46 x 38cm.
(Germann Auktionshaus) **$8,532 £5,688**

JOSEPH ANDERSON – Tiddlers – signed and dated 1866 – oil on canvas – 20 x 16in.
(Sotheby's) **$1,872 £1,265**

JAMES BELL ANDERSON – Self Portrait – signed and dated 1911 – oil on canvas – 29½ x 21¾in.
(Sotheby's) **$662 £462**

SOPHIE ANDERSON, Manner of – Little Red Riding Hood – on panel – 13 x 9¾in.
(Christie's) **$775 £518**

SOPHIE ANDERSON – Its Touch And Go To Laugh Or Not – signed, inscribed on a label on the reverse – 25 x 30in. *(Sotheby's)*   **$10,278 £7,040**

WILLIAM ANDERSON – A Horse And Cart Passing A Country Cottage; and Rustics And Cattle By A Country Church, A River Beyond – signed and dated 1818 – on panel – 11½ x 16½in. *(Sotheby's)*   **$11,550 £7,700 Pair**

WILLIAM ANDERSON – A Sail Barge
With Other Craft Offshore – pen and
black ink and watercolour – 7¼ x 9¼in.
(Sotheby's)   **$562   £396**

WILLIAM ANDERSON – Dutch Estuary
Scene With Fishing Barges – signed and
indistinctly dated – oil on panel – 7½ x
10¼in.
(Sotheby's)   **$3,157   £2,200**

MARIANO ANDREU – Femmes
Indolentes – signed and dated '43 – oil
on panel – 10 x 9in.
(Christie's)   **$2,185   £1,134**

FEDERICO ANDREOTTI – A Girl In
A Mop Cap – signed – oil on canvas –
25 x 20in.
(Sotheby's)   **$957   £660**

HENRY ANDREWS – A Friend Of
Nature – signed – 24 x 17in.
(Sotheby's)   **$1,072   £715**

HENRY ANDREWS – Courtship –
signed – oil on canvas – 10in. diam.
(Sotheby's)   **$578**   **£396**

P. ANGELLIS – A Fish Market By A
River – 28¼ x 24¼in.
(Christie's)   **$1,539**   **£1,026**

CAROLINE AMELIA ANGERSTEIN –
Four Sketchbooks Containing Drawings
Of The Angerstein Family – majority
inscribed and dated 1830-35 – pencil
with coloured washes .
(Sotheby's)   **$2,805**   **£1,870 Four**

ALBERT ANKER – Junge Frau Am
Spinnrad – signed and dated 1866 – oil
on canvas – 109 x 77cm.
*(Germann
    Auktionshaus)* **$76,347**   **£50,898**

RICHARD ANSDELL – In The Highlands – signed and dated 1856 – oil on canvas – 19¾ x 49½in.
(Sotheby's) **$7,892 £5,500**

RICHARD ANSDELL – The Victor – oil on canvas – 38 x 55in.
(Sotheby's) **$2,279 £1,540**

RICHARD ANSDELL – The Highland Shepherd – signed and dated 1870 – 27 x 20in.
(Sotheby's) **$2,970 £1,980**

RICHARD ANSDELL – Gathering The Flock – signed with initials and dated 1863 – oil on canvas – 56 x 31in.
(Sotheby's) **$6,186 £4,180**

RICHARD ANSDELL – The Rescue – signed and dated 1866 – oil on canvas – 54 x 41in.
(Sotheby's) **$6,699 £4,620**

RICHARD ANSDELL — A Highland
Cattle Fair, Isle of Skye — signed and
dated 1874 — 54 x 93in.
(Christie's)   **$8,791   £5,940**

THOMAS POLLOCK ANSHUTZ — A
Challenge — signed — pastel on canvas
— 30 x 24in.
(Christie's)   **$7,700   £5,130**

HENDRIK JOSEPH ANTONISSEN — An
Extensive River Landscape With A Farm-
house By A Path And A Drover With
Cattle In The Foreground — on panel —
25½ x 36¼in.
(Christie's)   **$5,670   £3,780**

KAREL APPEL — Untitled — signed and
dated '75 — acrylic on cardboard — 24¼ x
21¾in.
(Sotheby's)   **$2,475   £1,650**

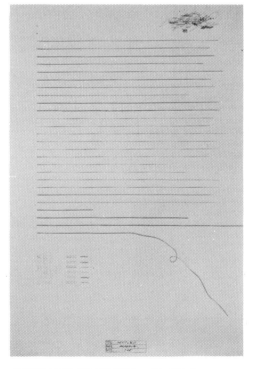

SHUSAKU ARAKAWA — Untitled —
signed, inscribed and dated 1968 — acrylic
on canvas — 71¼ x 48in.
(Christie's)   **$10,125   £6,750**

GEORGE ARMFIELD – 'Let Sleeping Dogs Lie' – signed and dated 1870 – on canvas – 9½ x 11½in.
(Sotheby's) **$1,815 £1,210**

GEORGE ARMFIELD – Terriers Rabbiting – signed and dated 18' – on board – 5¾ x 8in.
(Sotheby's) **$1,092 £748**

GEORGE ARMFIELD – Putting Up Mallard – signed and dated '84 – 17 x 22in.
(Sotheby's) **$1,525 £1,045**

GEORGE ARMFIELD – The Terriers' Meeting – signed and dated 1850 – 17¼ x 26in.
(Christie's) **$1,770 £1,188**

GEORGE ARMFIELD, Attributed to – Retrievers Putting Up Duck On A Moor – on board – 14½ x 24¾in.
(Sotheby's) **$462 £308 Pair**

MAXWELL ARMFIELD – Red Tape And Ceiling Wax (A Vision Of Elohim Gibor – 1944) (A Dance Of Shiva – 1946) – watercolour over pencil, squared for transfer – 28 x 23in.
(Sotheby's) **$943 £660**

ARMOUR

MARY NICOL NEILL ARMOUR –
Autumn Flowers – signed and dated
1944, inscribed on a label on the reverse
– oil on canvas – 17 x 22in.
(Sotheby's) $4,070   £2,750

JOHN ARMSTRONG – Surrealist Landscape – signed with monogram and
dated '47 – tempera on board – 22 x
18in.
(Sotheby's) $1,258   £880

THOMAS ARMSTRONG – Manchester
And Salford Children – signed and dated
1861 – 30 x 24in.
(Sotheby's) $4,290   £2,860

THOMAS ARMSTRONG – The Test –
signed with monogram and dated '65 –
31 x 23in.
(Sotheby's) $12,375   £8,250

ALOIS ARNEGGER – An Alpine Scene
– signed – on canvas – 24 x 36in.
(Sotheby's) $628   £418

VILHELM ARNESEN – Shipping Off
Kronborg Castle – signed and dated
1943 – oil on canvas – 18¾ x 28¾in.
(Sotheby's) $957   £660

ARNOLD – The Derby – signed and
dated 1887 – 42½ x 66in.
(Christie's) **$4,023** **£2,700**

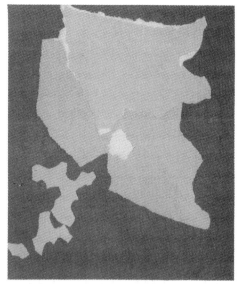

JEAN (HANS) ARP – Composition –
signed – papier dechire – 10 x 5½in.
(Christie's) **$2,592** **£1,728**

JOSE GALLEGOS Y ARNOSA – An
Arab Street Vendor – signed and dated
1881 – on panel – 15¾ x 8¼in.
(Christie's) **$9,590** **£6,480**

DAVID ADOLF CONSTANT ARTZ –
Dutch Girl In The Dunes At Sunset –
signed and dated 1870 – oil on canvas –
22 x 15½in.
(Sotheby's) **$1,183** **£825**

ARTZ

CONSTANT ARTZ – Ducks And Ducklings On A Pond – signed – on panel – 9½ x 11¾in.
(Sotheby's) **$1,237** **£825**

SAMUEL ATKINS – A Frigate Off Lisbon Harbour – signed – watercolour – 14¾ x 19¼in.
(Sotheby's) **$5,940** **£3,960**

SAMUEL ATKINS – 'Dover Castle' – signed – watercolour – 6½ x 9in.
(Sotheby's) **$561** **£374**

WILLIAM F. ASHBURNER – The Love Letter – signed and dated 1905 – oil on canvas – 29½ x 29¼in.
(Sotheby's) **$1,043** **£715**

G. F. ASHTON – Aldston – signed and inscribed on the reverse – 30 x 60in.
(Sotheby's) **$1,237** **£825**

THE REV. CHRISTOPHER ATKINSON – Mergus Merganser, Goosander – inscribed – pencil, watercolour and body-colour – 8¾ x 11¼in.
(Christie's) **$2,268** **£1,512**

THE REV. CHRISTOPHER ATKINSON –
Shoveller – pencil, watercolour and body-
colour – 11¼ x 8¾in.
(Christie's)   **$3,240   £2,160**

MABEL LUCIE ATTWELL – In The
School-Room – signed and inscribed on
the reverse – pencil, pen and brown ink
and watercolour heightened with white –
8¼ x 5¾in.
(Christie's)   **$1,879   £1,296**

MABEL LUCIE ATTWELL – On The
Cliff Top – signed, and inscribed on the
reverse – pencil, pen and brown ink and
watercolour heightened with white –
8½ x 5¾in.
(Christie's)   **$1,409   £972**

JOSEPH ATHANASE AUFRAY – Please
Mother – signed – on panel – 10½ x
8¼in.
(Sotheby's)   **$1,320   £880**

ALEXANDER AUSTEN – Card Games; and The Morning News – signed – 16 x 24in.
(Sotheby's) **$1,402** £935 Three

SAMUEL AUSTIN, Attributed to – A Coastal View With Figures And Shipping At Sunset – watercolour – 6¼ x 9¾in.
(Sotheby's) **$513** £352

AUSTRALIAN SCHOOL, circa 1840 – Port Jackson, Sydney – oil on board – 9 x 13in.
(Sotheby's) **$5,280** £3,520 Pair

MILTON AVERY – Two Harbour Views – oil on canvas – 7¼ x 11¼in. and 11¼ x 17¾in.
(Robert W. Skinner Inc.) **$650** £435 Two

JULES AVIAT – A Girl In A Doorway – oil on canvas – 21½ x 15in.
(Sotheby's) **$1,036** £715

PIETER VON AVONT, Follower of –
The Temptation In The Wilderness –
on metal – 19 x 25¼in.
(Sotheby's) $495   £330

MICHAEL AYRTON – Catalan Cage
Birds – signed and dated 1955 – oil on
canvas – 60 x 48in.
(Christie's) $4,050   £2,700

ALBERT WILLIAM AYLING – A
Card For The Races – signed and
inscribed – watercolour heightened
with bodycolour – 28 x 20in.
(Sotheby's) $429   £286

GEORGE AYLING – The Late H.M.S.
'Ark Royal The First' – signed – on
canvas – 26¾ x 36in.
(Sotheby's) $198   £132

MICHAEL AYRTON – Fox – inscribed
and dated '75 – pen and indian ink over
pencil – 10 x 7½in.
(Sotheby's) $297   £198

LUDOLF BACKHUYZEN – A Shipwreck
Off A Rocky Coast – 60 x 80¾in.
(Sotheby's) **$7,425** **£4,950**

S. BACKUS – 'Tropical Landscape' –
signed and dated 1950 – watercolour –
14½ x 21½in.
(Stalker &
Boos) **$90** **£53**

STANLEY ROY BADMIN – Mr Fox
Decides To Go Home – signed – watercolour over traces of pencil heightened
with bodycolour – 11½ x 7¾in.
(Sotheby's) **$4,404** **£3,080**

F. V. BAILLY, Follower of – A Still
Life Study Of Mixed Flowers In An Urn
– oil on canvas – 30 x 24in.
(Sotheby's) **$1,104** **£770**

THOMAS BAINES – Centre Rock Fall,
And The Eastern Cataracts, Victoria
Falls – signed and dated 1864 – oil on
canvas – 18¾ x 26½in.
(Sotheby's) **$25,806** **£18,700**

STANLEY ROY BADMIN – Skating
On Oakwood Pond, Sussex – signed –
watercolour over pencil heightened
with bodycolour – 10 x 7in.
(Sotheby's) **$2,202** **£1,540**

SAMUEL HENRY BAKER – The River
Derwent, Borrowdale – signed, inscribed
and inscribed and dated 1889 on the
reverse – 16 x 25in.
(Sotheby's) **$907** **£605**

WILLIAM GEORGE BAKER – Near Ohinemutu, Rotorua – signed and inscribed – oil on canvas on board – 14 x 18½in.
(Sotheby's)   **$528**   **£352**

LEON BAKST – Design For An Illustration, The Two Nymphs – signed in Russian – pen and indian ink – 6¼ x 10in.
(Sotheby's)   **$1,402**   **£935**

LEON BAKST – Portrait Of Boris Kochno – dated 1922 – pencil – 10 x 8in.
(Sotheby's)   **$330**   **£220**

CHARLES THOMAS BALE – Still Life With Game And Fruit – signed – 18 x 14in.
(Sotheby's)   **$528**   **£352**

GIOVANNI BALDUCCI – The Passover – oil on metal – 3¾ x 9¾in.
(Sotheby's)   **$2,604 £1,760**

THOMAS CHARLES BALE – Still Life
With Fruit – signed with monogram and
dated 1877 – 20 x 24in.
(Sotheby's)　　**$1,337**　　**£935**

JAN VAN BALEN – Minerva And The
Muses On Mount Helion – on copper –
35½ x 45½in.
(Christie's)　　**$10,038**　**£7,020**

EDMUND BALTHAZAR – Bathers –
signed and dated B/19 – oil on canvas –
15 x 17½in.
(Sotheby's)　　**$742**　　**£495**

**BALTHUS (Balthazar Klossowski De
Rola)** – Le Salon – oil on panel – 19½
x 23½in.
(Christie's)　　**$246,078　£167,400**

BALTHUS – La Sortie Du Bain – signed
and dated 1957 on the reverse – oil on
canvas – 78¾ x 78¾in.
(Sotheby's)　　**$1,270,500　£847,000**

BALTHUS – La Dormeuse – signed with
initials and dated '54 on the reverse – oil
on canvas – 18¼ x 21½in.
(Sotheby's)　　**$338,250 £225,500**

M. BALUNIN – Two Women By A
Sleigh – signed – gouache – 8¾ x
11¾in.
(Sotheby's)   **$1,754**   **£1,210**

ELIAS MOLLINEAUX BANCROFT –
A Shetland Webster – signed, signed
and inscribed on the reverse – 22 x 30in.
(Sotheby's)   **$629**   **£440**

BALTHUS – Portrait D'Helene Anavi
– signed with initials and dated 1952 –
oil on canvas – 42½ x 35¼in.
(Sotheby's)   **$148,500** **£99,000**

BALTHUS – Jeune Fille A La Fenetre
– signed and dated 1955 – oil on canvas
– 77¼ x 51¼in.
(Sotheby's)   **$891,000** **£594,000**

TOSHIO BANDO – Autoportrait –
signed and signed in Japanese – oil
on canvas – 12½ x 9in.
(Sotheby's)   **$1,402**   **£935**

JOHN BANTING – Spanish Shawl –
oil on canvas – 25 x 30in.
(Christie's)   **$1,539**   **£1,026**

BARATTI

FILIPPO BARATTI – The Surrender – signed and dated 1879 – 22½ x 32½in. *(Sotheby's)* **$39,600 £26,400**

WRIGHT BARKER – 'Crib' – signed and dated 1891 – on canvas – 11¾ x 23½in. *(Sotheby's)* **$883 £605**

GEORGE BARBIER – 'Le Crayon Aussi Est Une Arme' – signed and dated 1914 – pen and brush and ink and watercolour – 11 x 9½in. *(Sotheby's)* **$792 £528**

FRANCIS BARLOW – Landscape With A Milkmaid, Cattle And Deer – signed and dated 1684 – pen and brown ink and grey wash – 6¼ x 4¾in. *(Sotheby's)* **$6,930 £4,620**

THOMAS JONES BARKER – A Cricket Match At Pontypool, Monmouthshire – oil on canvas – 14 x 25in. *(Sotheby's)* **$7,425 £4,950**

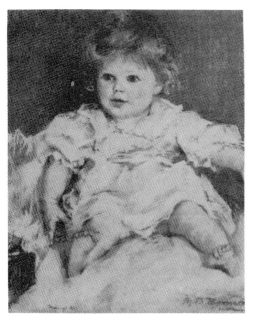

MARY B. BARNARD – One Year Old – signed and dated 1902 – oil – 23 x 19in.
(Sotheby's)   **$297**   **£198**

EDWARD CHARLES BARNES – The Morning Walk – signed with monogram – oil on canvas – 18 x 14in.
(Sotheby's)   **$797**   **£550**

EDWARD CHARLES BARNES – Building The Snowman – signed – 15¼ x 19¼in.
(Christie's)   **$1,780**   **£1,188**

SAMUEL JOHN BARNES – Highland
Scene With Sheep In A Wooded Landscape
– signed and dated '94/95 – oil on canvas
– 29½ x 49½in.
(Sotheby's)   **$662**   **£462**

JOSE TAPIRO Y BARO – Portrait Of A
Holy Man, Head And Shoulders – signed
– watercolour – 27 x 19in.
(Sotheby's)   **$660**   **£440**

**FEDERICO BAROCCI, Northern
Follower of** – The Adoration Of The
Shepherds – on metal – 12½ x 12½in.
(Sotheby's)   **$1,897**   **£1,265**

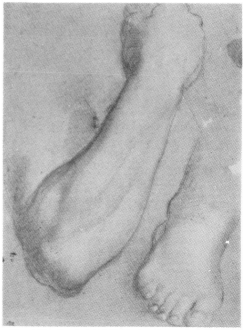

FEDERICO BAROCCI, Attributed to –
Study Of An Arm And A Foot – coloured
chalks on blue paper – 365 x 254mm.
(Sotheby's)   **$2,145**   **£1,430**

FRANCIS BARRAUD – After The
Fight – signed – watercolour over traces
of pencil heightened with bodycolour –
14 x 20½in.
(Sotheby's)   **$907**   **£605**

HENRY BARRAUD – A Hunter In A
Wooded River Landscape – signed –
17¼ x 23¼in.
(Christie's)   **$1,126**   **£756**

HENRY BARRAUD, Style of – An Artist With His Family In A Wood – oil on canvas – 21 x 25in.
(Sotheby's) **$1,485** **£990**

MAURICE BARRAUD – La Danseuse – signed and dated 1950 – oil on canvas – 116 x 89cm.
(Germann Auktionshaus) **$23,616** **£16,176**

WILLIAM BARRAUD, Circle of – The Rev. Michael Elwell Of Chester In His Gig – 19 x 23in.
(Sotheby's) **$1,484** **£1,045**

WILLIAM BARRAUD, Style of – 'Flirt', A Favourite Chichuahua – oil on canvas – 11¾ x 15¾in.
(Sotheby's) **$1,485** **£990**

JERRY BARRETT – The Lady And The Sweep – signed and dated 1869 – on canvas – 18 x 14in.
(Sotheby's) **$513** **£352**

WILLIAM BARRETT – Juvenile
Recruits – inscribed and dated 1836
– 21 x 24in.
(Lawrence) **$742** **£495**

JOHN BARWICK – A Black Hunter In
A Stable With A Spaniel – signed and
dated 1838 – 19½ x 24½in.
(Sotheby's) **$385** **£264**

JAMES BARRY – The Andover-London
Stage Passing A Sportsman On The Open
Road – signed and dated 1834 – oil on
canvas – 23½ x 29½in.
(Sotheby's) **$1,237** **£825**

JOHN BARWICK – An Appaloosa
Stallion In A Field – signed and
dated 1865 – 19½ x 24½in.
(Sotheby's) **$3,960** **£2,640**

CHARLES BARTLETT – Cabbage
Market – signed and dated 1900 –
watercolour over pencil – 24½ x
31½in.
(Sotheby's) **$3,300** **£2,200**

STEPHEN J. BATCHELDER – Yarmouth,
Haven Bridge – signed, inscribed and dated
1927 on the reverse – oil on canvas – 30
x 50in.
(Sotheby's) **$757** **£528**

FREDERICK S. BATCHELLER – Strawberries In A Basket – signed – oil on canvas – 14 x 18in.
(Robert W. Skinner Inc.) **$2,500 £1,666**

DAVID BATES – The Llugwy Below Capel Wrig Opposite Bryntick Hotel – signed, dated 1891 and inscribed on the reverse – on canvas – 28 x 38in.
(Sotheby's) **$5,445 £3,630**

JAMES BATEMAN – Tom Moody's Ghost – signed and dated '45 – oil on canvas – 23½ x 25¾in.
(Sotheby's) **$883 £605**

DAVID BATES – A Summers Day – signed – watercolour – 10¼ x 14¼in.
(Sotheby's) **$1,124 £770**

DAVID BATES – Bringing Home The Flock – signed and dated 1897 – oil on canvas – 24 x 36in.
(Sotheby's) **$2,970 £1,980**

DAVID BATES – Farmstead, Warwick – signed, inscribed on the reverse – oil on canvas – 17 x 24in.
(Sotheby's) **$2,145 £1,430**

DAVID BATES – Arab Girl Carrying
Pitcher – signed and dated 1892 – 21½
x 14½in.
(Lawrence)   **$660**   **£440**

DAVID BATES – Cowleigh Wood,
Malvern – signed, dated 1879 and
inscribed on the reverse – on canvas –
12¼ x 9½in.
(Sotheby's)   **$1,445**   **£990**

DAVID BATES – A View At Oadby,
Near Leicester – signed, inscribed and
dated 1904 – watercolour over traces
of pencil with scratching out – 10¼ x
14¼in.
(Sotheby's)   **$495**   **£330**

DAVID BATES – A Country Path –
signed – oil on canvas – 18 x 24in.
(Sotheby's)   **$2,227**   **£1,485**

DAVID BATES – An Old Bridge Near
Leicester – signed and dated 1888 –
oil on canvas – 20 x 30in.
(Sotheby's)   **$4,466**   **£3,080**

ARTHUR BATT – A Donkey Mare And
Her Foal – signed and dated 1897 – oil
on board – 9¾ x 12¾in.
(Sotheby's)   **$883**   **£605**

DOMENICO BATTISTA – Visage De Femme – signed and dated '82 – acrylic on canvas – 92 x 73cm.
(Germann
Auktionshaus) **$2,088** **£1,577**

JOSEPH BAUER – Watering The Geranium – signed, inscribed and dated 1875 – on panel – 11 x 8in.
(Sotheby's) **$1,073** **£715**

ANDRE BAUCHANT – Dans Un Bois – signed and dated 1930 – oil on canvas – 26 x 36in. *(Christie's)*
$5,670 £3,780

WILLI BAUMEISTER – Belebte Halde
Mit Farbinseln II – signed – oil on panel
– 31¼ x 25½in.
(Christie's)   **$21,870   £14,580**

CHARLES BAXTER – An Eighteenth
Century Beauty With A Posy – signed
and dated 1860 – 30 x 24½in.
(Sotheby's)   **$4,950   £3,300**

JOHAN BAUMGARTNER – Abraham And Melchizedek – oil on canvas – 10¼ x
14¾in. *(Sotheby's)*   **$13,350   £9,020**

ALFRED WALTER BAYES – In The
Stocks – signed – oil on canvas –
13½ x 20in.
(Sotheby's)   **$550**   **£385**

GEORGE TELFER BEAR – Daydreams,
(A Daughter Of The Hills) – signed –
23½ x 19½in.
*(Christie's &
    Edmiston's)*   **$450**   **£300**

WALTER JOHN BAYES – Outside St.
Mark's, Venice, Night – signed with
monogram and dated 1900 – watercolour and bodycolour – laid down on
card – 14 x 21¼in.
(Christie's)   **$469**   **£324**

JAMES PRINSEP BARNES BEADLE –
Lifeguards In Hyde Park – signed and
dated 1893 – on panel – 9½ x 11½in.
(Sotheby's)   **$1,815**   **£1,210**

GEORGE BEARE – Portrait Of A Lady,
Wearing A White Satin Dress – signed and
dated 1748 – oil on canvas – 29 x 24¼in.
(Sotheby's)   **$1,606**   **£1,100**

51

BEAVIS

RICHARD BEAVIS – Sussex Ox Wagon – signed, dated and inscribed – pencil and watercolour – 9¼ x 14¼in.
(Woolley &
Wallis)   **$1,380   £920**

LUIGI BECHI – The Pet Pigeons – signed – 15½ x 20in.
(Sotheby's)   **$3,300   £2,200**

JAMES CARROLL BECKWITH – Interior Of A Country Studio – signed and dated '93 – 28 x 20in.
(Sotheby's)   **$18,975   £12,650**

N. BECKER – A Girl And Her Corgi – signed and dated 1939 – oil on canvas – 43 x 33in.
(Sotheby's)   **$1,320   £880**

SIR WILLIAM BEECHEY – Portrait Of Vice-Admiral Sir Samuel Hood – 34½ x 26½in.
(Sotheby's)   **$11,550   £7,700**

CAPTAIN RICHARD BRYDGES BEECHEY – A Herdsman And Cattle In A Wooded River Landscape – signed and dated 1892 – 21½ x 29½in.
(Christie's)   **$2,413   £1,620**

JOHN BEER – The Middle Park Plate – signed, inscribed and dated 1901 – watercolour and bodycolour – 10 x 14¼in.
(Christie's)   **$405   £270**

ROBERT ANNING BELL – Cupid's Mirror – signed and dated '03 – 12 x 9½in.
(Sotheby's)   **$2,409   £1,650**

VANESSA BELL – Portrait Of Sir Leslie Stephen – oil on canvas – 28 x 35½in.
(Christie's)   **$1,377   £918**

LOUIS BELANGER – Views In Jamaica: View Of The Bridge Across The Rio Cobre Near Spanish Town; and View Of Port Antonio In The Parish Of Portland – 18¾ x 27in. *(Sotheby's)*   **$2,310   £1,540 Two**

BELLOTTO – The Pantheon, Rome,
With Numerous Figures In The Piazza –
28½ x 38in.
(Christie's)   **$6,480   £4,320**

FREDERIC MARLETT BELL-SMITH –
Prince's Street, Edinburgh – signed –
watercolour over pencil, with stopping
out – 9¼ x 12¼in.
(Sotheby's)   **$660   £440**

VANESSA BELL – Oriental Jar –
signed with initials on the reverse – oil
on canvas – 24 x 12in.
(Sotheby's)   **$2,202   £1,540**

SCHOOL OF BELLINI – Madonna
And Child With Saint John And Saint
Anne – on panel – 13½ x 18in.
(Lawrence)   **$3,719   £2,530**

DOMENICO BEMPO – A Trompe l'Oeil
Of A Framed Picture Of An Evangelist
Seen Behind A Curtain, Prints, Letters, A
Music Score And Other Objects With
Numerous Inscriptions – signed and dated
1767 – 28 x 24¾in.
(Christie's)   **$1,458   £972**

THOMAS C. S. BENHAM – The Confrontation – signed and dated '90 – 24 x 18¼in.
(Christie's)   **$1,528   £1,026**

FRANK MOSS BENNETT – The Reader – signed, dated 1938 and inscribed on stretcher – 14 x 10in.
(Sotheby's)   **$3,217   £2,145**

ALFRED BENNETT – Hampstead Heath – signed, inscribed and dated '99 – oil on canvas – 11 x 19¼in.
(Sotheby's)   **$449   £308**

FRANK MOSS BENNETT – Sticklepath, Dartmoor – signed, inscribed on the reverse – on board – 10 x 14in.
(Sotheby's)   **$429   £286**

FRANK MOSS BENNETT – The Fisherman's Return – signed and dated 1940 – on canvas – 13½ x 9½in.
(Sotheby's)   **$3,300   £2,200**

FRANK MOSS BENNETT – 'Singeing The King Of Spain's Beard' – signed, dated 1941-6 and inscribed on the reverse – on canvas – 14 x 20in. *(Sotheby's)*

$730   £484

FRANK MOSS BENNETT – The Ornithologists – signed and dated 1929 – 13½ x 19½in.
(Christie's) $4,210   £2,808

FRANK MOSS BENNETT – An Audience With Queen Elizabeth I – signed and dated 1942 – oil on canvas laid on board – 13½ x 19½in.
(Sotheby's) $1,320   £880

ALEXANDER BENOIS – Un Ballo In Maschera, (i) Costume Design For The Judge – signed and dated 1947 – 10 x 6¾in.; (ii) Costume Design For Two Noblemen Dressed As Sailors – both watercolour over pen and indian ink and pencil – 9½ x 7in.
(Sotheby's) $627   £418 Two

CHRISTIAN BERARD – Jeune Homme
En Bleu – signed and dated '26 – oil on
board – 41¼ x 29¼in.
(Sotheby's) **$6,600** **£4,400**

GIROLAMO DI BENVENUTO – Saint
Peter – on panel – 38½ x 13½in.
(Sotheby's) **$16,500** **£11,000**

JOHANN BERTHELSEN – Broadway
Church – signed – oil on canvasboard –
16 x 12in.
(Christie's) **$2,200** **£1,594**

ARMAND BERTON – La Seduction –
signed – 41 x 49in.
(Christie's)   **$13,586   £9,180**

CAREL BESCHEY – A Landscape With
Wagons By A Village – signed – on
panel – 25 x 32.2cm.
(Sotheby's)   **$12,540   £8,360**

FRANK BESWICK – Fishing A Still Pond
– signed and dated 1893 – watercolour
heightened with bodycolour – 17 x 28in.
(Sotheby's)   **$577   £385**

ROBERT BEVAN – Showing The Paces,
Aldridge's – watercolour and soft pencil
– 12 x 11½in.
(Christie's)   **$9,720   £6,480**

WILLIAM ROXBY BEVERLEY – Fisherfolk On The Beach At Scarborough –
signed with initials – watercolour – 6¾ x
12¾in.
(Sotheby's)   **$990   £660**

FRANK BESWICK – At The Cottage
Door – signed – watercolour, heightened
with bodycolour – 23½ x 15½in.
(Sotheby's)   **$513   £352**

ALBION HARRIS BICKNELL – Little
Reader Near The Sea – monogrammed,
signed, inscribed and dated 1868 on the
reverse – oil on panel – 8¾ x 6¼in.
*(Robert W. Skinner
Inc.)*   **$1,200   £800**

LAURENCE BIDDLE – Phlox Drum-
mondii, Pansies, Sweet Williams, Vir-
ginia Stocks, Lobelia And Wild Supple-
wort – signed and dated '57, also
inscribed on the reverse – canvas
mounted on board – 14 x 21in.
(Sotheby's)   **$865   £605**

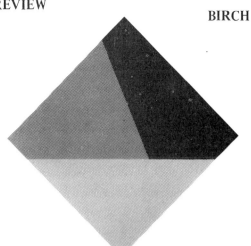

MAX BILL – Drei Gleichmassige Quanten
– signed and dated 1959 on the reverse –
oil on canvas – 16¾ x 16¾in.
(Christie's)   **$6,155   £4,104**

ALBERT BIERSTADT – Country Path
– signed – oil on canvas – 12¼ x 14½in.
(Christie's)   **$16,500 £11,000**

CARL BILLE – The Rescue – signed and
dated 1873 – on canvas – 24¾ x 37¼in.
(Sotheby's)   **$990   £660**

ALBERT BIERSTADT – 'Shoshonee
Indians: Rocky Mountains' – mono-
grammed – oil on paper – 5 x 7½in.
*(Robert W. Skinner
        Inc.)*   **$28,000 £18,666**

SAMUEL JOHN LAMORNA BIRCH –
Early June, Yorkshire – signed and
dated 1947 – oil on canvas – 20 x 24in.
(Christie's)   **$1,295   £864**

SAMUEL JOHN LAMORNA BIRCH –
Farm By A Swedish Lake – signed –
oil on canvas – 26 x 37in.
(Christie's) **$940** **£626**

SAMUEL JOHN LAMORNA BIRCH –
Bright Summer – signed – on panel –
11 x 13¾in.
(Sotheby's) **$595** **£396**

SAMUEL JOHN LAMORNA BIRCH –
Road By A Peaceful River – signed –
20 x 24in.
(Sotheby's) **$1,122** **£748**

THOMAS BIRCH – Wayside Inn On
Route To Philadelphia – oil on canvas
– 20¼ x 24½in.
(Christie's) **$22,000** **£15,068**

SAMUEL JOHN LAMORNA BIRCH
– Lamorna Cove – signed, inscribed
and dated 1917 on the reverse – on
board – 12¾ x 16½in.
(Sotheby's) **$353** **£242**

GIUSEPPE BERNARDINO BISON –
River Landscape With Fishermen By A
Cottage – gouache – 456 x 629mm.
(Sotheby's) **$1,815** **£1,210**

CORNELIS BISSCHOP, Attributed to — A Seamstress In An Interior — on panel —
22½ x 29in. *(Christie's)* $4,942 £3,456

ROGER BISSIERE — Jeune Femme Se Reposant — signed — oil on canvas — 38 x
55cm. *(Germann Auktionshaus)* $2,187 £1,458

WILLIAM KAY BLACKLOCK – On The
Dunes – signed – 13 x 18in.
(Sotheby's) **$3,212 £2,200**

WILLIAM KAY BLACKLOCK – Drawing Water By A Cottage – signed and
dated '17 – 24 x 20in.
(Sotheby's) **$3,372 £2,310**

WILLIAM KAY BLACKLOCK – The
Old Harbour, Porlock Weir – signed and
dated – 11 x 14½in.
*(Woolley &
Wallis)* **$870 £580**

MARIA BLANCHARD – La Gitane –
signed with initials – oil on canvas – 31½
x 20¾in.
(Sotheby's) **$16,500 £11,000**

JACQUES EMILE BLANCHE – A Portrait Of Charlotte Aman-Jean – signed
and dated 1917 – 37¾ x 30¼in.
(Sotheby's) **$4,125 £2,750**

JACQUES EMILE BLANCHE – Lovers-Amoureux, Dieppe – signed with initials, and signed, inscribed and dated 1939 on the reverse – 15 x 21½in. *(Christie's)*
$2,268   £1,512

THOMAS BLINKS – Showing Him Off – signed – 28 x 33in.
(Sotheby's)   **$5,280   £3,520**

THOMAS BLINKS – Full Cry – signed – 15½ x 23½in.
(Sotheby's)   **$6,424   £4,400**

THOMAS BLINKS, Manner of – Setters Hunting For A Pheasant – bears a signature – on canvas – 23 x 15½in.
(Sotheby's)   **$770   £528**

ABRAHAM BLOEMAERT, Circle of –
Moses And Aaron – oil on panel – 27½
x 45½in.
(Sotheby's) **$2,569 £1,760**

HENRY JOHN BODDINGTON – An
Overshot Mill – indistinctly signed on
the stretcher – 36 x 28in.
(Sotheby's) **$2,145 £1,430**

BERNARD JOHANNES BLOMMERS –
Woman Knitting With Child Seated In
The Dunes – signed – watercolour –
9½ x 13½in.
(Lawrence) **$1,485 £990**

BERNARDUS JOHANNES BLOMMERS
– At The Fireside – signed, inscribed
and dated '03 on an old label – oil on
canvas – 10 x 13¼in.
(Sotheby's) **$2,999 £2,090**

PIERRE LE BOEUFF – Continental
Market Square – signed – on canvas
– 16 x 21¼in.
(Sotheby's) **$674 £462**

JAKOB BOGDANI – Two Pairs Of Cocks And Hens, Doves And A Magpie – bears signature – 40 x 49½in.
(Sotheby's) **$19,800 £13,200**

BOHEMIAN SCHOOL, 18th century – A Music Party; and A Drinking Party – oil on canvas – 14½ x 17½in.
(Sotheby's) **$5,535 £3,740 Pair**

FRANK MYERS BOGGS – Notre-Dame de Paris – signed and inscribed – oil on canvas – 24 x 29¼in.
(Christie's) **$1,782 £1,188**

MAX BOHM – The Evening Meal – oil on canvas – 25¼ x 30¼in.
(Christie's) **$2,200 £1,465**

FRANK MYERS BOGGS – Village Lane – signed – oil on canvas – 22 x 15¼in.
(Christie's) **$3,850 £2,636**

LOUIS LEOPOLD BOILLY, Follower of – A Lady At Her Toilet – 18¼ x 15in.
(Sotheby's) **$1,567 £1,045**

GUY PENE DU BOIS — The Picnickers — signed and dated '29 — oil on canvas —
26 x 35½in. *(Christie's)* $20,900   £14,513

CHRISTIAN LUDWIG BOKELMANN — The Casino, Monte Carlo — signed and
dated 1884 — 36 x 50in.
(Christie's) $97,200   £64,800

FERDINAND BOL – David And
Jonathan – oil on canvas – 29½ x 23½in.
(Sotheby's) **$52,096 £35,200**

DAVID BOMBERG – Portrait Of A
Woman In Red – signed and dated 1931
– on panel – 24 x 19in.
(Sotheby's) **$2,310 £1,540**

BOLOGNESE SCHOOL, 17th century –
Head Of A Sibyl – pastel on blue paper
– 330 x 245mm.
(Sotheby's) **$1,402 £935**

DAVID BOMBERG – Portrait Of Lilian
(Greek Head), 1937 – inscribed – 20 x
16in.
(Sotheby's) **$1,155 £770**

BOND

RICHARD SEBASTIAN BOND – Mother
And Children On A River Bank – signed
and dated 1864 – oil on canvas – 19¼
x 29½in.
(Sotheby's)   **$417   £286**

PIERRE BONNARD – Soiree De
Campagne – signed – oil on canvas –
24½ x 18¾in.
(Christie's)   **$92,080   £62,640**

JULIETTE BONHEUR – Ducks &
Ducklings By A Stream – signed and
indistinctly dated – on panel – 9¾
x 12¾in.
(Sotheby's)   **$2,569   £1,760**

RICHARD PARKES BONINGTON –
French Coast With Fishermen – oil
on canvas – 17 x 21in.
(Sotheby's)   **$231,000 £154,000**

PIERRE BONNARD – Le Chapeau
Au Ruban Bleu – signed – on board
on canvas – 23¼ x 18¼in.
(Sotheby's)   **$153,120 £105,600**

PIERRE BONNARD – La Baignade Ou Les Enfants De La Famille Terrasse –
signed – oil on canvas – 13½ x 16in. *(Sotheby's)*   **$31,350   £20,900**

PIERRE BONNARD – Portrait De
Femme Blonde Au Corsage Bleu A Pois
– signed – oil on board laid down on
panel – 8¼ x 7½in.
(Sotheby's)   **$16,500   £11,000**

PIERRE BONNARD – Le Fiacre, Scene
de Rue – signed – oil on panel – 18 x
14½in.
(Christie's)   **$55,080   £36,720**

BONNARD

PIERRE BONNARD – Jardin En Dauphine – signed and dated 1901, also signed on the reverse – 20¾ x 25in. *(Sotheby's)* **$70,664 £48,400**

PIERRE BONNARD – St. Tropez – dated 1921 and inscribed – pencil on paper – 5 x 6½in. *(Christie's)* **$1,024 £702**

J. BONNY – Village Streets – signed – oil on canvas – 16 x 24in. *(Sotheby's)* **$1,808 £1,265 Pair**

J. BONNY – Abinger, Surrey – signed – oil on canvas – 20 x 29in. *(Sotheby's)* **$1,155 £770**

JAMES WILLIAM BOOTH – Ploughing Team – signed – watercolour – 10 x 15in. *(Sotheby's)* **$1,287 £858 Pair**

FRANCISCO BORES – Nu Aux Bras Croises – signed and dated '49 – oil on canvas – 45¼ x 31½in. *(Sotheby's)* **$5,610 £3,740**

ABRAHAM BOSSCHAERT – A Crown Imperial, Tulips And Other Flowers In A Vase – signed – on panel – 26 x 18½in. *(Sotheby's)* **$107,250 £71,500**

JAN BAPTIST BOSSCHAERT – Still
Life Of Summer Flowers – indistinctly
signed – oil on canvas – 34½ x 27¼in.
(Sotheby's)   **$3,854   £2,640**

DMITIR BOUCHENE – Les Gymnasts –
signed, signed, inscribed and dated 1939
– oil on board – 24½ x 18in.
(Sotheby's)   **$669   £462**

EUGENE BOUDIN – Environs D'Hon-
fleur – signed – on panel – 10¾ x 16in.
(Sotheby's)   **$17,666   £12,100**

EUGENE BOUDIN – Pleine Mer –
on board laid down on canvas – 6¾
x 9¼in.
(Sotheby's)   **$8,250   £5,500**

EUGENE BOUDIN – Femmes Breton-
nes Sur La Plage – signed – oil on
panel – 5¾ x 10¼in.
(Sotheby's)   **$11,550   £7,700**

EUGENE BOUDIN – Portrieux; Bateaux
a l'Ancre Dans Le Port – signed and
dated '73 – oil on canvas – 16 x 25¾in.
(Christie's)   **$45,360   £30,240**

EUGENE BOUDIN – Trouville, Le Port
– signed – on panel – 6¼ x 8¼in.
(Sotheby's)   **$32,120   £22,000**

SAMUEL BOUGH – Trawling On Loch
Fyne, Argyllshire – signed and dated
1878, and inscribed on the reverse –
watercolour – 8 x 12½in.
(Sotheby's)   **$561**   **£374**

SAMUEL BOUGH – A Highland Loch
Scene – signed and dated 1867 – water-
colour – 13 x 21in.
(Sotheby's)   **$280**   **£187**

GEORGE HENRY BOUGHTON – A
Rose Of New England – signed – on
panel – 23½ x 15¾in.
(Christie's)   **$4,023**   **£2,700**

WILLIAM ADOLPHE BOUGUEREAU –
A Dark Beauty – signed and dated 1898
– 18¼ x 15in.
(Christie's)   **$10,389**   **£7,020**

WILLIAM ADOLPHE BOUGUEREAU –
The First Kiss – signed and dated 1890 –
47 x 28in.
(Christie's)   **$55,944**   **£37,800**

FRANK WRIGHT BOURDILLON –
Across The Beach – signed and dated
1887, and inscribed on the reverse –
on canvas – 8¼ x 10¼in.
(Sotheby's) **$7,095 £4,730**

**LOUIS DE BOULLONGNE, The
Younger** – Male Nude Seated On A
Rock – signed – black and white chalk
on blue paper – 503 x 378mm.
(Sotheby's) **$7,425 £4,950**

JAMES E. BOURHILL – 'Just Caught';
and 'A Quiet Nibble' – signed and dated
1884 – 9½ x 14½in.
(Christie's) **$1,609 £1,080 Pair**

JOHN BOULTBEE – A Kennel Huntsman Letting His Hounds Out Of The Pen, A
View Of Beeston Castle Beyond – signed and dated 1803 – 27¾ x 35½in.
(Sotheby's) **$46,200 £30,000**

BOURHILL

JAMES E. BOURHILL – Caught; and
On The Riverbank – signed and dated
1884 – 10½ x 14½in.
(Christie's)   **$2,574   £1,728 Pair**

PIETER BOUT – A Winter Landscape
– oil on canvas – 13½ x 17½in.
(Sotheby's)   **$7,326   £4,950**

CORNELIS BOUTER – A Mother And
Child – signed – oil on canvas – 15¼
x 11¼in.
(Sotheby's)   **$715   £440**

DIERIC BOUTS, Follower of – Ecce
Homo – on panel – 18¼ x 13¾in.
(Sotheby's)   **$990   £660**

ANTOINE BOUVARD – Venetian
Canal Scene – signed – oil on canvas –
25 x 39in.
(Sotheby's)   **$2,409   £1,650**

ANTOINE BOUVARD – Venetian Canal
Scene With The Bell Tower Of St. Marco
In The Distance – signed – oil on canvas
– 19¼ x 25¾in.
(Sotheby's)   **$1,894   £1,320**

STEPHEN BOWERS – Wooded Landscape With Children By A Stream – signed and dated 1881 – watercolour – 29¼ x 20¼in.
(Dacre, Son & Hartley)   **$375**   **£250 Pair**

THOMAS SHOTTER BOYS – La Tour d'Eglise De Saint Jacques, Compiegne – pencil and watercolour – 11 x 8in.
(Christie's)   **$3,078**   **£2,052**

HERBERT BOYLE – View Of Skipton – signed – oil on board – 12 x 16in.
(Dacre, Son & Hartley)   **$637**   **£425**

JOHN BOYNE – Outside The Inn – watercolour over pencil – 13½ x 18¼in.
(Sotheby's)   **$495**   **£330**

THOMAS SHOTTER BOYS – Cowley Manor, The South Front – pen and brown ink, watercolour heightened with white, laid on linen – 10¾ x 7¼in.
(Christie's)   **$2,818**   **£1,944**

BRABAZON

HERCULES BRABAZON BRABAZON
— A River Estuary — signed with initials
— gouache — 6½ x 9½in.
*(Sotheby Beresford
        Adams)*   **$203   £121**

HERCULES BRABAZON BRABAZON —
Island Of San Giulio, Lake Orta — signed
with initials, and inscribed on the reverse
— pencil, watercolour and bodycolour on
grey-brown paper — 9¼ x 12½in.
(Christie's)   **$2,349   £1,620**

EMIL BRACK — A Young Girl In A
White Dress — signed and dated '86 —
36¼ x 24in.
(Sotheby's)   **$2,475   £1,650**

BASIL BRADLEY — The Ghillies
Return — signed — watercolour, height-
ened with white — 29 x 20in.
(Sotheby's)   **$3,960   £2,640**

HELEN BRADLEY — Our First Morning
In Blackpool — signed, and signed, inscribed and dated on a label — oil on canvasboard — 30 x 40in.
(Christie's)   **$9,590   £6,480**

ANTONIETTA BRANDEIS — Continental Lake Scene With Figures — signed
with monogram — on panel — 5 x 9¼in.
(Sotheby's)   **$1,518   £1,012**

ANTONIETTA BRANDEIS – Venice, The Doge's Palace – signed – oil on canvas – 30½ x 42½in.
(Sotheby's)   **$464**   **£320**

F. A. BRANDEL – Still Life Paintings With Dead Birds – one signed – 18¾ x 24½in.
(Sotheby's)   **$6,732**   **£4,400 Pair**

ANTONIETTA BRANDEIS – The Giants' Staircase, The Doge's Palace, Venice – signed – on board – 9½ x 7in.
(Sotheby's)   **$1,287**   **£858**

SIR FRANK BRANGWYN – The Adoration Of The Magi – signed with monogram – on board – 28¼ x 23¼in.
(Sotheby's)   **$694**   **£484**

ANTONIETTA BRANDEIS – San Trovaso, Venice – signed – on board – 6¾ x 9¼in.
(Sotheby's)   **$1,320**   **£880**

SIR FRANK BRANGWYN – Study For Stations Of The Cross – black and white chalk on blue paper, squared for transfer – 28 x 40½in.
(Sotheby's)   **$597**   **£418**

CHARLES BRANWHITE – Bridge Near Bettws-y-Coed, North Wales – inscribed on a label on the reverse – on panel – 12 x 17in.
(Sotheby's)   **$1,072**   £715

CHARLES BRANWHITE – Smelters Loading A Sailing Barge At Evening Near An Industrial Tow – signed and dated 1863 – watercolour heightened with white – 22¼ x 36½in.
(Christie's)   **$1,331**   £918

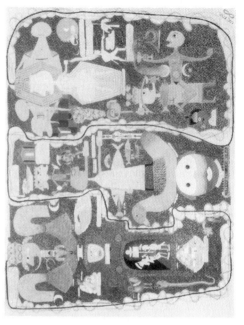

VICTOR BRAUNER – Tableau Auto-biographique – Ultratableau Biosensible – signed and dated 1948 – oil on canvas – 34¾ x 44½in.
(Sotheby's)   **$132,000   £88,000**

JOHN BRATBY – Stars And Stripes – signed and dated 1966 – on canvas – 52 x 32in.
(Sotheby's)   **$478**   £319

VICTOR BRAUNER – Eclipse – signed and dated '947 – oil on canvas – 8½ x 6¼in.
(Sotheby's)   **$11,550**   £7,700

VICTOR BRAUNER – Mitsi – signed
and dated 1939 – oil on canvas – 28¾
x 23½in.
(Sotheby's)   **$42,900   £28,600**

ERNEST R. BREACH – After The Shoot
– signed and dated 1885 – 49 x 73in.
(Sotheby's)   **$2,970   £1,980**

WILLIAM A. BREAKESPEARE – The
Fair Sitter – signed – on board – 7¾ x
11¼in.
(Christie's)   **$2,430   £1,620**

WILLIAM BREAKESPEARE – The Artist
And His Model – signed – on canvas –
17½ x 13½in.
(Sotheby's)   **$990   £660**

ALFRED DE BREANSKI – Snowdon,
North Wales – signed – oil on canvas –
30 x 50in.
(Sotheby's)   **$1,914   £1,320**

ALFRED FONTVILLE DE BREANSKI –
Borrowdale – signed – 16 x 24in.
(Sotheby's)   **$990   £660**

BREANSKI

ALFRED DE BREANSKI, SNR. — Henley Regatta — signed, inscribed on the reverse — 24 x 36in.
(Sotheby's) $10,725 £7,150

GUSTAVE DE BREANSKI — On The Coast Of Holland — signed and inscribed on a label — on canvas — 24 x 20in.
(Sotheby's) $513 £352

EMILE BRESSLER — Les Ecuyeres — signed and dated 1913 — oil on canvas — 62.5 x 115cm.
(Germann Auktionshaus) $4,939 £3,293

MAURICE BRIANCHON — Bouquet De Marguerites — signed — oil on canvas — 31¾ x 39¼in.
(Christie's) $29,959 £20,520

MAURICE BRIANCHON – Longchamps – signed – on board – 14¾ x 14¼in.
(Sotheby's) **$18,629 £12,760**

MAURICE BRIANCHON – Dimanche Au Bord de l'Eau a Chenneviere Sur Marne – signed – oil on canvas – 23¾ x 28¾in.
(Christie's) **$24,300 £16,200**

ELEANOR FORTESCUE BRICKDALE – 'Love And Its Counterfeits' – watercolour – 23 x 50in.
(Riddetts) **$5,700 £3,800**

FREDERICK LEE BRIDELL – The Grotto Of Neptune, Tivoli – signed and dated 1860 – oil on canvas laid on board – 47 x 72in.
(Sotheby's) **$1,485 £990**

MAURICE BRIANCHON – Femme Pensive – signed – oil on canvas – 36 x 24in.
(Christie's) **$15,768 £10,800**

FREDERICK ARTHUR BRIDGMAN – The Sultan's Favourite – signed – oil on canvas – 16 x 13in.
(Christie's) **$4,180 £3,028**

HARRY BRIGHT — An Eagle — signed
— oil on canvas — 23¾ x 17½in.
(Sotheby's) **$812 £572**

HENRY BRIGHT — Cattle Watering
By A Windmill On The Broads — signed
and dated 1860 — oil on canvas — 11½
x 26¾in.
(Sotheby's) **$8,351 £5,720**

HENRY BRIGHT — Windmill — pastel
heightened with white — 9.2 x 14in.
*(Woolley &
Wallis)* **$812 £560**

HENRY BRIGHT — Winter Landscape
With A Cottage And Figure — pastel
heightened with white — 8 x 12in.
*(Woolley &
Wallis)* **$609 £420**

HENRY BRIGHT — The River Thames
At Sheerness; and A Squall — one
signed and dated 1848, the other
inscribed on the reverse — oil on board
— 7 x 10in.
(Sotheby's) **$1,573 £1,100 Pair**

BRITISH SCHOOL — Workman Resting —
oil — 18 x 23in.
*(Capes, Dunn
& Co.)* **$384 £240**

WILLIAM BROCK – Apple Picking –
signed and dated 1911 – watercolour –
7¼ x 9¼in.
(Sotheby's) $248 £165

**VALENTINE WALTER LEWIS
BROMLEY** – Picking Wild Flowers –
signed and dated 1864 – watercolour
heightened with white and with gum
arabic – 8 x 12¾in.
(Christie's) $861 £594

NICHOLAS ALDEN BROOKS – Five
Note – signed and inscribed – oil on
panel – 7½ x 11in.
(Christie's) $7,920 £5,739

HARRY BROOKER – Teatime – signed
and dated '97 – 18 x 12in.
(Sotheby's) $2,264 £1,980

THOMAS BROOKS – Mauvais Temps
– signed, inscribed on the reverse –
37½ x 24½in.
(Sotheby's) $1,650 £1,100

THOMAS BROOKS – Pleasing Reflections – signed and dated 1873, inscribed on the reverse – oil on canvas – 19 x 30in. *(Sotheby's)*   **$8,772 £6,050**

JOHN BROWN – Roslin Castle On North Esk, Scotland – signed, dated 1860 and inscribed – oil on canvas – 25 x 30in. *(W. H. Lane & Son)*   **$1,372**   **£940**

JOHN GEORGE BROWN – The Confab – signed – oil on canvas – 24¾ x 29½in. *(Christie's)*   **$16,500 £11,458**

JOHN GEORGE BROWN – The Fisherman – signed – oil on canvas – 20½ x 15in. *(Robert W. Skinner Inc.)*   **$17,000 £11,335**

TOM BROWNE – The Queue For Alladin – signed – watercolour over pencil – 14 x 20¼in.
(Sotheby's)   **$1,365**   **£935**

PIETER BRUEGHEL, The Younger – A Wedding Dance – signed and dated 1621 – on panel – 16 x 22¼in.
(Sotheby's)   **$165,000 £110,000**

GEORGE WASHINGTON BROWNLOW – The Fisherman's Cottage – signed and dated 1861 – 12 x 16in.
(Christie's)   **$1,931**   **£1,296**

PIETER BRUEGHEL II, Studio of – The Bridegroom's Procession – on panel – 10½ x 14¾in.
(Sotheby's)   **$11,550**   **£7,700**

JENNIE BROWNSCOMBE – Love's Young Dream – signed and dated 1887 – oil on canvas – 21¼ x 32¼in. *(Christie's)*   **$20,900   £13,935**

PIETER BRUEGHEL, The Younger – Twelfth Night – oil on panel – 28½ x 40¼in. *(Sotheby's)*   **$84,656 £57,200**

EMMANUELE BRUGNOLI – St. Mark's Square, Venice – signed – on panel – 8¾ x 12½in. *(Sotheby's)*   **$2,649 £1,815**

ALFRED ARTHUR BRUNEL de Neuville – Kittens – signed – oil on oak panel – 4¼ x 5¾in.
(Robert W. Skinner Inc.) **$650** **£433**

EMMANUELE BRUGNOLI – Figures Outside The Basilica, Venice – signed – on panel – 12¼ x 7in.
(Sotheby's) **$5,139** **£3,520**

ALFRED ARTHUR BRUNEL de Neuville – Still Life, Peaches And Red And White Berries Spill From A Handled Basket – signed – oil on canvas – 21 x 25in.
(Robert W. Skinner Inc.) **$3,000** **£2,000**

LOUIS BURLEIGH BRUHL – A Mooring – signed – oil on canvas – 60 x 35in.
(Sotheby's) **$495** **£330**

FRANCOIS BRUNERY – An Eminent Gathering – signed – 29½ x 37½in.
(Christie's) **$16,200** **£10,800**

MARCEL BRUNERY – A Light Repast
– signed – oil on canvas – 19¼ x 23¾in.
(Sotheby's)   **$2,871   £1,980**

ADAM BUCK – Maternal Amusement
– signed and dated 1795 – pencil and
watercolour – 12 x 14¼in.
(Christie's)   **$1,539   £1,026**

H. C. BRYANT – Barn Interior With A
Donkey And Fowl – signed – oil on
canvas – 29¼ x 19½in.
(Sotheby's)   **$2,569   £1,760**

JOHN BUCKLER – The Principal, Dr
Macbride's House At Magdelen Hall,
Oxford – letter attached to the reverse
– watercolour over pencil – 9½ x 14in.
(Sotheby's)   **$594   £396**

H. C. BRYANT – Market Day,
Malmesbury – signed and dated 1868
– oil on canvas – 25 x 30½in.
(Sotheby's)   **$7,708   £5,280**

JOHN BUCKLER – South East View
Of Wraxhall Church, Wiltshire; Wraxhall
House; and Gateway To Wraxhall House
– signed and dated 1808 – watercolour
over pencil – 10¼ x 14½in.
(Sotheby's)   **$792   £528 Three**

JOHN CHESSEL BUCKLER – Durham
Cathedral – pencil and watercolour –
22½ x 31in.
(Christie's)   **$1,215**   **£810**

BERNARD BUFFET – Bouquet De
Dahlias – signed and dated '62 – oil
on canvas – 45½ x 35in.
(Sotheby's)   **$17,325   £11,550**

BERNARD BUFFET – La Place De
L'Opera – signed and dated '56 – oil
on canvas – 34¾ x 57in.
(Sotheby's)   **$13,875   £19,250**

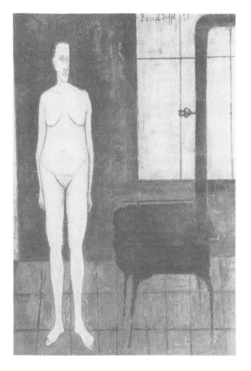

BERNARD BUFFET – Ne Debout Dans
L'Atelier – signed and dated '49, also
signed on the reverse – oil on canvas –
78 x 48½in.
(Christie's)   **$11,037   £7,560**

EDGAR BUNDY – Tending The Flowers
– signed and dated 1897 – 26 x 19in.
(Sotheby's)   **$4,175   £2,860**

EDGAR BUNDY – Discussing Strategy
– signed – oil on board – 20 x 30in.
(Sotheby's) **$1,650** **£1,100**

EDGAR BUNDY – At The Spinning
Wheel – signed – oil on canvas – 19½ x
24in.
(Sotheby's) **$1,420** **£990**

EDGAR BUNDY – A Celebration –
signed and dated 1900 – 36 x 27½in.
(Sotheby's) **$5,460** **£3,740**

HORACE ROBBINS BURDICK – 'A
Game Of Croquet, Stanstead, Canada'
– signed and dated 1875, inscribed on
the reverse – watercolour – 8¾ x 11¾in.
(Robert W. Skinner
Inc.) **$500** **£333**

EDGAR BUNDY – The Envoy – signed
and inscribed on the reverse – watercolour
heightened with white – 20 x 26¾in.
(Christie's) **$775** **£518**

ARTHUR J. W. BURGESS – Study Of
A Yacht – signed – watercolour – 8¾ x
17¾in.
(Sotheby's) **$561** **£374**

JOHN BURGESS – Antwerp Cathedral, With Figures By The Rubens Statue – signed and inscribed – pencil and water-colour heightened with white – 21¾ x 15½in.
(Christie's)   **$890   £594**

JOHN BAGNOLD BURGESS – La Sevilliana – signed and dated 1891 – 13½ x 10¼in.
(Lawrence)   **$1,980   £1,320**

JOHN BAGNOLD BURGESS – The Love Song – signed with monogram – oil on canvas – 30 x 24in.
(Sotheby's)   **$2,475   £1,650**

JOHN BAGNOLD BURGESS – A Spanish Girl – signed – on panel – 13 x 9½in.
(Sotheby's)   **$1,220   £814**

HEINRICH BURKEL – A Rest By The Wayside – signed – on board – 12½ x 15½in.
(Christie's) **$23,976 £16,200**

HEINRICH BURKEL – A Winter Landscape With Figures And Cattle By A Mill – signed – 17¼ x 23¼in.
(Christie's) **$30,369 £20,520**

DAVID BURLIUK – 'Kathleen' – signed – oil on panel – 7 x 6½in.
(Robert W. Skinner Inc.) **$350 £235**

AVERIL BURLEIGH – Mischief – signed and inscribed – watercolour, pen and black ink – 13½ x 11¼in.
(Christie's) **$615 £410**

SIR EDWARD COLEY BURNE-JONES – Study Of A Girl's Head Looking Down To The Left – pencil – 9¾ x 6½in.
(Christie's) **$2,590 £1,728**

JOHN BURNET, Attributed to — Meeting Daddy — bears signature — on panel — 8½ x 12in.
(Sotheby's)   **$396**   **£264**

ALEXANDER HOHENLOHE BURR — Good Doggie! — signed — 16 x 21½in.
(Christie's &
*   Edmiston's)*   **$1,125**   **£750**

JOHN P. BURR — The Young Farm Maid — signed and dated 1863 — oil on board — 10 x 7½in.
(Sotheby's)   **$455**   **£308**

EDWARD BURRA – Back Stage – signed
– pen and black ink – 16½ x 14½in.
(Christie's)   **$3,400**   **£2,268**

LUDOVICO BUTI, Attributed to – The
Martyrdom Of Saint Felicity And Her
Seven Sons – signed with a monogram
– oil on panel – 105 x 96in.
(Sotheby's)   **$1,284**   **£880**

EDWARD BURRA – Civilian Damage,
Spanish Civil War – signed – watercolour
– 40 x 27in.
(Christie's)   **$5,670**   **£3,780**

MILDRED ANNE BUTLER – Issie Butler,
Sister Of The Artist, At The Conservatory
Door, Kilmurry – signed, inscribed and
dated 1898 – watercolour heightened with
white – 9¾ x 7in.
(Christie's)   **$2,106**   **£1,404**

MILDRED ANNE BUTLER – Where The Sunshine And The Shadows Fell In Little Shiny Patches – signed, and signed and inscribed on the reverse – watercolour and bodycolour – 9¾ x 13¾in.
(Christie's)　　　**$1,017**　　**£702**

CHARLES ERNEST BUTLER – Fishing – signed and dated '93 – oil on canvas – 18 x 24in.
(Sotheby's)　　　**$829**　　**£572**

EDWARD BUTTAR – Interior – oil on canvas – 25 x 30in.
(Sotheby's)　　　**$660**　　**£440**

JAMES E. BUTTERSWORTH – British Men Of War And Other Shipping Possibly Off Portsmouth – signed – 17½ x 39¼in.
(Sotheby's)　　　**$4,950**　　**£3,300**

GIOVANNI MARIA BUTTERI, Attributed to – The Madonna And Child With Saint Anna And John – oil on panel – 34½ x 28½in.
(Sotheby's)　　　**$2,116**　　**£1,430**

A. BUZZI – The Pearl Necklace – signed – watercolour over pencil with scratching out – 21 x 28½in.
(Sotheby's)　　　**$4,555**　　**£2,970**

JAN VAN BYLERT – An Old Man With An Hour-Glass – signed – 25¼ x 22½in.
(Christie's)　　　**$6,486**　　**£4,536**

LOUIS SIMON CABAILLOT, Called
Lassalle — Washing Day — signed and
dated '76 — oil on panel — 13¾ x 10¾in.
(Sotheby's)　　**$1,914　£1,320**

ALEX. E. CADDY — View In An Indian
Street — signed and dated 1903 — oil
on canvas — 23½ x 17½in.
(Sotheby's)　　**$333　£242**

PAUL CADMUS — Male Nude — signed and inscribed — pastel on paper — 14½ x
20¾in. *(Christie's)*　　**$2,640　£1,760**

HECTOR CAFFIERI – 'On The Sands, Boulogne' – signed – watercolour – 13¾ x 20½in.
(Sotheby's) **$7,590 £5,060**

WALTER WALLER CAFFYN – 'Harvesting Near Reigate, Surrey' – signed, and inscribed on the reverse – 21 x 17in.
(Christie's) **$4,535 £3,024**

WALTER WALLER CAFFYN – Logging In The Surrey Hills – signed and dated 1895 – oil on canvas – 20 x 30in.
(Sotheby's) **$2,310 £1,540**

CHRISTIAN CAILLARD – La Jeune Eve – signed – oil on panel – 34½ x 49¼in.
(Christie's) **$7,095 £4,860**

ALEXANDER CALDER – Swirls And Spots – signed and dated '68 – gouache on paper – 22 x 30in.
(Christie's) **$1,375 £918**

WILLIAM FRANK CALDERON – How Four Queens Found Sir Lancelot Sleeping – signed and dated 1908 – 47 x 71½in.
(Sotheby's) **$11,550 £7,700**

A. CALDWELL – Landscape With Fishermen On A Lake – signed and dated 1797 – gouache – 24¼ x 35in.
(Sotheby's) **$660** **£440**

JOHN CALLOW – Summoning Help – signed – oil on canvas – 36 x 54in.
(Sotheby's) **$825** **£550**

WILLIAM CALLOW – View Of The Bay Of Naples – signed and inscribed on the reverse – watercolour – 12¾ x 18½in.
(Sotheby's) **$2,228** **£1,485**

LANCE CALKIN – Cleaning The Brass – signed – oil on canvas – 18½ x 23in.
(Sotheby's) **$1,595** **£1,100**

SIR AUGUSTUS WALL CALLCOTT – Fishermen On A Beach With Their Catch – 23½ x 32¼in.
(Sotheby's) **$1,485** **£990**

GEORGE D. CALLOW – Bonchurch, Isle Of Wight – signed and dated 1863 – oil on canvas – 12 x 23in.
(Sotheby's) **$1,237** **£825**

ABRAHAM CALRAET, Attributed to – Interior Of A Larder – bears the added signature of Aelbert Cuyp – 37 x 33½in.
(Sotheby's) **$11,880** **£7,920**

CLAUDE ANDREW CALTHROP –
Spinning – signed – 42 x 30in.
(Sotheby's) **$825** **£550**

EDWIN SHERWOOD CALVERT –
Fishing Boats Coming Inshore – signed
and dated 1891 – oil on canvas – 28 x
36in.
(Sotheby's) **$627** **£418**

SIR DAVID YOUNG CAMERON – A
Tower In Mar – signed – 13½ x 23in.
(Christie's &
Edmiston's) **$1,500** **£1,000**

CHARLES CAMOIN – La Crique Aux
Roches Rouges – signed – 25½ x 31¾in.
(Sotheby's) **$18,150 £12,100**

GOVERT DIRCKSZ. CAMPHUYSEN –
Peasants Carousing In A Barn – on panel
– 20¾ x 26¾in.
(Christie's) **$4,536 £3,024**

MASSIMO CAMPIGLI – Due Donne
Sulla Scala – signed and dated '66 –
oil on canvas – 14 x 16in.
(Christie's) **$13,402 £9,180**

CAMPO

FEDERICO DEL CAMPO – Venice, The Ca'D'Oro – signed and dated 1885 – 20 x 35¾in.
(Sotheby's) **$39,600 £26,400**

HENRY CAMPOTOSTO – Mother And Child In A Barn – signed and dated 1890 – on canvas – 18 x 25in.
(Sotheby's) **$6,745 £4,620**

DOMENICO CANTATORE – Study Of A Young Girl – oil on canvas – 97 x 60cm.
(Christie's) **$6,626 £4,508**

ANTONIO CANALETTO, Follower of – A View Of The Grand Canal Looking North East From Santa Croce To San Geremia – oil on canvas – 24¾ x 47½in.
(Sotheby's) **$5,781 £3,960**

J. VAN DE CAPPELLE – Dutch Fishing
Boats Offshore With Figures On The
Seashore – bears signature – 8 x 10½in.
(Christie's)   **$3,564   £2,376**

RAMON CARAZO – Carmen – signed
and dated 1931, also signed and dated
1932 on the reverse – oil on panel –
6 x 4¾in.
(Sotheby's)   **$510   £352**

GABRIEL CARELLI – Fishermen In
The Bay Of Naples – signed – on
panel – 5½ x 10in.
(Sotheby's)   **$738   £506**

GABRIELLI CARELLI – A View Of
Cairo – signed and inscribed – water-
colour – 6½ x 13¾in.; and another.
(Sotheby's)   **$615   £429**

GUISEPPE CARELLI – Napoli – signed
and inscribed – on panel – 8 x 14¾in.
(Sotheby's)   **$1,188   £792**

SOREN EMIL CARLSEN – Self Portrait
– oil on canvas – 31¾ x 23¼in.
(Christie's)   **$2,200   £1,465**

JAMES WILSON CARMICHAEL –
Shipping Off Dover In Choppy Seas –
signed and dated 1864 – 11 x 15in.
(Sotheby's)   **$1,485**   **£990**

JOHN WILSON CARMICHAEL –
Extensive Landscape With Figures And A
Cart On A Bridge, Mountains In The
Distance – signed and dated 1856 –
watercolour – 15 x 22in.
(Dreweatt Watson &
*   Barton)*   **$705**   **£480**

JAMES WILSON CARMICHAEL – Rear
Admiral Lord Collingwood Firing The
First Broadside At The Battle Of Trafalgar
– inscribed – pencil, pen and brown ink,
brown wash – 13 x 20¾in.
(Christie's)   **$453**   **£302**

JOHN WILSON CARMICHAEL – A
River Landscape With A Waterfall, And
Cattle Crossing A Bridge – signed and
dated 1858? – 12 x 18in.
(Christie's)   **$1,045**   **£702**

JOHN WILSON CARMICHAEL – On
A Swiss Lake – signed with initials,
inscribed and dated 1847 on the reverse
– on panel – 10 x 12in.
(Sotheby's)   **$797**   **£550**

JOHN WILSON CARMICHAEL –
Evening, The Pool Of London – signed
and dated 1858 – 26¾ x 39½in.
(Christie's)   **$15,390   £10,260**

JOHN WILSON CARMICHAEL – New Houses Of Parliament With Westminster Bridge Which They Are Pulling Down – signed, inscribed and dated 1846 – pencil and brown wash heightened with white on grey paper – 10 x 14¼in.
(Christie's) **$453** **£302**

JOHN WILSON CARMICHAEL – Shipping Off Tantallon Castle – signed and dated 1859 – 24 x 36in.
(Sotheby's) **$10,439** **£7,150**

JOHN WILSON CARMICHAEL – Ship In A Storm – signed and indistinctly dated – on canvas – 17 x 13½in.
(Sotheby's) **$1,518** **£1,012**

JOHN WILSON CARMICHAEL,
Follower of – Boats In Harbour, Roma – bears signature, dated 1863 and indistinctly inscribed – on canvas – 23½ x 35¾in.
(Sotheby's) **$3,693** **£2,530**

JOHN WILSON CARMICHAEL – Shipping Offshore With Fishermen By A Buoy – signed and dated 1839 – 23½ x 35½in.
(Christie's) **$6,114** **£4,104**

JEAN CAROLUS – A Proposal – signed, dated '48 and indistinctly inscribed – oil on panel – 31 x 24½in.
(Sotheby's) **$2,999** **£2,090**

JEAN CAROLUS – The Duet – signed –
on panel – 21¼ x 17¼in.
(Sotheby's)   **$2,310   £1,540**

DAVID CARR – Midi – signed – watercolour – 11¼ x 22¼in.
(Sotheby's)   **$445   £297**

SAMUEL S. CARR – Grazing Sheep
– signed – oil on canvas – 12 x 9in.
*(Robert W. Skinner
    Inc.)*   **$1,100   £733**

ANGELO CAROSELLI – A Necroman-
tic Subject – oil on canvas – 26 x 19¼in.
(Sotheby's)   **$6,512   £4,400**

TOM CARR – Spring In Strathmore –
signed – canvas on board – 24 x 30in.
(Sotheby's)   **$814   £550**

JOHN MULCASTER CARRICK – Kew Bridge – signed and dated 1884, and signed, inscribed and dated on the reverse – on board – 8¼ x 10¾in.
(Christie's)   **$2,413   £1,620**

JOHN MULCASTER CARRICK – St. Malo – signed and dated 1886 – on board – 8¼ x 10¾in.
(Christie's)   **$1,206   £810**

ROSALBA CARRIERA – Portrait Of A Young Woman As Ceres – pastel – 23½ x 19½in.
(Sotheby's)   **$11,396   £7,700**

JACOPO CARRUCI, Called Pontormo – Marcus Curtius Leaping Into The Pit – on panel – 21½ x 44¼in.
(Sotheby's)   **$10,725   £7,150**

ALEXANDER CARSE – Outside The Inn – signed and dated 1831 – oil on panel – 14 x 18½in.
(Sotheby's)   **$1,546   £1,045**

HENRY BARLOW CARTER – Durham From The River – watercolour – 12 x 17¾in.
(Christie's)   **$831   £540**

ROBERT CARRICK – The Anglers – signed – watercolour – 8¼ x 6¼in.
(Sotheby's)   **$544   £363**

FRANCESCO D'A CASADEMONT –
Cadaques Y La Barca – signed – oil
on canvas – 65 x 81cm.
*(Germann
Auktionshaus)* **$1,002**   **£668**

BRUNO CARUSO – Nudo Di Donna –
watercolour on card – 47 x 31cm.
(Christie's)   **$601**   **£409**

BRUNO CARUSO – Il Figliol Prodigo
(1966) – oil on canvas – 70 x 55cm.
(Christie's)   **$1,686**   **£1,147**

MARY CASSATT – Margot With A
Floppy Bonnet – signed – pencil on
paper – 11¾ x 8in.
(Christie's)   **$14,300**   **£9,530**

MARY CASSATT – Child Leaning Against Her Young Mother – signed – pastel on grey paper – 25½ x 18¾in. *(Christie's)* **$77,000 £53,472**

P. CASTEELS – Poultry And Doves In A Landscape – 30½ x 26¼in. *(Christie's)* **$1,944 £1,296**

CLAUDIO CASTELUCHI – Donna Orientale Seduta – signed – oil on canvas – 38¼ x 51¼in. *(Sotheby's)* **$693 £462**

CATTERMOLE

CHARLES CATTERMOLE – The Arrival
Of The King – signed – watercolour –
13¼ x 29¾in.
(Sotheby's)   **$313**   **£209**

LESLIE GIFFEN CAULDWELL – A
Breton Garden – signed and dated 1892,
and indistinctly inscribed on an old label
– oil on canvas – 21 x 17½in.
(Sotheby's)   **$2,052**   **£1,430**

LOUIS DE CAULLERY, Circle of –
A Square In An Imaginary Italian Town
– on panel – 28¾ x 41¼in.
(Sotheby's)   **$9,570**   **£6,380**

BERNARDO CAVALLINO, Circle of –
St. Matthew – oil on canvas – 43¾ x
36¾in.
(Sotheby's)   **$5,139**   **£3,520**

GIACOMO CAVEDONE, Circle of – The
Holy Family – 51 x 39in.
(Christie's)   **$2,316**   **£1,620**

JOHN CAWSE – The Village Musicians – bears another signature and date – 25 x 30in.
(Sotheby's)   **$1,980   £1,320**

GIACOMO CERUTI, Called Pitocchetto, Follower of – A Peasant Holding A Straw-Covered Flagon Of Wine – 30½ x 24½in.
(Christie's)   **$3,397   £2,375**

JAROSLAV CERMAK – The Widow – signed and dated 1858 – oil on canvas – 29¼ x 17½in.
(Sotheby's)   **$2,073   £1,430**

AUGUSTE CHABAUD – La Mere Au Foyer – signed, also signed and inscribed on the reverse – oil on canvas – 39¼ x 22¼in.
(Christie's)   **$1,261   £864**

NORA CHAESE – Bully Of The Block
– signed and dated 1884 – oil on canvas
– 20 x 15¼in.
(Christie's)   **$495   £358**

MARC CHAGALL – Le Loup, La Mere
Et L'Enfant – signed, inscribed and
dated '26 – gouache – 19¾ x 16in.
(Sotheby's)   **$54,450 £36,300**

MARC CHAGALL – La Cour d'une
Ferme – signed – gouache, watercolour
over pencil on buff paper – 24¾ x 18¾in.
(Christie's)   **$42,120 £28,080**

MARC CHAGALL – Le Rabbin –
signed – gouache on paper laid down on
board – 17¼ x 11in.
(Sotheby's)   **$79,200 £52,800**

MARC CHAGALL – Le Couple – signed
– watercolour – 14¼ x 11in.
(Sotheby's)   **$14,355**   **£9,900**

MARC CHAGALL – Le Corbeau Et Les
Amoureux – signed – gouache and brush
and ink – 12¼ x 9½in.
(Sotheby's)   **$5,775**   **£3,850**

MARC CHAGALL – Le Cosaque –
signed and dated '12 – gouache on paper
– 17¼ x 12½in.
(Christie's)   **$141,912**   **£97,200**

MARC CHAGALL – Fleurs De St. Jean-
Cap-Ferrat – signed and dated 1956-7 –
oil on canvas – 51¼ x 38¾in.
(Christie's)   **$396,900 £270,000**

MARC CHAGALL – Femme A La Pomme – signed – pen and indian ink – 8½ x 7¼in.
(Sotheby's)   **$19,800   £13,200**

GEORGE PAUL CHALMERS – Study For 'The Legend' – 25 x 30in.
(Christie's)   ·   **$2,250   £1,500**

ALFRED EDWARD CHALON, Circle of – Portrait Of Elizabeth And Maria Coles, Daughters Of James Coles – 45½ x 36½in.
(Sotheby's)   **$1,204   £825**

ALFRED EDWARD CHALON – Sophia Western Vide Tom Jones – oil on canvas – 25 x 29½in. *(Sotheby's)*
$1,237   £825

HENRY BERNARD CHALON – A Terrier Frightening A Mallard – signed and dated 1827 – on panel – 11¼ x 15¾in.
(Sotheby's)   **$1,650   £1,100**

GEORGE CHAMBERS, JNR., Attributed to – The Shipwreck – on panel – 10¼ x 15in.
(Sotheby's)   **$642   £440**

BENJAMIN CHAMPNEY – 'View At Woburn' – signed and dated, also dated 1863 on reverse – oil on board – 6 x 8in.
(Robert W. Skinner Inc.)   **$900   £600**

JAMES WILLS CHAMPNEY – At The Fireside – signed and dated '74 – oil on canvas – 22 x 18in.
(Sotheby's)   **$2,640   £1,760**

JOHN WESTBROOKE CHANDLER – Portraits Of Four Daughters Of A Gentleman At Play, As Macbeth And The Witches – 77 x 58in.
(Sotheby's)   **$9,570   £6,380**

CHARLES CHAPLIN – Sweet Dreams
– signed and dated 1886 – 31 x 55¼in.
(Sotheby's) **$37,950 £25,300**

CHARLES CHAPLIN – 'Devotion' –
signed – oil on canvas – 24½ x 19in.
(Sotheby's) **$610 £418**

JOHN GADSBY CHAPMAN –
'Shepherd Of The Campagna' – signed
and dated 1867 on reverse – oil on
board – 9¾ x 14in.
*(Robert W. Skinner
Inc.)* **$1,000 £666**

CHARLES CHAPLIN – The Pet Parrots
– signed – 41¼ x 30in.
(Christie's) **$7,992 £5,400**

WILLIAM CHAPPELL – Jumping The
Fence – signed – on canvas – 11½ x
13½in.
(Sotheby's) **$760 £506**

JAMES CHARLES – An Evening Gossip
– signed, dated 1899 and indistinctly
inscribed on reverse – oil on board –
23½ x 19½in.
(Sotheby's)   **$1,445   £990**

WILLIAM MERRITT CHASE – The
Yellow Blouse – signed – oil on canvas
– 19¾ x 16in.
(Christie's)   **$35,200   £24,444**

OMER CHARLET – An Allegory Of Time – signed and dated 1847 – 52½ x
74¼in. *(Sotheby's)*   **$7,425   £4,950**

WILLIAM MERRITT CHASE – Playing
Horse – signed – oil on canvas – 72¼ x
36¼in.
(Christie's) **$385,000 £267,361**

GAETANO CHIERICI – The Happy
Children – signed – 30 x 38¼in.
(Sotheby's) **$61,050 £40,700**

LILIAN CHEVIOT – Patrick A Terrier
– signed – oil on canvas – 18 x 13in.
(Sotheby's) **$1,485 £990**

SANDRO CHIA – Due Putti – signed,
also signed and dated 1977 on the reverse – oil on canvas – 47¼ x 35½in.
(Christie's) **$15,768 £10,800**

GEORGE CHINNERY – Portrait Of A Gentleman, A Member Of The Alexander Family – 29 x 24½in.
(Sotheby's) **$15,675 £10,450**

JACOPO CHIMENTI, Called Jacopo Da Empoli – Portrait Of A Lady As Saint Barbara (?) – oil on canvas – 29¼ x 21in.
(Sotheby's) **$35,816 £24,200**

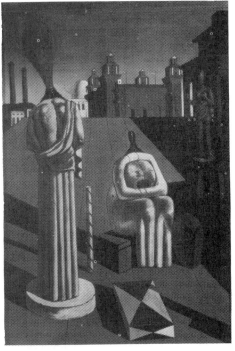

GEORGE CHINNERY – Portrait Of A Gentleman And His Wife – 18 x 14½in.
(Sotheby's) **$19,800 £13,200**

GIORGIO DE CHIRICO – Le Muse Inquietanti – signed – 31½ x 27½in.
(Sotheby's) **$95,700 £63,800**

GIORGIO DE CHIRICO – Due Cavalli
In Riva Al Mare – signed – 25¼ x 31¼in.
(Sotheby's)   **$89,320   £61,600**

GIORGIO DE CHIRICO – Dioscuri –
signed – gouache over pencil – 9½ x
13in.
(Sotheby's)   **$12,870   £8,580**

GIORGIO DE CHIRICO – Sera D'Estate
– signed – oil on canvas – 18 x 21¾in.
(Christie's)   **$44,452   £30,240**

GIORGIO DE CHIRICO – Cavallo In
Riva Al Mare, (circa 1973) – signed –
oil on canvas – 24 x 18cm.
(Christie's)   **$9,638   £6,557**

GIORGIO DE CHIRICO – Cavaliere A
Cavallo – signed, also signed on the
reverse – oil on canvas laid on board –
8¼ x 11½in.
(Christie's)   **$15,768   £10,800**

IWAN CHOULTSE – Sunset On The Peaks
– signed – 20¾ x 25¼in.
(Sotheby's)   **$2,145   £1,430**

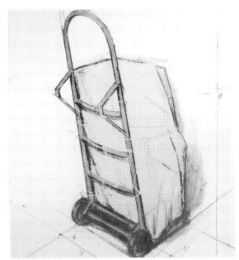

CHRISTO – Package On Handtruck (Project) – signed, inscribed and dated 1974 – mixed media on paper – 28¼ x 22½in.
(Christie's) **$6,155** **£4,104**

ALEXANDRE CINGRIA – La Villa Au Bord Du Lac – signed with monogram and dated 1912 – oil on board – 56 x 72.5cm.
(Germann Auktionshaus) **$1,795** **£1,197**

PIETER CLAESZ – Still Life With A Lobster – signed with monogram and dated 1641 – on panel – 25¼ x 34¾in.
(Sotheby's) **$173,250 £115,500**

GEORGE CLARE – Roses And Geraniums – signed and inscribed on label on the reverse – on canvas – 8¾ x 11¾in.
(Sotheby's) **$642** **£440**

OLIVER CLARE – A Still Life Of Fruit – signed and dated 1899 – on canvas – 17¾ x 13½in.
(Sotheby's) **$858** **£572**

OLIVER CLARE – Still Life With Grapes, Apples And Strawberries – signed and dated '89 – oil on canvas – 11 x 15in.
(Sotheby's) **$1,887** **£1,320**

ALBERT CLARK, SNR. – Mr Griffiths'
Grey 'Grenadier' – signed – 19½ x 23¼in.
(Sotheby's)   **$528**   **£352**

THOMAS CLARK – Portrait Of A Boy
– signed and dated 1767 – oil on canvas
– 29¼ x 24½in.
(Sotheby's)   **$9,570**   **£6,380**

ADOLPHE CLARY-BAROUX – Paris,
Le Pont De L'Estacade – signed – oil
on canvas – 23½ x 28½in.
(Sotheby's)   **$2,145**   **£1,430**

SIR GEORGE CLAUSEN – The Harvest
Moon – signed – oil on canvas – 13½ x
17¼in.
(Sotheby's)   **$2,489**   **£1,705**

SIR GEORGE CLAUSEN – A View
Across A Field – signed – watercolour –
8½ x 11¼in.
(Sotheby's)   **$495**   **£330**

SIR GEORGE CLAUSEN – Haystacks
On A Summers Day – signed – a
pastel sketch – 8¼ x 9¾in.
(Sotheby's)   **$353**   **£242**

ROBERT CLEMINSON – Gundogs –
signed – oil on canvas – 16 x 24in.
(Sotheby's)   **$1,058   £715 Pair**

ROBERT CLEMINSON – Watching; and
Resting – signed – oil on canvas – 36 x
28in.
(Sotheby's)   **$2,145   £1,430 Pair**

HENDRIK DE CLERCK, Circle of –
The Virgin And Child Surrounded By
Dancing Putti In A Wooded Landscape
With A Town Beyond – on panel – 20
x 28in.
(Christie's)   **$3,088   £2,160**

CORNELIS VAN CLEVE, Circle of –
The Virgin And Child By A Window –
oil on panel – 13¼ x 9½in.
(Sotheby's)   **$17,666   £12,100**

JOOS VAN CLEVE – Portrait Of A Gentleman Holding A Staff Of Office – on
panel – 20 x 14½in.
(Sotheby's)   **$39,600   £26,400**

EDWARD JOHN COBBETT – Fisher-girls – oil on canvas – 18 x 24in.
(Sotheby's)   **$1,754   £1,210**

FRANCOIS CLOUET, Studio of –
Charles IX, King Of France – on panel –
14¼ x 10in.
(Sotheby's)   **$16,500 £11,000**

EDWARD JOHN COBBETT – Little Red
Riding-Hood – signed – 24¼ x 20in.
(Christie's)   **$2,106   £1,404**

JEAN CLOUET, Follower of – Portrait
Of A Lady – on panel – 12 x 8½in.
(Sotheby's)   **$5,940   £3,960**

EDWARD JOHN COBBETT – Welsh
Peasants – signed and dated 1852 – 30
x 42in.
(Sotheby's)   **$6,102   £4,180**

EDWARD JOHN COBBETT – The Daisy
Chain – signed and dated 1868 – 25 x
30in.
(Sotheby's)   **$4,620   £3,080**

EDWARD JOHN COBBETT – Windsor
Forest – signed and dated 1846 – 34 x
44in.
(Sotheby's)   **$8,250   £5,500**

EDWIN COCKBURN – The New Toy –
signed and indistinctly dated, also
signed and dated 1865 on the reverse –
oil on canvas – 18 x 24in.
(Sotheby's)   **$2,145   £1,430**

EDWIN COCKBURN – One For The
Pot – signed and dated 1861 – oil on
panel – 16 x 24in.
(Sotheby's)   **$1,650   £1,100**

EDWIN COCKBURN – 'Our Grandchild'
– signed and dated 1848 on the reverse –
on canvas – 14 x 12in.
(Sotheby's)   **$363   £242**

**MAJOR GENERAL JAMES PATTISON
COCKBURN** – London From One Tree
Hill, Greenwich – watercolour – 13 x
20in.
(Sotheby's)   **$792   £528**

GEORGE COCKRAM – When The West With Crimson Glows – signed and inscribed on an old label to reverse – watercolour – 30 x 48in.
(Sotheby's) **$789** £550

ISAAC MICHAEL COHEN – Portrait Of A Young Boy – signed and dated '28 – oil on canvas – 61½ x 29½in.
(Sotheby's) **$707** £495

GEORGE COLE – Grazing Among The Bracken And Heather – signed and dated 1874 – 20 x 30in.
(Sotheby's) **$1,650** £1,100

GEORGE VICAT COLE – A Mountainous Lake Landscape – signed with monogram – on board – 16 x 24in.
(Christie's) **$405** £270

GEORGE VICAT COLE – Falling Leaves – signed with monogram and dated 1880 – oil on canvas – 49 x 35in.
(Sotheby's) **$2,392** £1,650

GEORGE VICAT COLE – A View Of Windsor Castle – signed with monogram and dated 1892 – 38¼ x 59¼in.
(Christie's) **$11,340** £7,560

J. W. COLE – Lightfoot, A Bay Hunter
And A Terrier In A Landscape – signed
– oil on canvas – 16½ x 20½in.
(Sotheby's)   **$1,485**   **£990**

REX VICAT COLE – Wren's Fleet Street
Gatehouse To The Middle Temple – sig-
ned – on board – 10½ x 13½in.
(Sotheby's)   **$660**   **£440**

WILLIAM STEPHEN COLEMAN –
Listening To The Sea – signed – oil
on canvas – 30 x 20in.
(Sotheby's)   **$1,132**   **£792**

FRANCESCO COLEMAN – 'The Dusky Queen' – signed and inscribed – watercolour
– 13¾ x 21in. *(Sotheby's)*   **$546** **£374**

EVERT COLLIER – A Vanitas Still Life –
signed and dated 1692 – on panel – 14¼
x 11½in.
(Sotheby's)   **$7,068   £4,620**

WILLIAM STEPHEN COLEMAN – The
Swing – signed – 21½ x 12½in.
(Sotheby's)   **$7,066   £4,840**

SAMUEL D. COLKETT – 'The Stone
Bridge', With Thatched Cottage, Figures
And Country Lane – oil on canvas –
oval 11 x 13in.
(Hilhams)   **$368   £230**

ARTHUR BEVAN COLLIER – View
Near Launceston – signed – oil on canvas
– 15 x 23½in.
*(Dreweatt Watson &
    Barton)*   **$823   £560**

JAMES COLLINSON – The Writing Lesson
– signed and dated 1855 – on panel – 21¼
x 17in.
(Christie's)   **$29,160 £19,440**

SEBASTIANO CONCA, Attributed to –
Samson And Delilah – 26 x 35½in.
(Sotheby's) **$4,207** **£2,750**

JOHN CONSTABLE – The Young Waltonians, Stratford Mill – full-scale sketch
– 51½ x 72½in.
(Sotheby's) **$363,000 £242,000**

NICHOLAS MATTHEW CONDY,
Follower of – An Estuary Scene With
Fishermen Bringing In Their Nets – oil
on panel – 5¼ x 7½in.
(Sotheby's) **$2,087** **£1,430**

WILLIAM CONOR – Woman And Child
With Donkey – signed – pastel – 13 x
17in.
(Sotheby's) **$1,485** **£990**

JOHN CONSTABLE – Girl In A White
Bonnet – board on panel – 12¾ x 6¼in.
(Sotheby's) **$16,500 £11,000**

JOHN CONSTABLE — The Grace Adorning Venus, After Niccolo dell'Abate — signed and dated 1805 on verso — pencil — 13 x 10¼in.
(Sotheby's)   **$990**   **£660**

CONTINENTAL SCHOOL, 17th century — Portrait Of Claudia Felizitas, Empress Of Austria, 1673-76 — oil on canvas — 43 x 31in.
(Dreweatt Watson & Barton)   **$1,264**   **£860**

GIUSEPPE CONSTANTINI — Italian Peasant Woman Sewing — signed and dated — oil on panel — 7 x 4.2in.
(Woolley & Wallis)   **$812**   **£560**

CONTINENTAL SCHOOL, 18th century — Three Figures On Horseback With Vendors Tempting The Travellers With Fish And Liquor — oil on canvas — 14 x 12in.
(Andrew Grant)   **$750**   **£500**

CONTINENTAL SCHOOL, Late 18th century – Cattle, Sheep And Peasant By A Tree – bears signature and date – oil on panel – 14½ x 20in.
(Dreweatt Watson & Barton) **$396** **£270**

HUBERT COOP – The Brimming River – signed – watercolour and bodycolour – 13¾ x 21in.
(Christie's) **$861** **£594**

EBENEZER WAKE COOKE – Sorrento, Italy – signed and inscribed on the reverse – watercolour – 21½ x 32in.
(Sotheby's) **$2,446** **£1,705**

ALFRED EGERTON COOPER – Lord John Torpichen – signed with initials, inscribed on the reverse – oil on canvas – 50 x 40in.
(Sotheby's) **$455** **£308**

EDWARD WILLIAM COOKE – On The Scheldt – signed and dated 1867 – 23¼ x 33½in.
(Christie's) **$17,820** **£11,880**

EDWIN COOPER, Follower of – The London-Cheltenham Coaches Passing On The High Road – 18¼ x 30in.
(Sotheby's) **$1,650** **£1,100**

GERALD A. COOPER – Vase On A Mantelpiece – signed and inscribed on labels on the reverse – on canvas board – 23½ x 19¾in.
(Sotheby's)   **$2,248   £1,540**

GERALD COOPER – Summer Flowers In A Vase – signed and dated '52 – oil on board – 23¾ x 20in.
(Christie's)   **$4,210   £2,808**

THOMAS SIDNEY COOPER – Sheep In A Landscape Resting At Riverside With Reed Beds And Farm In Distance – signed – watercolour – 12 x 18in.
(Morphets)   **$1,281   £890**

THOMAS SIDNEY COOPER – Cattle Watering At A Ford – signed and dated 1876 – 28 x 36in.
(Christie's)   **$2,105   £1,404**

THOMAS SIDNEY COOPER – Peaceful Moments, Cattle Resting In A Water Meadow, Sheep Beyond, The Scene Illuminated By Evening Sunlight – signed and dated 1873 – oil – 29 x 41½in.
(Neales)   **$6,000   £4,000**

THOMAS SIDNEY COOPER – In The Meadows, Cow And Two Sheep In Landscape – signed and dated 1890 – oil on board – 10 x 16¼in
(Dacre, Son &
Hartley) **$2,145 £1,500**

THOMAS SIDNEY COOPER – Four Cows In River Landscape – signed and dated 1882 – oil on panel – 10 x 14in.
(Dacre, Son &
Hartley) **$2,175 £1,450**

THOMAS SIDNEY COOPER – A Study Of Sheep – signed, inscribed and dated 1869 – on panel – 14½ x 10½in.
(Sotheby's) **$858 £572**

THOMAS SIDNEY COOPER – The End Of November – signature and date 1872 – 48 x 72½in.
(Christie's) **$7,992 £5,400**

WILLIAM SIDNEY COOPER – Fordwich, Kent – signed, dated 1886 and inscribed on the reverse – on canvas – 20 x 36in.
(Sotheby's) **$1,320 £880**

WILLIAM SIDNEY COOPER – Spring Blossoms – signed and dated 1919 – 27 x 20in.
(Christie's) **$1,287 £864**

WILLIAM SIDNEY COOPER – Cattle Watering From A River – signed and dated 1883 – watercolour – 16½ x 24in.
(Sotheby's) **$584** **£407**

CHARLES WEST COPE – Naval Pensioners At Greenwich – signed and dated 1846 – watercolour over pencil – 12¾ x 17½in.
(Sotheby's) **$561** **£374**

WILLIAM COPLEY – Portrait Of The Artist As A Young Expatriot – signed and dated '51 on the reverse – oil and mixed media on canvas – 20¾ x 28in.
(Sotheby's) **$4,450** **£3,300**

EDWARD HENRY CORBOULD – The Lesson – signed and dated 1862 – watercolour heightened with white – 15¾ x 12in.
(Christie's) **$548** **£378**

EDWARD HENRY CORBOULD – A Girl By A Gate – signed and dated 1850 – watercolour heightened with body-colour and gum arabic – 24¾ x 17¾in.
(Sotheby's) **$1,072** **£715**

EDWARD HENRY CORBOULD – After The Duel – signed and dated 1852 – watercolour heightened with white – 17 x 24¾in.
(Christie's) **$2,413 £1,620**

JOSE VILLEGAS Y CORDERO – The Siesta – signed and dated 1870 – 41¾ x 25¾in.
(Sotheby's) **$72,600 £48,400**

JOHN CORDREY – The Royal Mail Carriage And Eight In An Open Road – signed and dated 1812 – 21 x 35¾in.
(Sotheby's) **$7,260 £4,840**

LOVIS CORINTH – Zwei Weibliche Akte – signed and dated 1910 – oil on canvas – 90 x 75cm.
(Germann Auktionshaus) **$21,469 £14,705**

MICHEL CORNEILLE – Studies Of Heads, recto; and Figure And Composition Studies, verso – bears inscription – red and black chalk, recto; red and white chalk, verso – 272 x 446mm.
(Sotheby's) **$7,425 £4,950**

ANDRE CORTEZ – On The Way Home
– signed – oil on canvas – 9½ x 13in.
*(Robert W. Skinner
   Inc.)*   **$300   £200**

AGNOLO DI COSIMO, Called Il Bronzino
– Head Of A Saint – oil on panel – 22¼
x 19¼in.
(Sotheby's)   **$45,584   £30,800**

ANTONIO MARIA FABRES Y COSTA –
The Prisoner – signed and dated 894 –
35½ x 27¼in.
(Christie's)   **$40,500   £27,000**

JAN COSSIERS – Granida And Daifilo
– oil on canvas – 70 x 76in.
(Sotheby's)   **$11,396   £7,700**

F. COTES – The Death Of Sophonisba –
30 x 25in.
(Christie's)   **$615   £410**

COTES – Rebecca, Lady Powell, Wife Of Sir Alexander Powell – oil on canvas – oval 27½ x 22½in.
(Geering & Colyer)   **$1,875   £1,250**

HORATIO HENRY COULDERY – A Proud Mother – signed in monogram – 18 x 24in.
(Christie's)   **$4,183   £2,808**

HORATIO HENRY COULDERY – Study Of A Tabby Cat On A Red Cushion – signed – oil on canvas – 12½ x 18½in.
(Sotheby's)   **$1,136   £792**

JOHN SELL COTMAN – 'The Castle Of Gerville' – signed – pencil drawing – 12½ x 9in.
(Reeds Rains)   **$1,305   £900**

GUSTAVE COURBET – La Vague – signed – 13 x 18½in.
(Sotheby's)   **$23,100   £15,400**

VINCENT-JOSEPH-FRANCOIS COURDOUAN – Hauling In The Nets – signed and dated 1894 – oil on canvas – 19¼ x 29½in.
(Sotheby's) $1,766   £1,210

ROBERT McGOWN COVENTRY – The Bruges Fish Market – signed and inscribed on the reverse – watercolour over pencil, heightened with white – 14½ x 21in.
(Sotheby's) $976   £660

REINIER COVEYN, Circle of – A Lace-Maker With A Child Seated Beside Her – on panel – 18½ x 14¼in.
(Christie's) $1,467   £1,026

ROBERT McGOWAN COVENTRY – A Dutch Fishing Town With Peasants At The Quayside, Fishing Boats, And A Church – signed – 15 x 20½in. *(Christie's)*
$1,275   £850

MICHAEL VAN COXCIE – The Annunciation – on panel – 24 x 30in.
(Sotheby's)   **$9,570   £6,380**

MARMADUKE CRADDOCK – Study Of Peacock, Peahen And Fowl In Garden Scene – oil on canvas – 25 x 30in.
(Edgar Horn)   **$3,450   £2,300**

FRANCESCO COZZA – A Peasant Girl With A Carnation – oil on canvas – 24¾ x 19¾in.
(Sotheby's)   **$7,326   £4,950**

MARMADUKE CRADDOCK, Attributed to – An Intruder In The Duck Pond – oil on canvas – 18½ x 30¾in.
(Sotheby's)   **$1,320   £880**

FREDERICK SCHILLER COZZENS – Race Between The Bedoinn, Katrina And Emerald – signed and dated 1890 – watercolour and gouache on paper on board – 13½ x 21½in.
(Christie's)   **$4,400   £2,933**

MARMADUKE CRADDOCK, Circle of – Peacocks, Swans, Hens And Other Varieties Of Birds In A River Landscape – oil on canvas – 40 x 50in.
(Sotheby's)   **$5,445   £3,630**

CRADDOCK

MARMADUKE CRADDOCK – A Peacock, Turkey And Other Fowl In A Landscape – 21 x 55½in.
(Sotheby's) **$4,620 £3,080**

LAURENS CRAEN, Follower of – A Still Life Of A Basket Of Fruit And An Ornate Cup And Cover – bears signature and date – oil on canvas – 23 x 29½in.
(Sotheby's) **$4,558 £3,080**

LUCAS CRANACH, After – Portrait Of Frederick The Magnanimous – inscribed – on panel – 14½ x 11in.
(Sotheby's) **$2,692 £1,760**

WALTER CRANE – The Renaissance of Venus – signed and dated – ink on tracing paper laid down on paper – 13½ x 10¼in.
(Sotheby's) **$722 £495**

JOSEPH CRAWHALL – Study Of A Cock – signed – watercolour heightened with white on brown paper – 6¼ x 8½in.
(Christie's) **$4,070 £2,808**

JOSEPH CRAWHALL, JNR. – Donkeys – watercolour – 11 x 14¾in.
(Christie's & Edmiston's) **$1,350 £900**

WILLIAM CRAWHALL – Istanbul, The Dolmabahce Palace On The Bosphorus – signed and dated 1871 – oil on canvas – 35½ x 60in.
(Sotheby's)   **$9,900   £6,600**

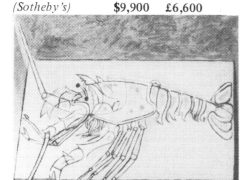

JOHN CRAXTON – Crayfish On A Table – signed and inscribed '58, inscribed on the backboard – oil and gouache on board – 20 x 23½in.
(Sotheby's)   **$660   £440**

PIERRE CREIXAMS – Le Joueur De La Flute – signed – oil on canvas – 92 x 73cm.
(Germann Auktionshaus)   **$4,723   £3,235**

LORENZO DI CREDI, Workshop of – The Madonna And Child – on panel – 25 x 19in.
(Christie's)   **$11,340   £7,560**

LUIGI CRESPI – Portrait Of A Lady Holding A Parasol – oil on canvas – 13¾ x 10¼in.
(Sotheby's)   **$1,221   £825**

THOMAS CRESWICK – Barnard Castle
– signed – oil on canvas – 21 x 28in.
(Sotheby's)   **$1,155   £770**

SANTA CROCE, Attributed to a member of the family – The Virgin And
Child With Saint Sebastian And Saint
James The Great – oil on panel – 14½
x 18½in.
(Sotheby's)   **$1,606   £1,100**

JOSHUA CRISTALL – The Bracken Girl
– signed and dated 1830 – watercolour
– 10¼ x 8¼in.
(Sotheby's)   **$1,567   £1,045**

CAPTAIN JAMES CROCKETT – West
View Of Clarmont House And Bungalow
With The Islamabad River Beyond,
Chittagong; and View Of George
Dowdswell's And Lieut. Bourkes House,
Chittagong – inscribed on the reverse –
watercolour and bodycolour – 15½ x
20¼in.
(Sotheby's)   **$1,485   £990 Two**

**VITTORE CRIVELLI, Circle of, Called
Crivellone** – Birds Mobbing An Owl –
oil on canvas – 14 x 17¼in.
(Sotheby's)   **$1,058   £715**

RAY CROOKE – 'Aborigine Figures,
North Queensland' – signed – oil on
board – 30 x 38cm.
*(Australian Art
     Auctions)*   **$650   £432**

ANTHONIE JANSZ. VAN DER CROOS
— An Extensive Landscape With A Distant
Town — oil on panel — 21¾ x 19in.
(Sotheby's) **$10,582 £7,150**

JAMES SHAW CROMPTON — An Arab
Wedding Procession Through Cairo —
signed — watercolour and bodycolour —
29½ x 22½in.
(Christie's) **$4,698 £3,240**

J. D. CROOME — Study Of Monkeys
— inscribed on a label on the reverse —
oil on board — 10¾ x 9in.
(Sotheby's) **$990 £660**

WILLIAM CROSBY — A Dell On The
Greta, Yorkshire — signed and dated
1864, and signed and inscribed on the
reverse — 17½ x 13½in.
(Christie's) **$1,367 £918**

WILLIAM CROSBY – Lost And Found
– signed and dated 1890 – 23 x 30in.
(Sotheby's)   **$1,980   £1,320**

THE REV. DR. WILLIAM CROTCH – A
Collection Of Drawings And Watercolours
Of London – majority signed with initials
and dated, and all inscribed on the reverse
– pencil, pen and grey ink and watercolour or black and coloured chalks, the
first two on blue paper – 5¼ x 9¼in. and
smaller, twenty-one in all.
(Christie's)   **$3,564   £2,376**

HENRI-EDMOND CROSS – La Terrasse
– 26¾ x 36¼in.
(Sotheby's)   **$95,700 £63,800**

WILLIAM CROUCH – Views In Calabria
– one signed with initials, dated 1884
and inscribed – watercolour – 14¼ x
20½in.
(Sotheby's)   **$905   £638 Pair**

HENRI-EDMOND CROSS – Mere
Jouant Avec Son Enfant – signed – oil
on canvas – 28¾ x 39½in.
(Sotheby's)   **$99,000   £66,000**

WILLIAM CROUCH – Rome, Capriccio
Views With The Temple Of Vesta, Ponte
Rotto, and Other Buildings – pencil and
watercolour – 15¾ x 23¼in.
(Christie's)   **$1,252   £864 Pair**

NICHOLAS JOSEPH CROWLEY – The
First Step – oil on canvas – 39½ x
49¼in.
(Sotheby's)   **$4,125   £2,750**

ROBERT CROZIER of Manchester –
Portrait Of Messrs, Goodyear, Chapman
And William Hunt, Gardeners To Sir
Benjamin Heywood, Bt., Claremont,
Manchester – signed and dated 1847 –
26 x 31in.
(Sotheby's)   **$6,600   £4,400**

ROBERT CROZIER – Mother And Child
– signed and dated 1868 – oil on canvas
– 25½ x 20in.
(Sotheby's)   **$1,036   £715**

C.T.R. – The Virgin And Child With An
Attendant Angel – signed in monogram
and dated 1577 – on panel – 19¼ x
13in.
(Christie's)   **$5,405   £3,780**

CUIT

GEORGE CUIT, SNR. – View Of The East End Of Lincoln Cathedral – gouache – 25½ x 37¼in.
(Sotheby's)   **$1,452**   **£968**

NORA LUCY MOWBRAY CUNDELL – L'Ennui – signed and dated '22 – oil on panel – 16 x 14in.
(Christie's)   **$972**   **£648**

JANET AGNES CUMBRAE-STEWART – Seated Nude – signed and dated '19 – pastel – 21¾ x 15¾in.
(Sotheby's)   **$3,036**   **£2,200**

CHARLES CUNDALL – The Bear Pit – signed and dated 1926 – on panel – 15 x 17in.
(Sotheby's)   **$1,072**   **£715**

NORA LUCY MOWBRAY CUNDELL – The Old Navajo – inscribed – oil on canvas – 29¾ x 23¾in.
(Sotheby's)   **$792**   **£528**

JAMES CURNOCK – Two Ballet Dancers – signed and dated 1845 – watercolour over pencil heightened with touches of bodycolour with stopping out – 27 x 22½in.
(Sotheby's) **$1,815 £1,210**

CECIL E. L. CUTLER – The Royal Diamond Jubilee Procession, Tuesday 22nd June 1897 – signed, inscribed and dated – watercolour and bodycolour – 13½ x 19¾in.
(Christie's) **$375 £259**

J. G. CUYP, After – A Shepherdess With Doves – oil.
(Andrew Grant) **$1,800 £1,200**

H. CUSTODIS – Portrait Of Lady Bennet, Standing Three-Quarter Length – inscribed – on panel – 38¾ x 29¾in.
(Christie's) **$3,888 £2,592**

JACOB GERRITSZ. CUYP – Portrait Of Three Children With A Lion, A Leopard And A Goat – 45 x 49½in.
(Sotheby's) **$6,600 £4,400**

LEON DABO – Quiet Sailboats On
The Water – signed – oil on canvas –
21 x 14½in.
(Robert W. Skinner
Inc.)   **$700   £465**

RICHARD DADD – A Castle On A
Cliff Overlooking A Lake – watercolour
– 14½ x 19½in.
(Sotheby's)   **$18,150   £12,100**

**COUNT HENRI DE MONTPEZAT
D'AINECY** – A Spring Outing – signed
– 27 x 38¾in.
(Sotheby's)   **$16,500   £11,000**

RICHARD DADD – Bacchanalian Scene
– inscribed, dated 1862 on the reverse –
on panel – 14 x 9½in.
(Sotheby's)   **$132,000 £88,000**

JOHN DALBY – Mares And Foals In A
Landscape – signed and dated 1850 –
10 x 12in.
(Christie's)   **$8,910   £5,940**

SALVADOR DALI — Le Mannequin —
signed and dated 1939 — brush and ink
and gouache on pink paper — 13 x 10¼in.
(Sotheby's)   **$20,735 £14,300**

HERBERT DALZIEL — Withered And
Strewn — signed and dated 1879,
inscribed on the reverse — oil on canvas
— 40 x 50in.
(Sotheby's)   **$957   £660**

PIETRO DANDINI — Bacchus And
Ariadne — on copper — 12 x 14½in.
(Sotheby's)   **$3,372   £2,310**

SALVADOR DALI — A Fable Is Only A
Fable But A Pretty Leg Is A Bite — signed
and dated 1947 — pen and indian ink and
watercolour — 13 x 9¾in.
(Sotheby's)   **$36,300 £24,200**

**BARTHOLOMEW DANDRIDGE, Circle
of** — Portrait Of John, 2nd Viscount
Dudley And Ward, As A Child — 49 x
39in.
(Sotheby's)   **$2,475   £1,650**

147

WILLIAM DANIELL – A View Of Plymouth Showing The Royal William Victualling Yard – 14½ x 24¼in.
(Sotheby's)   **$8,580   £5,720**

FELIX OCTAVIUS CARR DARLEY – 'Sailors Bound For Sea' – signed – sepia and ink wash – 14½ x 10½in.
(Robert W. Skinner Inc.)   **$650   £433**

HONORE DAUMIER – Le Fardeau – oil on panel – 18¼ x 14¾in.
(Christie's)   **$47,628   £32,400**

ALLAN DAVIDSON – A Lady Warrior – signed – oil on board – 25 x 11in.
(Sotheby's)   **$1,237   £825**

ALLAN D. DAVIDSON – An Old Salt – signed – oil on board – 20½ x 17in.
(Butterfield's)   **$200   £118**

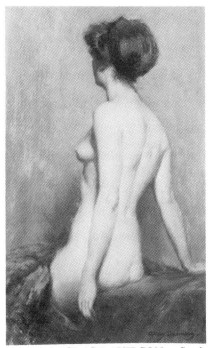

ALLAN DOUGLAS DAVIDSON – Study Of A Nude Girl – signed – on board – 12 x 7½in.
(Sotheby's) **$1,188** **£792**

NORMAN PRESCOTT DAVIES – Simon And Dorothea, The Children Of William Richmond Newburn – signed and dated 1886 – oil on canvas – 44 x 34in.
(Sotheby's) **$3,190** **£2,200**

HARRY DAVIES – Sunset Landscape With Shepherd By Gate With His Flock Of Sheep – watercolour – 14½ x 10½in.
(Andrew Grant) **$675** **£450**

ARTHUR A. DAVIS – The Kill – signed and dated 1905 – watercolour – 14¼ x 21½in.
(Sotheby's) **$417** **£286**

H. B. DAVIS – An Angler Fishing From A River, With A Woman Feeding Poultry In The Garden Of A Cottage On The Further Bank – signed and dated 1903 – 19¾ x 29½in.
(Anderson & Garland) **$100** **£60**

HENRY T. DAVIS – Robert The
Devil, Tom Cannon Up – signed,
inscribed and dated 1880 – oil on
canvas – 28 x 36in.
(Sotheby's)   **$1,101**   **£770**

J. PAIN DAVIS – Moth Robbing The
Squirrel's Nest, Peas-Blossom Alarmed –
56 x 43½in.
(Sotheby's)   **$1,650**   **£1,100**

LUCIEN DAVIS – At The Rose Garden
Gate – signed – watercolour heightened
with bodycolour – 13½ x 8½in.
(Sotheby's)   **$1,567**   **£1,045**

JOHN SCARLETT DAVIS – The Library At Tottenham, The Seat Of B. G.
Windus, Esq – signed and dated 1835, also inscribed – watercolour with
stopping out, heightened with gum arabic – 11½ x 22in.
(Sotheby's)   **$46,200 £30,800**

WILLIAM HENRY DAVIS – A White
Shorthorn Heifer In A Landscape – 19¼
x 23¼in.
(Sotheby's)   **$1,445   £990**

NORA DAVISON – View Outside The
Theatre Royal, Drury Lane – signed –
13½ x 11½in.
(Lawrence)   **$517   £352**

WILLIAM HENRY DAVIS – Study Of A
Spaniel – signed and dated 1839 – oil on
paper – 8 x 21in.
(Sotheby's)   **$462   £308**

**WILLIAM HENRY DAVIS, Attributed
to** – A Prize Short Horn Bull In A Landscape – 15½ x 21¼in.
(Sotheby's)   **$330   £220**

NORA DAVISON – View At The Corner
Of King's Bench Walk, London – signed
– 12 x 9in.
(Lawrence)   **$242   £165**

HEINRICH MARIA DAVRINGHAUSEN
– Portrat, Mann Im Frack – signed – oil
on canvas – 26 x 26in.
(Christie's)   **$7,095**   **£4,860**

HENRY DAWSON, Attributed to –
A Busy Harbour – oil on canvas – 18 x
24in.
(Sotheby's)   **$707**   **£495**

HENRY THOMAS DAWSON –
Rotterdam, Old Haven – signed, dated
1878 and inscribed on a label on the
reverse – on canvas – 10 x 14in.
(Sotheby's)   **$792**   **£528**

MONTAGUE DAWSON – The Melbourne
Trader, 'The Antelope', 1443 tons, built
1866 – signed – oil – 24 x 36in.
(Woolley &
Wallis)   **$24,650**   **£17,000**

MONTAGUE DAWSON – H.M.S. Victory
Sweeping The Seas – signed – oil on
canvas – 28 x 32½in.
(Christie's)   **$24,300**   **£16,200**

MONTAGUE DAWSON – Taking It
Green – signed – watercolour heightened
with bodycolour – 16¼ x 26¼in.
(Sotheby's)   **$2,475**   **£1,650**

MONTAGUE DAWSON – A Sailing
Barge – signed – watercolour height-
ened with bodycolour – 16¼ x 26¼in.
(Sotheby's)   **$3,300**   **£2,200**

EDWARD DAYES − A Skating Scene With Numerous Figures In The Foreground −
29 x 42in.
(Sotheby's) $12,375 £8,250

EDWARD DAYES − St Peter's Church,
Conisbrough, Yorkshire − watercolour
over pencil − 7¼ x 9¼in.
(Sotheby's) $1,419 £946

PERCY DEACON − Haymakers Above
The Sea − signed − 24 x 42in.
(Sotheby's) $3,960 £2,640

PETER DEAN − Star Gazers − oil on
canvas − 60 x 50in.
(Christie's) $7,884 £5,400

DEAN

SAMUEL DEAN – Farmyard Ricks –
signed and dated 1916 – oil on canvas
– 34 x 48in.
(Sotheby's) **$865 £605**

ALEXANDRE DEFAUX – Poirier En
Fleurs – signed and inscribed on label to
reverse – oil on board – 16 x 12¾in.
(Sotheby's) **$1,499 £1,045**

CORNELIS DECKER, Style of –
Figures On A Roadway Near A Windmill
– on panel – 13 x 16in.
(Sotheby's) **$1,980 £1,320**

JOSEPH DECKER – Greenings –
signed – oil on canvas – 9 x 11in.
(Christie's) **$220,000 £152,777**

FRANZ VON DEFREGGER – A Tyrolean Peasant – signed and dated '98 –
19½ x 14½in.
(Christie's) **$31,968 £21,600**

EDGAR DEGAS – Femme Nue Couchee
– stamped with signature – charcoal
heightened with white pastel – 20½ x
20½in.
(Sotheby's) **$24,750 £16,500**

ALFRED DEHODENCQ – Les Prisonniers
Marocains – signed – 97 x 64½in.
(Sotheby's) **$42,900 £28,600**

EDGAR DEGAS – Deux Danseuses –
21½ x 15¾in.
(Sotheby's) **$319,000 £220,000**

ADELCHI DEGROSSI – In The Tavern
– signed and inscribed – on panel – 12
x 9in.
*(Sotheby Beresford
Adams)* **$739 £440**

**ALEXANDER ALEXANDROVITCH
DEINEKA** – The Song – signed – oil
on canvas – 39¼ x 39¼in.
(Christie's) **$2,838 £1,944**

EUGENE DELACROIX – Le Christ Sur
Le Lac De Genezareth – 17½ x 21in.
(Sotheby's) **$156,750 £104,500**

PAUL DELVAUX – Nu Couche – signed
and inscribed – pen and indian ink and
wash – 13¼ x 10¼in.
(Sotheby's) **$4,950 £3,300**

JULIUS DELBOS – Harbour View –
signed, also signed and inscribed on the
reverse – oil on canvas – 40 x 50in.
(Christie's) **$2,090 £1,514**

HIPPOLYTE CAMILLE DELPY – River
Landscape With Boats – signed – oil on
panel – 21 x 12in.
*(Dacre, Son &
Hartley)* **$2,700 £1,800**

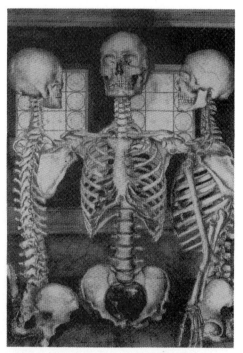

PAUL DELVAUX – Les Squelettes –
signed and inscribed 1942 – brush and
pen and ink and watercolour – 39 x
27¼in.
(Sotheby's) **$17,545 £12,100**

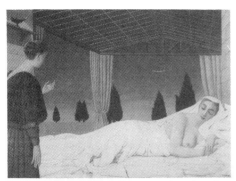

PAUL DELVAUX – Songe – signed and dated 12-52 – on panel – 43¼ x 59in.
(Sotheby's) **$75,900 £50,600**

PAUL DELVAUX – Deux Dryades – signed and dated 9-66 – watercolour, pen and ink on paper – 23½ x 18¾in.
(Christie's) **$48,880 £33,480**

PAUL DELVAUX – Trois Filles De Cirque – signed and dated '34 – watercolour and indian ink – 23 x 29in.
(Sotheby's) **$13,200 £8,800**

PAUL DELVAUX – Femme Nue Assise – signed and dated '33 – pencil on paper – 12½ x 9½in.
(Christie's) **$2,365 £1,620**

JEAN DELVILLE – La Meduse – signed and dated 1893 – pen and ink, blue crayon, pastel, watercolour and gold paint – 5¾ x 14in.
(Sotheby's) **$31,350 £20,900**

MAURICE DENIS – L'Autoportrait De L'Artiste Avec Sa Famille – signed and dated 1923 – oil on canvas – 39¼ x 48½in.
(Christie's) **$6,307 £4,320**

ANDRE DERAIN – Paysage De Provence – signed – oil on canvas – 23¼ x 28¼in.
(Sotheby's) **$29,700 £19,800**

ANDRE DERAIN – Le Pecheur –
watercolour – 6 x 5in.
(Sotheby's)   **$858**   **£572**

CLAUDE DERUET, Attributed to –
Portrait Of A Child Said To Be Louis XIV
– 41¾ x 26¾in.
(Sotheby's)   **$1,402**   **£935**

ANDRE DERAIN – Nu Assis – signed
– oil on canvas – 15¼ x 10½in.
(Christie's)   **$5,518**   **£3,780**

GEORGES D'ESPAGNAT – Fille Avec
Chien – signed – oil on canvas – 51½ x
38½in.
(Christie's)   **$1,261**   **£864**

GEORGES D'ESPAGNAT – Portrait D'Une Femme – signed with initials – 23½ x 19in.
(Sotheby's) **$825** **£550**

LOUIS PAUL DESSAR – 'The Wood-chopper' – signed and dated 1906 – oil on canvas – 28 x 36in.
(Robert W. Skinner Inc.) **$1,800** **£1,200**

THOMAS DESSOULAVY – An Extensive River Landscape In Italy – signed and dated 1853 – oil on canvas – 31¼ x 46½in.
(Sotheby's) **$3,960** **£2,640**

THOMAS DESSOULAVY – The Roman Campagna – signed and dated 1841 – 20½ x 28in.
(Sotheby's) **$1,650** **£1,100**

JEAN-BAPTISTE-EDOUARD DETAILLE – Planning Manoeuvres – signed and dated 1876 – watercolour – 13 x 10in.
(Sotheby's) **$995** **£682**

EDWARD JULES DETMOLD – Chickens – signed and dated '19 – watercolour – 23¼ x 20¼in.
(Sotheby's) **$5,280** **£3,520**

LUDWIG DEUTSCH – The Harem
Guard – signed – on panel – 31¼ x
23¼in.
(Christie's)   **$135,864 £91,800**

A. DEVIS – Portrait Of A Gentleman,
In A Dark Coat And White Waistcoat In
A Landscape – 26½ x 19¼in.
(Christie's)   **$1,134**   **£756**

LUDWIG DEUTSCH – A Standing Arab
– signed and dated 1909 – oil on canvas
– 28¼ x 20½in.
(Sotheby's)   **$5,104   £3,520**

ANTHONY DEVIS – Rent Day; A
Family Resting; Raking; and A Rustic
Family – pencil, pen and grey ink and
watercolour – 5¼ x 8in. and smaller.
(Christie's)   **$453   £302** Four

ARTHUR DEVIS – Portrait Of Wrightson
Mundy Of Markeaton, Derbyshire In A
Landscape – signed and dated 1748 –
29½ x 24½in.
(Christie's) **$13,770** **£9,180**

ARTHUR DEVIS – A Conversation Piece
With Figures Gathered Around A Harpsi-
chord In An Interior – 49¼ x 39in.
(Sotheby's) **$24,750** **£16,500**

A. W. DEVIS – Arabs Playing Chess –
13 x 17in.
(Christie's) **$2,106** **£1,404**

ARTHUR DEVIS – Portrait Of A Lady
Of The Lister Family, In A Blue And
White Satin Dress – 19 x 13½in.
(Christie's) **$3,078** **£2,052**

MELCHIOR D'HONDECOETER,
Follower of – Goats And Fowl In A Land-
scape – 58½ x 79in.
(Sotheby's) **$11,880** **£7,920**

THOMAS COLMAN DIBDIN – Abbeville – signed – watercolour heightened with bodycolour – 30½ x 21½in.
(Sotheby's) **$660** **£440**

THOMAS COLMAN DIBDIN – Amiens Cathedral, Northern France – signed, inscribed and dated 1876 – watercolour over pencil heightened with bodycolour – 30 x 21in.
(Sotheby's) **$781** **£550**

THOMAS COLMAN DIBDIN – A Street Scene In Rouen – signed and dated 1865 – watercolour heightened in white – 10 x 15in.
(Dreweatt Watson & Barton) **$514** **£350**

SIR FRANK DICKSEE – Sylvia – on panel – 12 x 9in.
(Sotheby's) **$14,850** **£9,900**

SIR FRANK DICKSEE – A Mother Reading To Her Children By A Window – watercolour and bodycolour – 10½ x 13¾in.
(Christie's) **$861** **£594**

JOHN ROBERT DICKSEE – Returning
From Church – signed with monogram,
signed and inscribed on the reverse –
oil on canvas – 14 x 12in.
(Sotheby's) **$1,815 £1,210**

FRANK DILLON, Circle of – Temple
Ruins, Karnak – oil on canvas – 35½ x
27½in.
(Sotheby's) **$1,214 £880**

THOMAS FRANCIS DICKSEE –
'Cordelia' – inscribed on the reverse –
oil – 19¼ x 15¼in.
*(Anderson &
Garland)* **$3,000 £2,000**

G. DINET – The Orange Seller – signed
and dated 1900 – oil on canvas – 39¼
x 29¼in.
(Sotheby's) **$2,552 £1,760**

CHARLES DIXON – Shipping At Greenwich – signed – watercolour – 14¾ x 23in.
(Sotheby's)   **$2,970   £1,980**

OTTO DIX – Selbstbildnis Mit Modell – signed and dated 1923, also signed and dated on the reverse – 41¼ x 35½in.
(Sotheby's)   **$330,000 £220,000**

GASPARE DIZIANI – The Arming Of Erminia – 31½ x 49½in.
(Sotheby's)   **$26,400   £17,600**

OTTO DIX – Ritratto Di Martens, 1921 – signed and dated – 40 x 34cm.
(Christie's)   **$3,012   £2,049**

CHARLES EDWARD DIXON – The Pool Of London – signed and dated '17 – watercolour with bodycolour over pencil – 22 x 44in.
(Sotheby's)   **$2,890   £1,980**

WILLIAM CHARLES THOMAS DOBSON – Little Red Riding Hood – signed with monogram – on panel – 12 x 10in.
(Sotheby's)   **$825   £550**

WILLIAM CHARLES THOMAS DOBSON – Meditation – signed with monogram and dated 1873 – watercolour – 20 x 16in.
(Lawrence) $726   £484

ANTON DOLL – Winter Landscape With Figures Sledging – signed – oil – 23 x 34.5in.
(Woolley & Wallis) $10,440   £7,200

WILLIAM CHARLES THOMAS DOBSON – Meditation – signed with monogram and dated 1873 – watercolour – 21 x 16¾in.
(Christie's) $1,722   £1,188

CARLO DOLCI – Ecce Homo – 19¼ x 15in.
(Christie's) $1,853   £1,296

WILLIAM ANSTEY DOLLOND – Fresh From The Garden – signed – watercolour – 17¼ x 8in.
(Sotheby's) $1,023   £682

JOHN CHARLES DOLLMAN – Gold – signed and dated 1894 – oil on canvas –
42 x 69in. *(Sotheby's)*   **$15,675   £10,450**

CHRISTIAN DOMMERSEN – The Bay
Of Naples – signed and dated 1877 –
on canvas – 19½ x 33½in.
(Sotheby's)   **$2,087   £1,430**

W. R. DOMMERSEN – On The Zuyder
Zee, Holland – signed and dated 1889,
and indistinctly inscribed on reverse – oil
on canvas – 10½ x 14½in.
(Sotheby's)   **$1,420   £990**

KEES VAN DONGEN – Les Peripateti-
ciennes – inscribed – oil on canvas –
51½ x 32in.
(Christie's)   **$174,636 £118,800**

KEES VAN DONGEN – Portrait De Marie Van Dongen – signed – charcoal and pastel – 24¼ x 20½in.
(Sotheby's)   **$27,115   £18,700**

KEES VAN DONGEN – Fatma – signed – oil on canvas – 25½ x 18¼in.
(Sotheby's)   **$103,950   £69,300**

KEES VAN DONGEN – Le Restaurant De La Paix – signed – oil on canvas – 19¾ x 28¾in.
(Christie's)   **$193,687 £131,760**

KEES VAN DONGEN – La Promenade Du Chien Sous La Pluie – signed – 18¼ x 15in.
(Sotheby's)   **$27,302   £18,700**

KEES VAN DONGEN – La Soiree – signed – watercolour and brush and ink – 16¾ x 22½in.
(Sotheby's)   **$24,722   £17,050**

J. W. DONNE – A Man O' War Off
Plymouth – signed and dated 1838 –
watercolour over pencil – 10½ x 14¼in.
(Sotheby's)   **$593**   **£418**

LAMBERT DOOMER – The Expulsion
Of The Prodigal Son From The Brothel –
signed and dated 1695 – 25¼ x 32in.
(Sotheby's)   **$9,570**   **£6,380**

JEAN M. DOTT – Interrupted Reading,
Portrait Of Peter McOmish Dott – signed and dated 1916, also inscribed on
a label – 26 x 32in.
(Sotheby's)   **$528**   **£352**

GERARD DOU – An Astronomer By
Candlelight – signed – on panel – 12½
x 8¼in.
(Sotheby's)   **$1,815,000 £1,210,000**

GERARD DOU, After – The Violin
Player – oil on panel – 13½ x 10½in.
(Sotheby's)   **$5,209**   **£3,520**

PARKE-CUSTIN DOUGHERTY – 'L'Entree Du Village' – signed – oil on canvas – 35 x 44½in. *(Robert W. Skinner Inc.)* **$5,700 £3,800**

ARTHUR GARFIELD DOVE – Swans – signed – watercolour and pen and ink on paper on board – 4¾ x 6½in. *(Christie's)* **$4,620 £3,080**

EDWIN ALGERNON STEWART DOUGLAS – At High Pressure – signed and dated 1893 – inscribed on the reverse – oil on panel – 7 x 12in. *(Sotheby's)* **$3,630 £2,420**

PATRICK DOWNIE – Gathering Wrack – signed – oil on canvas – 30 x 50in. *(Sotheby's)* **$2,116 £1,430**

DOUW, After, 19th century Continental School – The Dentist – oil on canvas – 13½ x 11in. *(W. H. Lane & Son)* **$730 £500**

NATHAN DRAKE, Attributed to – A Gentleman On His Horse With A Hound Passing A Rustic In A Landscape – 23½ x 19½in. *(Sotheby's)* **$1,237 £825**

DREUX

ALFRED DE DREUX – The Young
Horseman – signed – 21½ x 17½in.
(Christie's)   **$31,968 £21,600**

AMY JULIA DRUCKER – A Street
Market In Marchmont Street, E.1., At
Night – signed – oil on canvas – 24 x
28in.
(Sotheby's)   **$963   £660**

JAMES DRUMMOND – Returning From
The Fields – signed – oil on canvas –
29 x 24¼in.
(Sotheby's)   **$1,846   £1,265**

ARTHUR DRUMMOND – Making Attar
Of Roses In Ancient Greece – signed and
dated 1894 – 36 x 26in.
(Sotheby's)   **$4,950   £3,300**

MALCOLM DRUMMOND – The Princess
Of Wales Pub, Trafalgar Square, Mrs
Francis Behind The Bar – oil on canvas –
26 x 17in.
(Christie's)   **$2,557   £1,728**

SIR RUSSELL DRYSDALE – 'Pearl Fisherman At Broome' – signed – oil on canvas – 76 x 127cm.
(Australian Art Auctions) **$56,781 £37,854**

ADOLPHE HENRI DUBASTY – A Gypsy Girl Holding A Tambourine – signed and dated 1868 – oil on board – 15¾ x 12¼in.
(Geering & Colyer) **$660 £440**

ALBERT DUBOIS-PILLET – Falaises a Yport – signed – oil on canvas – 10¼ x 16½in.
(Christie's) **$19,440 £12,960**

GUY PENE DUBOIS – Adolph Lewisohn's Party – signed, dated '30 and inscribed, also signed and inscribed on the reverse – watercolour and pen and black ink on paper – 15¾ x 12¼in.
(Christie's) **$6,160 £4,105**

JEAN DUBUFFET – Corps De Dame Peau De Lapin – signed and dated '50 – oil on panel – 31¾ x 25½in.
(Sotheby's) **$239,250 £159,500**

171

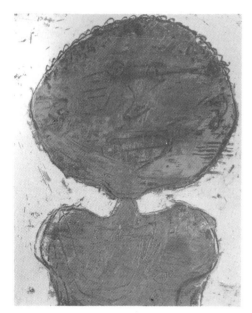

RAOUL DUFY – La Plage Aux Naiades
– signed – watercolour – 19 x 24¾in.
(Sotheby's)   **$25,575 £17,050**

JEAN DUBUFFET – Mademoiselle Mine
Orange – signed and dated 1950 – oil
on board – 28¾ x 23½in.
(Sotheby's)   **$89,100 £59,400**

CHARLES DUFRESNE – La Famille Ou
Le Bebe En Maillot – signed – 40¾ x
40¾in.
(Sotheby's)   **$7,920 £5,280**

RAOUL DUFY – Cannes – signed and
dated 1940 – watercolour – 19¾ x 25¾in.
(Sotheby's)   **$40,672 £28,050**

RAOUL DUFY – Batiment Decore De
Pilastre Entre Quatre Palmiers – signed
– watercolour – 19¼ x 25in.
(Sotheby's)   **$28,050 £18,700**

RAOUL DUFY – Arlequin A La Lyre –
signed – watercolour and gouache –
25¾ x 19½in.
(Sotheby's)   **$28,875 £19,250**

RAOUL DUFY – Les Moissons a Langres
– signed – gouache and watercolour on
paper – 19 x 25½in.
(Christie's)   **$24,300 £16,200**

RAOUL DUFY – Vue de Langres –
signed and dated 1934 – oil on canvas –
18¼ x 22in.
(Christie's)   **$42,120   £28,080**

**HIPPOLYTE-FRANCOIS-LEON
DULARD** – Cavalier – signed – oil on
panel – 16 x 13in.
*(Robert W. Skinner
    Inc.)*   **$325   £216**

GASPAR DUGHET, Follower of –
Figures In A Landscape By A Monastery
– gouache – 238 x 308mm.
(Sotheby's)   **$247   £165**

PIETER JACOBSZ. DUIFHUIZEN,
Called Colinckhovius – An Interior With
A Peasant Family – on panel – 14 x
19½in.
(Sotheby's)   **$5,940   £3,960**

DUMONSTIERS, Studio of the – Portrait
Of A Lady – on panel – 10½ x 8in.
(Sotheby's)   **$1,093   £715**

DUMONSTIERS

DUMONSTIERS, Studio of the — Portrait Of A Child — oil on canvas — 24 x 19in.
(Sotheby's) $2,930   £1,980

LAWRENCE DUNCAN — The Young Shipwright — inscribed on the reverse — watercolour heightened with white — 17½ x 15in.
(Christie's) $704   £486

LAWRENCE DUNCAN — The Pedlar — signed with a monogram and dated 1861 — 19¼ x 15in.
(Lawrence) $727   £495

HENRY TREFFREY DUNN, After Rossetti — The Loving Cup — 17½ x 12in.
(Christie's) $1,053   £702

JOSEPH DUNN OF WORCESTER –
Pointers Putting Up A Pheasant In Woodland – signed – oil on canvas – 13¼ x
17¼in.
(Sotheby's)   **$1,485**   **£990**

GEORGE HENRY DURRIE – Jones
Inn – signed with initials and inscribed
– oil on canvas – 21¾ x 30¼in.
(Christie's)   **$77,000   £53,472**

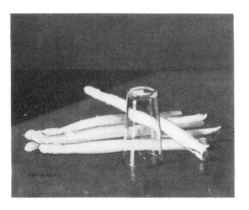

RAPHAEL DURANCAMPS – Bodegon
Con Esparragos – signed – oil on canvas
– 14½ x 17½in.
(Sotheby's)   **$1,237**   **£825**

DUTCH SCHOOL, Late 17th century –
Winter Landscape With Figures Skating
On A River – signed with initials – oil
on panel – 12½ x 14½in.
(Dreweatt Watson &
Barton)   **$2,058   £1,400**

GODEFROY DURAND – Lambeth
Market – signed and dated 1873 – pencil
and watercolour heightened with white –
12¼ x 19½in.
(Christie's)   **$1,174**   **£810**

DUTCH SCHOOL, 17th Century – A
Village Fair In Summer With Musicians,
Dancers And Players – oil on canvas –
38 x 62in.
(Andrew Grant)   **$6,000   £4,000**

DUTCH SCHOOL

DUTCH SCHOOL, circa 1720 – An Interior Of A Picture Dealer's Shop – on panel – 16 x 24½in.
(Sotheby's)   **$2,356**   **£1,540**

DUTCH SCHOOL, 17th century – Peasants Drinking In An Interior – oil on panel – 14½ x 12in.
(Sotheby's)   **$674**   **£462**

JOHN DUVALL – Cup Bearer III, A Chestnut Horse In A Stable – signed – oil on canvas – 16½ x 21½in.
(Sotheby's)   **$627**   **£418**

DUTCH SCHOOL, circa 1610 – Portrait Of A Child, Small Full Length Standing By A Table In A Pink And White Embroidered Dress – on copper – 5½ x 4¼in.
(Christie's)   **$2,106**   **£1,404**

CORNELIS DUYSTER, Circle of – An Interior With A Card Party – oil on panel – 8 x 8½in.
(Sotheby's)   **$10,093**   **£6,820**

PHILIPS VAN DYCK – An Elegant
Couple – oil on canvas – 15¾ x 12¾in.
(Sotheby's) **$6,424 £4,400**

MARCEL DYF – Voilier Au Vent –
signed – oil on canvas – 23¼ x 28½in.
(Christie's) **$1,620 £1,080**

MARCEL DYF – La Baie – signed – oil
on canvas – 21 x 25½in.
(Christie's) **$1,540 £1,026**

H. ANTHONY DYER – The Open Door
– signed – watercolour and gouache –
30 x 22in.
(Robert W. Skinner
Inc.) **$1,100 £735**

MARCEL DYF – La Gitane – signed –
oil on canvas – 29 x 24in.
(Sotheby's) **$2,073 £1,430**

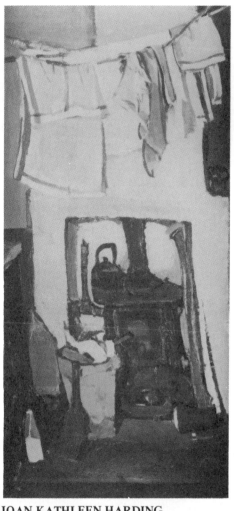

THOMAS COWPERTHWAIT EAKINS –
Portrait Of Frank Macdowell – oil on
canvas – 24 x 20¼in.
(Christie's)   **$88,000   £61,111**

**JOAN KATHLEEN HARDING
EARDLEY** – Autumn Landscape –
inscribed on the reverse – on board
– 25½ x 20½in.
(Sotheby's)   **$1,237   £825**

**JOAN KATHLEEN HARDING
EARDLEY** – The Stove – signed –
oil – 35 x 16in.
(Sotheby's)   **$4,950   £3,300**

**JOAN KATHLEEN HARDING
EARDLEY** – Sleeping Boy In Blue
– inscribed – coloured chalks, 10
x 11½in.
(Sotheby's)   **$990   £660**

MAUD EARL – Mother's Dog, Tommy
– signed and dated '99 – oil on canvas –
18 x 24in.
(Sotheby's)   **$1,595   £1,100**

HENRY EARP, SNR. – Cattle In A Field
With A Castle Beyond – signed – oil on
panel – 11¾ x 9½in.
(Sotheby's) **$710** **£495**

HENRY EDRIDGE – Portrait Of Miss
Morice The Younger As A Child – signed
and dated 1797 – pencil and brown wash
– 8½ x 6in.
(Christie's) **$1,944** **£1,296**

SIR ALFRED EAST – Village On The
Great Canton High Road Between Kioto
And Yeddo – signed, inscribed on the
reverse – oil on panel – 9 x 6in.
(Sotheby's) **$1,894** **£1,320**

HENRY EDRIDGE – A Naval Officer By
A Breakwater Holding A Telescope –
pencil and watercolour heightened with
white – 16¼ x 11in.
(Christie's) **$1,134** **£756**

EDWARDS

LIONEL EDWARDS – Golden Miller And Insurance – signed and dated 1950 – 29½ x 39½in.
(Sotheby's) **$7,590 £5,060**

LIONEL EDWARDS – The Hunt – signed and dated '07 – grisaille watercolour over pencil, heightened with bodycolour – 14 x 20½in.
(Sotheby's) **$1,287 £858**

LIONEL DALHOUSIE ROBERTSON EDWARDS – Salmon Fishing On The Spey – signed with monogram – watercolour – 4¾ x 9½in.
(Sotheby's) **$835 £572**

LIONEL DALHOUSIE ROBERTSON EDWARDS – 'In At The Kill' – signed and dated 1904 – watercolour – 14 x 20¾in.
(Sotheby's) **$1,650 £1,100**

JOHN WILLIAM EDY – A View Across The Thames With Westminster Abbey In The Distance – signed and indistinctly dated – watercolour – 10½ x 17¾in.
(Sotheby's) **$770 £528**

GERBRANDT VAN DEN EECKHOUT – Soldiers In A Guardroom – signed and dated 1662 – 21½ x 17in.
(Sotheby's) **$44,550 £29,700**

GEORGE EGAN – A View Of Edmundsham In The County Of Dorset, The Seat Of John Frye Hussey, Esq. – signed and inscribed – gouache – on laid paper – 13 x 16½in.
(Sotheby's) **$1,650 £1,100**

NICK EGGENHOFER – Pony Express
– signed – watercolour on artist's board
– 15 x 20in.
(Christie's)   **$4,400**   **£3,055**

SAMUEL EGLINGTON – A Mishap –
signed – oil on panel – 23½ x 16¾in.
(Sotheby's)   **$3,372**   **£2,310**

ERWIN EICHINGER – Man With A Jug
– signed – oil on board – 10.7 x 8in.
(Woolley &
Wallis)   **$493**   **£340**

ERWIN EICHINGER – The Connoisseur –
signed and inscribed – on panel – 10 x
12in.
(Sotheby's)   **$957**   **£638**

ERWIN EICHINGER – Portraits Of
Elderly German Gentlemen – signed –
oil on panel – 9½ x 7½in.
(Edgar Horn)   **$1,020**   **£680 Pair**

FERENCZ FRANZ EISENHUT – The Pet
Monkey – signed and dated 88 – 23½ x
33in.
(Christie's) **$27,540 £18,360**

JOHANN ANTON EISMAN – A Coastal
Scene With Shipping – 32¾ x 46½in.
(Sotheby's) **$4,558 £3,080**

ERWIN EICHINGER – Planning the
Campaign – signed and inscribed – on
panel – 12¼ x 10¼in.
(Sotheby's) **$990 £660**

SUZANNE EISENDIECK – Deux
Danseurs – signed – 23¾ x 19½in.
(Sotheby's) **$1,595 £1,100**

EMILE EISMAN-SEMENOWSKY – An
Odalisque – signed and dated '18 – oil
on canvas – 14 x 10½in.
(Sotheby's) **$1,435 £990**

GEORGE SAMUEL ELGOOD – The Terrace, Berkeley Castle, Gloucestershire – signed and dated 1887 – watercolour over pencil – 12 x 19¾in.
(Sotheby's) **$2,310 £1,540**

KNUT EKWALL – The Fisherman And The Siren – signed – 77½ x 59¼in.
(Christie's) **$12,150 £8,100**

NICHOLAES ELIASZ, Called Pickenoy – Portrait Of A Woman Holding A Kerchief – on panel – 46 x 33½in.
(Sotheby's) **$17,820 £11,880**

MILDRED E. ELDRIDGE – Study Of A Wheatear; Study Of A Yellow Necked Mouse; and Dyke At Ynyslas Bog, Wales – signed and dated between 1965 and 1969 – watercolour over pencil – 13½ x 17¼in.
(Sotheby's) **$385 £264 Three**

PAUL H. ELLIS – The Thames At Gatehampton – signed – oil on canvas – 24 x 42in.
(Sotheby's) **$1,515 £1,045**

PAUL H. ELLIS — Arabs And Camels
In The Desert -- signed — 22 x 32in.
(Christie's)   **$1,540   £1,026**

LOUWYS-AERNOUTS ELSEVIER –
The Interior Of A Barn With A Peasant
Smoking — signed and dated 1641 — on
panel — 18¼ x 23in.
(Christie's)   **$2,316   £1,620**

FRED ELWELL — A Polisher's Shop
— signed — 39½ x 29½in.
(Christie's)   **$5,632   £3,780**

JOHN EMMS — A Dispute — signed and
dated 1896 — 14 x 18in.
(Sotheby's)   **$1,237   £825**

JOHN EMMS — New Forest Buck
Hounds, The Whip Holding Up The Pack
— signed and dated 1895 — on canvas —
30 x 43in.
(Sotheby's)   **$13,200   £8,800**

JOHN EMMS — Study Of The Terrier
'Nettle' — signed, inscribed and dated
1891 — 11¾ x 14¾in.
(Sotheby's)   **$907   £605**

JOHN EMMS — 'Joey, Brag, Jackie And
Dick' — signed, inscribed and dated 1901
— on canvas — 30 x 40in.
(Sotheby's)   **$1,567   £1,045**

LT. COL. EVELYN L. ENGLEHART – The Cafe Of The Casbah, Tunis – signed and dated '08 – watercolour – 10¼ x 16in.
(Sotheby's)   **$683**   **£495**

ROSALIE EMSLIE – Portrait Of A Girl In A Landscape – signed – oil on canvas – 16 x 11¼in.
(Christie's)   **$1,377**   **£918**

ENGLISH SCHOOL, circa 1830 – View Of St. George's Circus From The Black-friar's Road, Looking South – oil on canvas – 24½ x 29½in.
(Sotheby's)   **$5,280**   **£3,520**

KARL ENDERLEIN – Riunione – monogram – pencil – 37 x 32cm.
(Christie's)   **$540**   **£368**

ENGLISH SCHOOL, circa 1750 – A Hound – gouache – 11¼ x 17¼in.
(Sotheby's)   **$1,650**   **£1,100**

ENGLISH SCHOOL

ENGLISH SCHOOL, circa 1770 – Views Of The Park At Oatlands, Surrey, The Seat Of The Earl Of Lincoln – gouache on paper – 17½ x 25¼in.
(Sotheby's) **$1,402** **£935 Pair**

DELPHIN ENJOLRAS – Evening On The Terrace – signed – on canvas – 19½ x 25½in.
(Sotheby's) **$1,237** **£825**

ENGLISH SCHOOL, 19th century – 'Sportsmen With Spaniels Flushing Game' – oil – 20 x 24in.
(Reeds Rains) **$1,087** **£750**

JOHN JOSEPH ENNEKING – 'Squall Over Ogunquit' – signed and dated '80(?) – oil on canvas – 18 x 24in.
(Robert W. Skinner Inc.) **$3,500** **£2,335**

ENGLISH SCHOOL, 19th century – A Harvesting Scene – indistinctly signed – oil on canvas – 19½ x 29½in.
(Sotheby's) **$947** **£660**

AUGUSTUS WILLIAM ENNESS – The Edge Of The Village – signed – on canvas – 14½ x 19½in.
(Sotheby's) **$264** **£176**

ARTHUR HENTY ENOCK – H.M.S.
Enterprise In Dartmouth Harbour, Misty
Morning – signed – watercolour – 15¾
x 23½in.
(Sotheby's)   **$1,718   £1,210**

JAMES ENSOR – Les Pochards –
signed – 33 x 41in.
(Sotheby's)   **$62,700   £41,800**

MAX ERNST – Aus: Oiseau En Peril
– signed – etching and collage in colour
– 33 x 27cm.
*(Germann
    Auktionshaus)* **$1,002   £668**

SIR JACOB EPSTEIN – Girl And
Kitten – signed – pencil – 22½ x 17½in.
(Sotheby's)   **$1,980   £1,320**

MAX ERNST – Monument Aux Oiseaux
– signed and dated 1927, also signed and
dated on the reverse – oil on canvas – 63¼
63¼ x 51¼in.
(Sotheby's)   **$313,500 £209,000**

RUDOLF ERNST – An Odalisque –
signed and inscribed – on panel – 23½ x
15½in.
(Christie's)   **$31,968   £21,600**

RUDOLF ERNST – On The Steps Of The
Throne – signed – on panel – 28 x 36in.
(Christie's)   **$16,200   £10,800**

FREDERICK ETCHELLS – Portrait Of
A Girl – oil on canvas – 20 x 16in.
(Christie's)   **$7,192   £4,860**

RUDOLF ERNST – The Dealer In Guns
– signed – watercolour – 14 x 9½in.
(Sotheby's)   **$1,320   £880**

WILLIAM ETTY – A Female Nude
Seated By A Table Of Flowers – on
panel – 20½ x 16¾in.
(Christie's)   **$724   £486**

WILLIAM ETTY, Attributed to —
Portrait Of An Indian Wearing A Turban
— 23¼ x 19¼in.
(Sotheby's)   **$578**   **£396**

PHILIP EVERGOOD — Portrait Of Mrs
Charles Edward Smith — signed — blue
chalk and charcoal on paper — 22¼ x
14½in.
(Christie's)   **$825**   **£597**

PHILIP EVERGOOD — Two Miners —
signed — oil on canvas — 49 x 30¼in.
(Christie's)   **$12,100**   **£8,065**

ADRIANUS EVERSEN — A Busy Street
— signed — oil on canvas — 27¼ x 23¼in.
(Sotheby's)   **$11,962**   **£8,250**

FABRIS

PIETRO FABRIS – A View Of Naples –
oil on canvas – 21 x 39¾in.
(Sotheby's) **$29,304 £19,800**

JOHN FAED – William Pitt, Charles
James Fox And Two Statesmen –
signed – canvas on board – 6 x 8in.
(Sotheby's) **$825 £550**

BARENT FABRITIUS – Abraham
Banishing Hagar And Ishmael – 38½ x
51½in.
(Christie's) **$6,177 £4,320**

JOHN FAED – A Gentle Critic – signed
and dated '60? – 18½ x 14½in.
(Christie's) **$7,992 £5,400**

JOHN FAED – The Stirrup Cup –
signed and dated 1868 – oil on canvas –
36 x 46in.
(Sotheby's) **$5,104 £3,520**

JOHN FAED – At The Spring, Or Gossip
– signed and dated '83 – 20¾ x 16¾in.
(Christie's) **$10,389 £7,020**

THOMAS FAED – The Fisherman's Daughter – signed and dated 1864 – 31 x 20in.
(Sotheby's) **$10,725** **£7,150**

EDWARD HENRY FAHEY – A West Country Harbour – signed – oil on canvas – 50 x 40in.
(Sotheby's) **$1,402** **£935**

G. FALL – Still Life Of Dead Wood Pigeons, A Hare And Raven – signed and dated – oil on canvas – 18 x 24in.
(Morphets) **$285** **£190**

HENRI FANTIN-LATOUR – Vase De Roses – signed – 16½ x 14in.
(Sotheby's) **$98,890** **£68,200**

HENRI FANTIN-LATOUR – Trois Peches Sur Une Assiette – signed and dated '68 – oil on paper laid on canvas – 7¾ x 10in.
(Christie's) **$47,628** **£32,400**

WALTER FARMER – Home From Work
– signed and dated 1905 – oil on canvas –
16 x 20in.
(Sotheby's)　　**$1,320**　　**£880**

DAVID FARQUHARSON – Boscastle
– signed – watercolour over pencil –
18 x 13in.
(Sotheby's)　　**$651**　　**£440**

DAVID FARQUHARSON – In The Fields
– signed and dated '85 – oil on canvas –
12 x 19in.
(Sotheby's)　　**$1,276**　　**£880**

DAVID FARQUHARSON – Loch Achray,
Well Wooded Track Beside The Loch With
A Man Walking Under The Shade Of The
Trees, A Mare And Foal Grazing By A Wire
Fence – signed and dated (18)90 – oil on
canvas – 39 x 60cm.
(Henry Spencer &
Sons)　　**$930**　　**£520**

JOSEPH FARQUHARSON – Days
Departing Glory, Shepherd And Sheep
In Snowy Landscape – signed – oil –
12 x 18in.
(Dacre, Son &
Hartley)　　**$3,750**　　**£2,500**

HENRI LE FAUCONNIER – Nature Morte
– signed with initials – watercolour – 29
x 20¼in.
(Sotheby's)　　**$492**　　**£330**

ANTOINE DE FAVRAY, Circle of — A Carnival Scene — oil on canvas — 20½ x 25in.
(Sotheby's)　　$3,051　£2,090

LYONEL FEININGER — Ostsee Fischer — signed, inscribed and dated '31 — watercolour, pen and black ink on paper — 11¼ x 17¾in.
(Christie's)　　$16,200　£10,800

GIACOMO FAVRETTO — A Courting Couple — signed — on panel — 18 x 14½in.
(Sotheby's)　　$27,225　£18,150

CONRAD FELIXMULLER — Der Blinde Korbflechter — signed and dated '50 — 27¼ x 19¼in.
(Sotheby's)　　$14,025　£9,350

PEREGRINE M. FEENEY — The Lonely Sea And The Sky — signed and dated 1901 — oil on canvas — 38 x 44in.
(Sotheby's)　　$377　£264

FRANZ DE PAULA FERG — A River Landscape — signed — 18 x 24½in.
(Sotheby's)　　$20,625　£13,750

FERGUSSON

JOHN DUNCAN FERGUSSON –
Teapot And Daffodil – signed on
the reverse – oil on panel – 12 x
9½in.
(Sotheby's)   **$8,954**   **£6,050**

JOHN DUNCAN FERGUSSON –
Study Of Margaret Morris – black
chalks and coloured wash – 13 x 10in.
(Sotheby's)   **$846**   **£572**

JOHN DUNCAN FERGUSSON –
Woman On A Bench – canvas on
board – oil – 9 x 7in.
(Sotheby's)   **$3,135**   **£2,090**

JOHN FERNELEY, SNR. – Portrait Of
Frank Hall Standish Esq., On Horseback –
signed and dated 1819 – 39 x 49in.
(Sotheby's)   **$75,900**   **£50,600**

JOHN FERNELEY, SNR. – Portrait Of
Charles Neil Hogg On His Grey Hunter,
Alice Grey, A View Of Gumley Hall,
Leicestershire, Beyond – signed and dated
1839 – 33½ x 41½in.
(Sotheby's)   **$52,800**   **£35,200**

JOHN FERNELEY, SNR. – The Quorn, Sir Harry Goodricke's Hounds At The Whaw-Hoop – oil on canvas – 58½ x 107¼in.
(Sotheby's) $85,800 £57,200

GEORGES DE FEURE – Le Pecheur Et Le Moulin A Vent – signed – oil and tempera on canvas – 13 x 18¼in.
(Christie's)   **$6,307   £4,320**

HARRY FIDLER – A Plough Team – signed – 26.5 x 30.5cm.
(Sotheby Beresford Adams)   **$1,253   £700**

DOMENICO FIASELLA, Attributed to – The Flight Into Egypt – 24½ x 29¼in.
(Sotheby's)   **$907   £605**

ANTHONY VANDYKE COPLEY FIELDING – A Mediterranean Coastal Landscape – signed – watercolour – 9 x 12½in.
(Sotheby's)   **$594   £396**

FIELDING

ANTHONY VANDYKE COPLEY FIELDING – Sailing Vessels Out Of Harbour – watercolour with scratching out – 16¾ x 22½in.
(Sotheby's)   **$825**   **£550**

NEWTON SMITH LIMBIRD FIELDING – Ducks On The Banks Of A River; and Poultry In A Yard – signed – watercolour over pencil heightened with gum arabic, with scratching out – one 6½ x 9¾in., the other 6¾ x 10in.
(Sotheby's)   **$1,732**   **£1,155 Two**

NEWTON SMITH LIMBIRD FIELDING – Gun Dogs; and A Stag Near A Waterfall – signed and dated 1854 – watercolour heightened with bodycolour – 5 x 7¼in.
(Sotheby's)   **$718**   **£506 Two**

SIR SAMUEL LUKE FILDES – A Venetian Flower – signed and dated '87 – oil on panel – 17 x 13in.
(Sotheby's)   **$3,135**   **£2,090**

JOHN FINNIE – The Young Anglers – signed – watercolour – 16½ x 12½in.
(Sotheby's)   **$330**   **£220**

WILLIAM MARK FISHER – 'Cherry Blossom' – signed and inscribed – oil on canvas – 14¾ x 19¼in.
(Sotheby's) $915   £638

FRANCESCO FIORENTINO, The Pseudo Pier – The Madonna And Child Adored By Angels – on panel – 22½ x 11in.
(Sotheby's) $24,750   £16,500

GEORG FLEGEL – A Still Life Of Fruit And Nuts With A Stag Beetle – signed and dated 1630(?) – oil on panel – 12 x 19½in.
(Sotheby's) $89,540   £60,500

JANET FISHER – On The Breezy Hillside – signed – oil on canvas – 20 x 36in.
(Sotheby's) $2,145   £1,430

FLEMISH SCHOOL

FLEMISH SCHOOL – A King Or Emperor Dispensing Justice – inscribed and dated 1560 – oil on panel – 46½ x 58in.
(Sotheby's) **$9,442 £6,380**

FLEMISH SCHOOL, 18th century – Ornamental Birds In A Landscape – on metal – 7½ x 9½in.
(Sotheby's) **$875 £572**

FLEMISH SCHOOL, Late 17th century – The Colosseum – 47¾ x 66in.
(Sotheby's) **$4,290 £2,860**

FLEMISH SCHOOL, 17th century – Portrait Of A Lady – on panel – 10¼ x 7½in.
(Sotheby's) **$841 £550**

FLEMISH SCHOOL, circa 1700 –
Winter Landscape – gouache on vellum
– 173 x 231mm.
(Sotheby's)   **$1,536**   **£1,045**

FLEMISH SCHOOL, Early 17th century
– Solomon Before The Queen Of Sheba
– oil on panel – 30 x 44in.
(Sotheby's)   **$2,409**   **£1,650**

BLANDFORD FLETCHER – Bosham
Estuary, Sussex – signed – oil on canvas –
15½ x 25¾in.
(Sotheby's)   **$757**   **£528**

EDWIN HENRY EUGENE FLETCHER –
Sunset Over The Thames, St. Paul's –
signed – 40 x 60in.
(Sotheby's)   **$2,805**   **£1,870**

EDWIN FLETCHER – Shipping On
The Thames – signed – oil on canvas –
19¼ x 30in.
(Sotheby's)   **$883**   **£605**

WILLIAM BLANDFORD FLETCHER –
Harbour At Low Tide – signed – oil on
canvas – 16 x 18in.
(Sotheby's)   **$1,101**   **£770**

WILLIAM BLANDFORD FLETCHER –
Quimperle – on panel – 6½ x 9½in.
(Sotheby's)   **$693**   **£462**

SIR WILLIAM RUSSELL FLINT – The
Collection Of Studies – signed – water-
colour – 10½ x 14½in.
(Christie's)   **$12,787**   **£8,640**

SIR WILLIAM RUSSELL FLINT –
Models Of Anticoli – signed, inscribed
on the backboard – watercolour over
pencil – 13 x 15½in.
(Sotheby's)   **$3,300**   **£2,200**

SIR WILLIAM RUSSELL FLINT –
Melinda – signed – watercolour –
12 x 9in.
(Sotheby's)   **$4,455**   **£2,970**

SIR WILLIAM RUSSELL FLINT –
Hispano Moresque – signed – water-
colour – 13 x 24in.
(Sotheby's)   **$6,600**   **£4,400**

SIR WILLIAM RUSSELL FLINT – Rocks
And Pools – signed – watercolour – 13¾
x 18¾in.
(Christie's)   **$4,535**   **£3,024**

SIR WILLIAM RUSSELL FLINT –
Evening Gold – signed, and signed
and inscribed on the backboard – watercolour – 14¾ x 21½in.
(Christie's) **$4,860 £3,240**

SIR WILLIAM RUSSELL FLINT –
'Seated Lady' – signed and inscribed
on a label on the reverse – pastel –
6½ x 10in.
(Sotheby's) **$754 £517**

SIR WILLIAM RUSSELL FLINT –
Across A Green Bay – signed, inscribed on the backboard – watercolour
– 13 x 19½in.
(Sotheby's) **$4,620 £3,080**

SIR WILLIAM RUSSELL FLINT – The
Tired Princess, Ray Fuller As Madame du
Barry – signed – red chalk on pink
washed paper – 9¼ x 14in.
(Christie's) **$1,620 £1,080**

EUGENE-VICTOR DE FLOGNY –
'Keeping Watch – signed, inscribed and
dated 1865 – on canvas – 29 x 21in.
(Sotheby's) **$2,392 £1,595**

EUGENE-VICTOR DE FLOGNY –
Keeping Watch – signed, inscribed and
dated 1865 – oil on canvas – 29 x 21in.
(Sotheby's) **$4,554 £3,300**

FRANS FLORIS, Studio of – Adam And
Eve Lamenting The Death Of Abel –
bears monogram and dated 1563.
(Sotheby's) **$3,135 £2,090**

FLORIS

FRANS FLORIS, Circle of – Faith, Hope
And Charity – on panel – 38 x 48½in.
(Sotheby's)   **$4,620   £3,080**

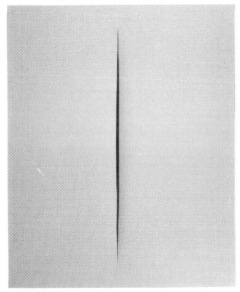

LUCIO FONTANA – Concetto Spaziale
– signed and inscribed – 25½ x 21¼in.
(Sotheby's)   **$13,200   £8,800**

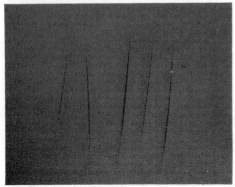

LUCIO FONTANA – Concetto Spaziale
– circa 1964 – 18¼ x 21½in.
(Sotheby's)   **$15,950   £11,000**

PROSPERO FONTANA – Portrait Of
A Gentleman – 46½ x 35in.
(Sotheby's)   **$11,880   £7,920**

FRANCESCO FONTEBASSO – Two
Soldiers, One Holding A Medal – 22¼ x
18¼in.
(Christie's)   **$7,776   £5,184**

FRANCESCO FONTEBASSO – The Continence Of Scipio – 14½ x 31½in.
(Christie's) **$4,860** **£3,240**

JAMES G. FORBES – The Cobbler – signed and dated 1859 – oil on canvas – 20 x 16in.
(Sotheby's) **$1,320** **£880**

STANHOPE FORBES – A Conversation – signed and dated 1911 – 25½ x 21½in.
(Sotheby's) **$2,970** **£1,980**

JEAN-LOUIS FORAIN – Homme Galant – signed – watercolour and coloured crayons over pen and ink – 10½ x 4¼in.
(Sotheby's) **$4,950** **£3,300**

STANHOPE FORBES – The White Gate – signed and dated 1937 – 19¾ x 24¾in.
(Sotheby's) **$1,320** **£880**

MYLES BIRKET FOSTER – Ben Venue
And Ellen's Isle, Loch Katrine – signed
with monogram – watercolour – 6 x 8in.
(Sotheby's)　　　　**$1,284**　　**£880**

STANHOPE FORBES – The Munitions
Girls, Forging 4.5 shells At Kilnhurst
Steelworks – signed and dated 1918 –
40 x 50in.
(Sotheby's)　　**$26,400**　**£17,600**

MYLES BIRKET FOSTER – The
Donkey Ride – signed with monogram
– watercolour – 7 x 5½in.
(Sotheby's)　　　　**$2,649**　**£1,815**

STANHOPE ALEXANDER FORBES –
Waiting For The Fleet – signed – on
board – 12½ x 9¼in.
(Christie's)　　　　**$4,212**　**£2,808**

MYLES BIRKET FOSTER – View Of
Tewkesbury Abbey With Trees, Figures,
Cattle And Sheep – signed with a mono-
gram – 4 x 5½in.
(Lawrence)　　　　**$4,068**　**£825**

MYLES BIRKET FOSTER – The
Watering Place – signed with monogram
– watercolour and bodycolour – 7 x
11¼in.
(Christie's)　　　　**$5,185**　**£3,456**

MYLES BIRKET FOSTER – Perth –
signed with monogram – pencil and watercolour heightened with white – 6 x 8in.
(Christie's)　　　　**$7,047**　**£4,860**

TSUGUHARU FOUJITA — Lesconil,
Finistere — signed and dated 1950 —
10½ x 8½in.
(Sotheby's)   **$18,150   £12,100**

MYLES BIRKET FOSTER — The
Lover's Footsteps — signed with mono-
gram — watercolour — 6½ x 4¾in.
(Sotheby's)   **$2,805   £1,870**

TSUGUHARU FOUJITA — La Madone
— signed — 15¾ x 12¼in.
(Sotheby's)   **$119,625   £82,500**

TSUGUHARU FOUJITA — L'Athlete
— signed and signed in Japanese — pencil
and charcoal — 35½ x 22½in.
(Sotheby's)   **$4,620   £3,080**

TSUGUJI FOUJITA – Le Chat – signed and dated 1926 – pen and black ink and ink wash – 9¼ x 14¼in.
(Christie's)   **$6,480   £4,320**

TSUGUJI FOUJITA – Portrait De Jeune Fille Avec Son Chat Et Son Chien – signed and dated 1952 – oil on canvas – 18 x 15½in.
(Christie's)   **$63,504   £43,200**

ROBERT FOWLER – Contemplation – signed – on canvas – 27½ x 35½in.
(Sotheby's)   **$957   £638**

TSUGUJI FOUJITA – Jeune Fille Aux Pommes de Terre – signed and inscribed – oil on canvas – 13 x 9½in.
(Christie's)   **$89,100 £59,400**

CHARLES JAMES FOX – Trafalgar Square; and Cleopatra's Needle On The Embankment – signed – oil on canvas – 20 x 14in.
(Sotheby's)   **$550   £385 Pair**

HENRY CHARLES FOX – 'End Of A
Hard Day' – signed – 29½ x 12½in.
(Reeds Rains)   **$420**   **£280**

HENRY CHARLES FOX – The Farm
Pool – signed and dated 1917 – watercolour heightened with bodycolour –
14½ x 21¼in.
(Sotheby's)   **$710**   **£495**

EDWARD REGINALD FRAMPTON –
Love In The Alps – signed, and signed
and inscribed on the reverse – 30 x 36in.
(Christie's)   **$10,530**   **£7,020**

HENRY CHARLES FOX – A Surrey
Farmstead – signed and dated 1891 –
on canvas – 16 x 24in.
(Sotheby's)   **$1,606**   **£1,100**

COUNT ALEXANDRE T. FRANCIA –
Venice – signed – watercolour over pencil heightened with gum arabic with
stopping out – 14 x 22in.
(Sotheby's)   **$1,402**   **£935**

HENRY CHARLES FOX – Crossing A
Ford; and On The Arun – signed and
dated 1907 – watercolour heightened
with bodycolour – 15 x 22in.
(Sotheby's)   **$825**   **£550 Pair**

FRANCOIS-THOMAS-LOUIS FRANCIA
– Low Tide – signed and dated 1839 –
sepia and blue watercolour – 5 x 7½in.
*(Robert W. Skinner
    Inc.)*   **$425**   **£283**

FRANCKEN – Elegant Figures On A Venetian Quay – on panel – 17¾ x 26½in.
(Christie's)   **$1,458   £972**

FRANS FRANCKEN, The Younger – Judith Feasting With Holofernes – on panel – 10½ x 17¼in.
(Christie's)   **$2,916   £1,944**

FRANS FRANCKEN, The Younger, Attributed to – Death And The Miser – oil on metal – 6½ x 5in.
(Sotheby's)   **$2,604   £1,760**

MALCOLM FRASER – Sheep On A Wintry Eve – signed – 30 x 40in.
(Sotheby's)   **$1,452   £968**

FRANS FRANCKEN, The Younger – Christ In The House Of Martha And Mary – signed – 19½ x 28¾in.
(Christie's)   **$4,050   £2,700**

FRENCH SCHOOL, 17th century – An Allegory Of Summer Or Abundance – oil on canvas – 33¼ x 28½in.
(Sotheby's)   **$4,070   £2,750**

FRENCH SCHOOL, 18th century — A
Chaffinch — gouache — 172 x 122mm.
(Sotheby's) **$6**93 **£46**2 Pair

PIERRE-EDOUARD FRERE — 'Making
Cider' — signed and dated 1883 — on
canvas — 24 x 19¼in.
(Sotheby's) **$16,381 £11,220**

ROGER DE LA FRESNAYE — Tetes
D'Homme — signed and dated '21 — brush
and indian ink on paper — 10½ x 7¾in.
(Christie's) **$946 £648**

FREDERICK CARL FRIESEKE —
Woman At A Dressing Table — signed
— oil on canvas — 32 x 32in.
(Christie's) **$33,000 £22,916**

EMILE OTHON FRIESZ — Dans Le Parc
— signed — oil on canvas — 65 x 54cm.
*(Germann
Auktionshaus)* **$4,939 £3,293**

ALFRED DOWNING FRIPP — Lovers
Tiff — signed and dated 1845 — water-
colour — diameter 23¼in.
(Sotheby's) **$610 £407**

FRIS

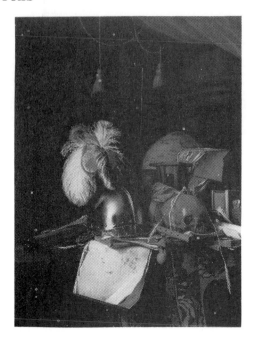

JAN FRIS – A Vanitas Still Life –
signed and dated 1666 – 42½ x 33¼in.
(Sotheby's)   **$12,375   £8,250**

WILLIAM POWELL FRITH – Lovers By
A Waterfall – signed twice, and indist-
inctly dated – 14 x 11½in.
(Sotheby's)   **$12,375   £8,250**

FRISIAN SCHOOL, 1619 – Portrait Of
A Girl – on panel – 50 x 38in.
(Sotheby's)   **$9,424   £6,160**

WILLIAM POWELL FRITH – The
Courtship – signed and dated 1898 –
12¾ x 9½in.
(Christie's)   **$965   £648**

GEORGE FROST – A Cottage By
Trees – charcoal and stump – 6½ x 9¼in.
(Christie's)   **$70   £48**

WILLIAM EDWARD FROST –
Sabrina – signed, also signed and dated
1871 on the reverse – oil on canvas –
28 x 36in.
(Sotheby's)   **$2,552**   **£1,760**

**WILLIAM EDWARD FROST, Attributed
to, After Correggio** – Madonna And Child
– indistinctly inscribed – oil on canvas –
32 x 32in.
(Sotheby's)   **$426**   **£297**

**RUELAND FRUEAUF, The Elder,
Follower of** – The Flagellation – oil
on panel – 42 x 33½in.
(Sotheby's)   **$32,560**   **£22,000**

JAMES FROTHINGHAM – Portrait Of
A Gentleman (Said To Be J. A. Haskell
Of Perth Amboy) – oil on panel – 9¼
x 7in.
(Christie's)   **$825**   **£550**

JOHN FULLEYLOVE – A Busy Market
In A Continental Town – signed and
dated 1886 – watercolour over pencil
– 14¼ x 10¼in.
(Sotheby's)   **$742**   **£495**

DAVID FULTON – The Travelling
Musician – signed and dated 1880 –
oil on canvas – 20 x 26in.
(Sotheby's)　　**$1,058**　　**£715**

HELGE FUNKE – Stilleben Mit Fischen
– signed and dated '20 – oil on canvas
– 14¾ x 17¾in.
(Sotheby's)　　**$990**　　**£660**

DAVID FULTON – At The Beehives
– signed and dated 1888 – oil – 24 x
19in.
(Sotheby's)　　**$1,485**　　**£990**

JOHANN HEINRICH FUSELI – Medea
– inscribed and dated '71 – brushpoint
and grey wash over pencil with some
brown wash; verso, An Assassin Fleeing
– inscribed and dated '74 – grey washes
over pencil – on paper – 17½ x 25¼in.
(Sotheby's)　　**$62,700**　**£41,800**

SAMUEL FULTON – A Springer Spaniel
– signed – 14 x 18in.
(Sotheby's)　　**$495**　　**£330**

JAN FYT – Foxes At Bay – signed and
dated 1653 – oil on canvas – 66 x 103in.
(Sotheby's)　　**$32,560 £22,000**

BARENT GAEL – Travellers At A Village Farrier – signed – 17 x 21¼in.
(Christie's)   **$7,776   £5,184**

GIUSEPPE GABANI – An Arab Horseman In The Desert – signed and inscribed – watercolour over pencil – 21 x 14in.
(Sotheby's)   **$1,290   £935**

GAINSBOROUGH, Circle of – 'Joseph Nice Of Cotton Hall, Cambridge' – 23½ x 19½in.
(Reeds Rains)   **$360   £250**

WILLIAM HIPPON GADSBY – The Little Thief; and Detected – signed, one with monogram – oil on canvas – 24 x 20in.   *(Sotheby's)*   **$6,061   £4,180 Pair**

THOMAS GAINSBOROUGH – Portrait
Of Lambe Barry – 13½ x 11½in.
(Sotheby's) **$82,500 £55,000**

EUGENE GALIEN-LALOUE – La
Madelaine – signed – gouache – 7 x
12in.
*(Woolley &
Wallis)* **$5,800 £4,000**

EUGENE GALIEN-LALOUE – Les
Grandes Boulevards Sous La Niege –
signed – gouache – 7 x 12in.
*(Woolley &
Wallis)* **$5,510 £3,800**

FRANCOIS GALL – Scene A La Plage
– signed – oil on board – 26.5 x 34.5cm.
*(Germann
Auktionshaus)* **$1,201 £823**

SEARS GALLAGHER – Winter Romance
– signed – gouache on ivory board – 17
x 16in.
*(Robert W. Skinner
Inc.)* **$1,400 £933**

PIETER GALLIS – A Still Life Of Roses,
A Tulip, A Crown Imperial Lily In A
Glass Bowl On A Ledge – signed – 18 x
15in.
(Christie's) **$11,340 £7,560**

ROBERT GALLON – 'A Surrey Village'
– signed – oil on canvas – 19¾ x 30½in.
(Sotheby's) **$7,066 £4,840**

ROBERT GALLON – View Of The
Thames With Haymakers, And Children
Gathering Flowers – signed – oil – 20
x 30in.
*(Dacre, Son &
Hartley)* **$3,000 £2,000**

MAURO GANDOLFI – The Artist's
Dream – inscribed and dated 1811 –
watercolour on vellum – 705 x 523mm.
(Sotheby's) **$22,638 £15,400**

MAURO GANDOLFI – Sheet Of Studies
Of Heads – bears signature – pen and
brown ink – 208 x 290mm.
(Sotheby's) **$2,970 £1,980**

COSIMO GAMBERLUCCI – Jephtha's
Return – 42 x 33in.
(Sotheby's) **$2,524 £1,650**

WILLIAM FRASER GARDEN – View
Of A Church Spire, From A Quiet Backwater – signed and dated '04 – watercolour over traces of pencil – 7 x 10½in.
(Sotheby's) **$1,204 £825**

215

DANIEL GARDNER – A Young Child Embracing A Pet Deer – 24½ x 29in.
(Sotheby's) **$3,135** **£2,090**

DANIEL GARDNER – A Little Girl Playing With A Dog On A Woodland Bank – pastel and bodycolour on paper laid down on canvas – 20½ x 16¼in.
(Christie's) **$3,078** **£2,052**

DEREK GARDNER – The Tea Clipper Spindrift – signed, also inscribed on the reverse – oil on canvas – 28 x 42in.
(Sotheby's) **$2,359** **£1,650**

WILLIAM BISCOMBE GARDNER – Looking Up The Creek From Tomlin's Wharf, Old Leigh, Essex – signed and inscribed on the reverse – watercolour – 7¾ x 13¾in.
(Sotheby's) **$674** **£462**

HENRY GARLAND – Waiting For A Ride – signed and dated 1885 – on canvas – 13¾ x 12in.
(Sotheby's) **$825** **£550**

VALENTINE GARLAND – Three Puppies – signed – on canvas – 20 x 15in.
(Sotheby's) **$1,947** **£1,298**

HENRY GARLAND – Highlanders
Going South – signed and dated and
inscribed on reverse – oil on canvas –
28 x 36in.
(Morphets) $942 £650

**RAIMUNDO DE MADRAZO Y
GARRETA** – A Portrait Of A Seated
Woman – signed and dated '87 – oil
on panel – 58¼ x 39½in.
(Sotheby's) $4,785 £3,300

**RAIMUNDO DE MADRAZO Y
GARRETA** – An Evening Out – signed
– oil on canvas – 37 x 22½in.
*(Robert W. Skinner
Inc.)* $8,500 £5,666

WALTER BONNER GASH – A Sketch
Near Warkton Plank – inscribed on a
label on the reverse – on board – 10 x
7in.
(Sotheby's) $642 £440

GUSTAV-ADOLF GAUPP – Galante Szene – signed and dated 1893 – oil on canvas – 100 x 72cm.
(Germann Auktionshaus) **$6,736 £4,491**

A. HANDEL GEAR – The Doll – signed – 40 x 30in.
(Sotheby's) **$1,124 £770**

ELLEN A. GAYLER – Lionel, Great Grandson Of John Constable – signed and inscribed on a label – oil on canvas – 30 x 20in.
(Sotheby's) **$346 £242**

ANDREW GEDDES – Portrait Of A Lady – 36 x 28in.
(Sotheby's) **$1,284 £880**

W. GEDDES – The Day's Catch – signed – on board – 9½ x 13½in.
(Sotheby's) **$462 £308**

WYNBRAND SIMONSZ. DE GEEST,
Follower of – Portrait Of Adriaen
Verkins As A Child – bears inscription –
on panel – 32 x 21¼in.
(Sotheby's) **$9,570 £6,380**

BENEDETTO GENNAR, Circle of – Portrait Of A Lady – oil on canvas – 35 x
27¼in.
(Sotheby's) **$2,569 £1,760**

LUCIEN GENIN – Rouen – signed –
on board – 55 x 46cm.
(Germann
Auktionshaus) **$1,366 £911**

S. LUIGI GENTILE – Eruption Of
Vesuvius, 1822 – signed – en gouache
– 33 x 22½in.
(Lawrence) **$957 £638**

ABRAHAM VAN GERWEN – Interior Of A Church – signed and dated 1643 – oil on canvas – 37½ x 43½in.
(Sotheby's) **$4,496** **£3,080**

JEAN LEON GEROME – In The Doorway – signed – 32¼ x 26in.
(Christie's) **$28,771** **£19,440**

FRANCESCO GESSI, Circle of – Cupid And Psyche – 53½ x 64in.
(Sotheby's) **$1,155** **£770**

MARK GERTLER – Portrait Of A Young Boy – signed – oil on canvas – 15¼ x 11½in.
(Sotheby's) **$1,387** **£935**

F. GEERHARTS – A British Man-Of-War And Other Shipping Off A Mediterranean Coast – indistinctly signed and dated 1662 – 37 x 51in.
(Christie's) **$6,177** **£4,320**

GIOVANNI GHISOLFI, Attributed to –
The Tower Of Babel – 64 x 47½in.
(Christie's)   **$3,397**   **£2,376**

MARCUS GHEERAERTS, The Younger
– Portrait Of Henry Brooke, Lord
Cobham – inscribed by a later hand –
oil on canvas – 73½ x 45¾in.
(Sotheby's)   **$7,920**   **£5,280**

PIER LEONE GHEZZI – Two Musicians
– bears two inscriptions – oil on canvas
– 77½ x 59½in.
(Sotheby's)   **$26,862** **£18,150**

ALBERTO GIACOMETTI – Tete De
Jeune Homme – oil on board – 10½ x
8¼in.
(Christie's)   **$10,249** **£7,020**

GIANNI

GIAN GIANNI – Fishing Boats Off
Valetta Harbour At Night – signed and
dated 1892 – oil on board – 7¼ x 19in.
(Sotheby's) $578   £396

JOHN GIFFORD – 'Two Retrievers With
Dead Game Waiting By A Stile' – signed
and dated 1889 – oil on canvas – 42 x
38in.
(Andrew Grant) $1,650   £1,100

JOHN GIFFORD – A Hunter, Springers
And A Day's Bag – signed – oil on can-
vas – 49 x 39½in.
(Sotheby's) $4,466   £3,080

REGIS FRANCOIS GIGNOUX – 'Ice
Skating' – oil on canvas – 18 x 24in.
*(Robert W. Skinner
   Inc.)* $1,600   £1,066

MAJOR GODFREY DOUGLAS GILES
– The Jockey Club Stakes, October 1st,
1903, 'Sceptre' Beating 'Rock Sand' By
Four Lengths – signed, inscribed and
dated 1903 – 22 x 30in.
(Sotheby's) $2,475   £1,650

WILLIAM WARD GILL – The Forge
Bridge, Downton, Near Ludlow –
inscribed – on canvas – 15½ x 26½in.
(Sotheby's) $478   £319

JAN PAUWEL GILLEMANS, The
Younger – Still Life With Figures In A
Landscape – 22½ x 32¾in.
(Sotheby's) $4,290   £2,860

SIR WILLIAM GEORGE GILLIES –
Still Life Of Summer Flowers In A Blue
And White Vase – signed – 30 x 33in.
(Christie's) **$2,100 £1,400**

CHARLES GINNER – On Hampstead
Heath – signed – watercolour, pen and
black ink – 11¾ x 8½in.
(Christie's) **$2,430 £1,620**

HENRY GILLARD GINDONI – The
Duel – signed and dated 1881 – water-
colour – 31 x 21½in.
(Sotheby's) **$757 £528**

BELISARIO GIOJA – Unveiling The
Portrait – signed and inscribed – water-
colour – 20¾ x 14in.
(Sotheby's) **$1,092 £748**

GIORDANO

LUCA GIORDANO, Follower of – The
Marriage Of The Virgin – oil on canvas
– 39 x 49in.
(Sotheby's) **$1,628** **£1,100**

ANNE LOUIS GIRODET-TRIOSON,
Attributed to – Portrait Of A Young
Lady, Said To Be The Actress Mme.
Mars, As A Bacchante – 19½ x 16in.
(Christie's) **$1,467** **£1,026**

ALFRED AUGUSTUS GLENDENING –
Herding The Flock – signed and dated
'09 – oil on canvas – 12 x 20in.
(Sotheby's) **$1,237** **£825**

ALFRED AUGUSTUS GLENDENING –
A Shepherd And Sheep By A River In A
Wooded Landscape – signed and dated
'99 – 12 x 22in.
(Christie's) **$2,755** **£1,836**

ALFRED AUGUSTUS GLENDENING,
SNR. – Glyn Gwynnant, North Wales –
signed – 16 x 26in.
(Sotheby's) **$1,072** **£715**

ALFRED AUGUSTUS GLENDENING –
Punting On A River – signed – oil on
canvas – 15½ x 25in.
(Sotheby's) **$2,640** **£1,760**

CHARLES GLEYRE, Follower of –
Classical Maidens In A Boat – oil on
canvas – 30¾ x 53in.
(Sotheby's) **$1,136** **£792**

FRANK GLINDON – A Florist's Workshop – signed – oil on canvas – 31 x 43in.
(Sotheby's)   **$1,402**   **£935**

HENRY GILLARD GLINDONI – First In The Field – signed and dated 1903 – oil on canvas – 34 x 44in.
(Sotheby's)   **$2,805**   **£1,870**

HENRY GILLARD GLINDONI – Conversation Piece With A Lady And An Elderly Male Companion Outside An Antique Dealer's Shop – signed and dated 1894 – watercolour – 62 x 50cm.
(Henry Spencer &
Sons)   **$905**   **£620**

JOHN GLOVER – Boatmen On A River Near A Ruined Abbey – watercolour over pencil – 8½ x 11½in.
(Sotheby's)   **$577**   **£385**

VINCENT VAN GOCH – Paysanne A La Cuvette – signed – pen and sepia ink, pencil, black chalk and wash – 12½ x 10¼in.
(Sotheby's)   **$108,900** **£72,600**

JOHN WILLIAM GODWARD – Ismenia – signed and dated 1908, also signed and dated on the reverse – 31½ x 25½in.
(Sotheby's)   **$44,550**   **£29,700**

JOHN WILLIAM GODWARD – Contemplation – signed with monogram and dated 1906 – on panel – 7½ x 4in.
(Sotheby's)   **$1,815**   **£1,210**

GODWARD

COLONEL ROBERT CHARLES GOFF
– Venice, Santa Maria Della Salute
From The Giudecca Canal – signed and
dated 1910 – pencil and watercolour
heightened with white on grey paper –
10¼ x 14½in.
(Christie's)   **$650**   **£432**

JOHN WILLIAM GODWARD – Reverie
– signed with initials – 10 x 9in.
(Sotheby's)   **$1,284**   **£880**

WALTER H. GOLDSMITH – 'Bray On
Thames' – signed and dated '92 – watercolour – 17¼ x 35in.; together with an
engraving.
(Sotheby's)   **$1,136**   **£792**

JOHN WILLIAM GODWARD – On The
Balcony – signed and dated 1911 – 32
x 16in.
(Sotheby's)   **$23,100**   **£15,400**

HENDRIK GOLTZIUS, Circle of – Venus
And Adonis – oil on panel – 21¾ x 16½in.
(Sotheby's)   **$3,745**   **£2,530**

NATALIA GONTCHAROVA – (i)
Costume Design For A Peasant Woman;
(ii) Costume Design For A Shrimp
Seller – signed, inscribed on the reverse
– watercolour over pencil – 18½ x
12¼in.
(Sotheby's) **$660** **£440**

FREDERICK GOODALL – Travellers –
signed and dated 1864 – watercolour
over pencil heightened with bodycolour
– 15¾ x 21½in.
(Sotheby's) **$19,877** **£14,300**

FREDERICK GOODALL – On The
Banks Of The Nile With The Pyramids
Beyond – signed with monogram and
dated 1886 – oil on canvas – 13½ x
17½in.
(Sotheby's) **$2,732** **£1,980**

FREDERICK GOODALL – The Flower
Festival – signed with monogram and
dated 1867 – canvas laid on board –
29 x 21in.
(Sotheby's) **$5,621** **£3,850**

FREDERICK GOODALL – Beggars Outside A Mosque – signed with monogram
and dated 1858-70 – on canvas – 21½ x
15in.
(Sotheby's) **$4,620** **£3,080**

WALTER GOODALL – Feeding The
Chickens – signed and dated 1856 –
watercolour – 11½ x 9¾in.
(Sotheby's) **$1,124** **£770**

EDWARD ALFRED GOODHALL –
Riverside Scene With Buildings On The
Loire – signed – 20 x 28in.
(Lawrence) **$1,455** **£990**

ROBERT GWELO GOODMAN – The
Weir – signed with initials and dated
1909 – pastel – 23¼ x 28½in.
(Sotheby's) **$2,884** **£2,090**

ALBERT GOODWIN – Pastoral Sym-
phony, Guernsey – signed and dated
'92 – oil on board – 25 x 35in.
(Sotheby's) **$9,075** **£6,050**

ALBERT GOODWIN – St. Michael's
Mount – signed and inscribed –
pencil, oil, pen and black ink – laid on
card – 9¾ x 7¾in.
(Christie's) **$1,566** **£1,080**

ALBERT GOODWIN – A Devonshire
Fishing Village – signed – oil on can-
vas – 27 x 42in.
(Sotheby's) **$24,750** **£16,500**

ALBERT GOODWIN – Venetian Butterfly – signed, inscribed and dated 1920 – mixed media, on board – 14 x 20½in.
(Sotheby's)   **$757**   **£528**

ALBERT GOODWIN – Engelberg – signed and inscribed – pencil, pen and grey ink, watercolour and bodycolour – 10¼ x 15in.
(Christie's)   **$2,818**   **£1,944**

SYLVIA GOSSE – Out Shopping – signed – 20 x 16in.
(Sotheby's)   **$2,805**   **£1,870**

MICHELE GORDIGIANI – Portrait Of A Young Girl – oil.
(Andrew Grant)   **$4,650**   **£3,100**

SYLVIA GOSSE – The Vegetable Market, Dieppe – signed – 30 x 20in.
(Sotheby's)   **$3,630**   **£2,420**

JAN VAN GOYEN, Follower of – A
River Landscape – oil on panel – 7 x
9¾in.
(Sotheby's)   **$1,365**   **£935**

SYLVIA GOSSE – Souvenir Of Venice
– signed – 33½ x 21¾in.
(Sotheby's)   **$1,650**   **£1,100**

COLIN GRAEME – Cocker Spaniel
With Dead Game – both signed, one
dated 1904 – on canvas – 26½ x 19½in.
(Sotheby's)   **$957**   **£638 Pair**

THOMAS COOPER GOTCH – A Breton
Family – signed with monogram – oil
on canvas – 20 x 13in.
(Sotheby's)   **$820**   **£572**

COLIN GRAEME – Putting Up A Duck
– signed and dated 1903 – on canvas –
19 x 28¾in.
(Sotheby's)   **$1,980** **£1,320**

COLIN GRAEME – Putting Up A Pheasant – signed and dated 1903 – on canvas – 30 x 50in.
(Sotheby's)   **$1,254   £836**

ANTON GRAFF – The Head Of Christ – inscribed on the reverse – 19 x 15¼in.
(Sotheby's)   **$1,178   £770**

DUNCAN GRANT – Roman Model, Portrait Of A Young Man, Naked To The Waist – signed and dated 1935 – oil on board – 24½ x 18½in.
(Christie's)   **$1,438   £972**

ANTIVEDUTO GRAMATICA – The Virgin And Child – 37 x 28¼in.
(Sotheby's)   **$6,600   £4,400**

DUNCAN GRANT – Portrait Of Paul Roche In The Studio At Charleston – signed – on board – 23½ x 18½in.
(Sotheby's)   **$1,320   £880**

DUNCAN GRANT – A Still Life Study
Of Fruit, Flowers And A Bottle –
signed and dated 1929 – on canvas –
14 x 10½in.
(Sotheby's) **$1,927 £1,320**

WILLIAM JAMES GRANT – A Visit To
The Old Soldier – signed and inscribed
on a label – 32 x 53in.
(Christie's) **$3,078 £2,052**

ALFRED H. GREEN – Dancing At
Gypsy Encampment – signed and dated
1874 – 27½ x 36in.
(Lawrence) **$1,320 £880**

CHARLES GREEN – Dick Swiveller And
The Little Marchioness – signed with
initials – pencil and watercolour – 6¾ x
9¾in.
(Christie's) **$1,620 £1,080**

JAMES GREEN – Indian Jugglers –
signed – watercolour over pencil heightened with white – 32½ x 25in.
(Sotheby's) **$2,887 £1,925**

JEAN-BAPTISTE GREUZE, After –
L'Accordee De Village – 19¾ x 25¼in.
(Lawrence) **$679 £462**

JEAN-BAPTISTE GREUZE, After — A Small Girl With A Dog — oil on canvas — 24 x 27½in.
(Sotheby's)   **$1,286   £880**

JEAN-BAPTISTE GREUZE — A Girl With A Dove — on panel — 25½ x 21¾in.
(Sotheby's)   **$34,650   £23,100**

ORAZIO GREVENBROECK — A Moonlit Capriccio Of A Mediterranean Harbour — on silvered copper — 11 x 16¾in.
(Christie's)   **$4,324   £3,024**

EDITH F. GREY — Playing With The Kittens — signed and dated '97 — oil on canvas — 24 x 15½in.
(Sotheby's)   **$2,552   £1,760**

BERNARD FINEGAN GRIBBLE — Pirates Boarding A Ship — signed — on board — 21½ x 26½in.
(Sotheby's)   **$412   £275**

BERNARD FINEGAN GRIBBLE — A State Procession, Venice — signed — on board — 19 x 29½in.
(Sotheby's)   **$693   £462**

BERNARD F. GRIBBLE – The Pirate's Prize – signed and dated 1901(?) – 54 x 72½in.
(Christie's) **$2,265 £1,512**

WILLIAM GRIFFIN – 'Wanderer' And Other Shipping In A Rough Sea – signed and dated 1839 – on canvas on board – 28½ x 41in.
(Christie's) **$12,150 £8,100**

BORIS GRIGORIEV – Portrait Of A Man Reading – signed – oil on canvas – 52 x 41¾in.
(Christie's) **$3,942 £2,700**

SAMUEL HIERONYMUS GRIMM – Gentlemen Conversing Below A Waterfall – signed and dated 1778 – pen and grey ink and watercolour – 5½ x 8¼in.
(Sotheby's) **$1,155 £770**

BORIS GRIGORIEV – Portrait D'Homme – signed and dated 1921 – 35½ x 29¼in.
(Sotheby's) **$2,475 £1,650**

ABEL GRIMMER, Follower of – A Landscape With A View Of A Country House – on panel – 19¾ x 26in.
(Sotheby's) **$5,890 £3,850**

ARTHUR GRIMSHAW – Whitby Harbour By Night – signed and dated 1899, and signed and inscribed on the reverse – 12 x 18in.
(Christie's)   **$2,755   £1,836**

JOHN ATKINSON GRIMSHAW – Whitby – signed and dated 1883, inscribed on the reverse – 19½ x 29½in.
(Sotheby's)   **$6,424   £4,400**

ATKINSON GRIMSHAW – A Village Street By Moonlight – signed and dated 1874 – on board laid down on panel – 22 x 17½in.
(Christie's)   **$4,827   £3,240**

JOHN ATKINSON GRIMSHAW – Fair Maids Of February – signed and dated 1862, inscribed on the reverse – oil on board – 14 x 12in.
(Sotheby's)   **$16,747   £11,550**

JOHN ATKINSON GRIMSHAW – Whitby – signed and dated 1882 and inscribed on the reverse – oil on canvas – 19½ x 29½in.
(Sotheby's)   **$6,314   £4,400**

JOHN ATKINSON GRIMSHAW – A Moonlit Lane – signed and dated 1883 – on panel – 12 x 20in.
(Sotheby's)   **$2,310   £1,540**

235

JOHN ATKINSON GRIMSHAW – A
Street In Old Chelsea – signed and dated
'93, inscribed on the reverse – 7 x 15in.
(Sotheby's)   **$2,640   £1,760**

JOHN ATKINSON GRIMSHAW –
Courting Time – signed and dated 1880
– oil on canvas – 12 x 19in.
(Sotheby's)   **$6,061   £4,180**

LOUIS H. GRIMSHAW – Kings Bench
Walk, Temple Gardens – signed and
dated 1902, inscribed on the reverse – on
board – 12 x 18in.
(Sotheby's)   **$4,125   £2,750**

JUAN GRIS – Scene Mondaine –
signed with monogram – gouache and
pen and indian ink on paper – 9¾ x
8¼in.
(Christie's)   **$2,522   £1,728**

JUAN GRIS – Puisque Je Te Jure, Mon
Cheri, Que C'Est Pour Moi Que Les
Autres Se Sont Suicides – brush and
ink and blue crayon over pencil – 13¼
x 10½in.
(Sotheby's)   **$2,073   £1,430**

JUAN GRIS – Au Cafe – coloured
crayons and watercolour over pen and
ink – 15½ x 12½in.
(Sotheby's)   **$2,640   £1,760**

JUAN GRIS – La Femme Au Tableau –
signed – oil on canvas – 24 x 19½in.
(Christie's) **$55,566 £37,800**

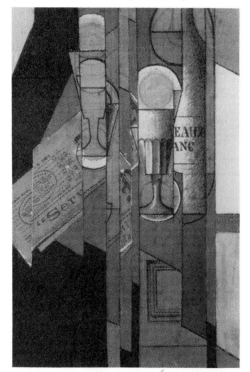

JUAN GRIS – Verresm Journal Et Bouteille De Vin – collage, gouache, watercolour, coloured chalks and charcoal on
paper – 17¾ x 11¾in.
(Christie's) **$259,200 £172,800**

FRANCOIS ADOLPHE GRISON –
L'homme A La Pipe – signed – oil on
wood – 18 x 13.5cm.
*(Germann
Auktionshaus)* **$2,469 £1,646**

KONRAD GROB – Taufe In Meiringen
– signed and dated 1891 – oil on canvas
– 85 x 107cm.
*(Germann
Auktionshaus)* **$17,065 £11,377**

A. J. GROENWEGEN – Milking Time –
signed – watercolour – 7 x 10in.
(Sotheby's) **$536 £374**

MARCEL GROMAIRE – Nu Blond Pres D'Une Fenetre – signed and dated 1950 – 40 x 32½in.
(Sotheby's)   **$31,317 £21,450**

GEORGE GROSZ – Das Paar – signed – watercolour on paper – 22½ x 18in.
(Christie's)   **$61,560 £41,040**

PH. GRONDARD – A Cottage Interior With Figures By The Fireside – signed – oil on canvas – 10¾ x 18½in.
(Sotheby's)   **$803 £550**

WILLEM P. DE GROOT – A Couple In A Landscape With A Distant View Of Dordrecht – signed and dated 1783 – 33½ x 35in.
(Christie's)   **$6,156 £4,104**

GEORGE GROSZ – Elsa Rat Mit Promenadenkleid – watercolour over pen and ink – 12½ x 7¾in.
(Sotheby's)   **$5,901 £4,070**

GEORGE GROSZ – Erschiessung Eines
Gefangenen – signed – pen and black
ink on paper – 6½ x 10in.
(Christie's) $388   £259

GEORGE GROSZ – Pferderennen –
signed – charcoal – 19¼ x 14½in.
(Sotheby's) $3,509   £2,420

GEORGE GROSZ – Kapital Gegen China
– brush and indian ink – 20½ x 25½in.
(Sotheby's) $2,805   £1,870

FRANCIS GRUBER – Belle Isle, Vue de
la Fenetre – signed and dated 1940 – oil
on canvas – 40 x 42in.
(Christie's) $3,890   £2,592

HANS JULIUS GRUDER – Neapolitan
Peasants – signed with monogram and
dated 1858 – oil on canvas – 25½ x
21in.
(Sotheby's) $1,276   £880 Pair

NORBERT JOSEPH KARL GRUND –
A Village In Winter With Figures By A
Frozen River – on panel – 7¾ x 11in.
(Christie's) **$4,324** **£3,024**

BASILIUS GRUNDMANN – Elegante
Gessellschaft – signed with monogram
and dated 1776 – oil on wood – 37 x
43cm.
*(Germann
Auktionshaus)* **$7,633** **£5,089**

ELIOTH GRUNER – 'Windsor Farmyard'
– signed – oil on canvas – 38 x 55cm.
*(Australian Art
Auctions)* **$7,096** **£4,731**

E. GRUTTEFIENS – 'Moonlight In The
Fresian Islands' – oil – 40 x 61in.
(Reeds Rains) **$600** **£400**

GIACOMO GUARDI – Sta. Maria Degli
Angeli, Murano – signed and inscribed
on verso – gouache – 103 x 178mm.
(Sotheby's) **$2,073** **£1,430**

GIACOMO GUARDI – View Of Piazza
San Marco – signed and inscribed on the
verso – gouache – 147 x 236mm.
(Sotheby's) **$2,145** **£1,430**

GIACOMO GUARDI – The Piazza S.
Marco – signed and inscribed –
gouache – 154 x 240mm.
(Sotheby's) **$2,310** **£1,540**

MAX GUBLER – Sitzende Madchen Mit Mandoline, Um 1925 – oil on paper – 91 x 61cm.
(Germann Auktionshaus) **$2,097   £1,398**

CHARLEMAGNE-OSCAR GUET – The Dutch Fish Girl – signed and dated 1821 – paper – 16 x 12¾in.
(Sotheby's)   **$760   £506**

JEAN ANTOINE THEODORE GUDIN – A Coastal Landscape With Arab Fishermen Launching A Boat At Sunset – signed and dated 1844 – 41 x 53in.
(Christie's)   **$15,984 £10,800**

PARIS VON GUTERSLOH – Scene On A Cafe Terrace – signed and dated 1920 – watercolour – 4 x 5¼in.
(Lawrence)   **$3,072   £2,090**

RENATO GUTTUSO – Disegno Erotico – charcoal and white on paper – 50 x 35cm.
(Christie's)   **$1,445   £983**

241

GUTTUSO

SEYMOUR JOSEPH GUY — Peaceful
Afternoon — signed with initials and
dated 1882 — oil on canvas — 24 x 18in.
(Christie's) **$41,800 £29,027**

RENATO GUTTUSO — Due Nude In
Piedi — signed — pen and brush and ink —
19¼ x 11½in.
(Sotheby's) **$1,485 £990**

ALLAN GWYNNE-JONES — Saw Mills
Near Parkstone — on board — 21 x 23in.
(Sotheby's) **$990 £660**

NICOLAS GYSIS — The Village Barber
— signed — 35¼ x 25¾in.
(Sotheby's) **$62,700 £41,800**

CARL HAAG – An Italian Girl Beside A Spring – signed and dated 1857 – watercolour over pencil with scratching out – 19¾ x 13¾in.
(Sotheby's)   **$693   £462**

ARTHUR TREVOR HADDON – A Spanish Street Scene – signed – oil on canvas – 29½ x 24½in.
(Sotheby's)   **$1,043   £715**

CORNELIS VAN HAARLEM – Sophonisba – 26 x 18in.
(Sotheby's)   **$2,145   £1,430**

ARTHUR TREVOR HADDON – A Spanish Street Scene – signed – 30 x 22in.
(Christie's)   **$2,590   £1,728**

ARTS REVIEW

TREVOR HADDON – Venetian Fruit Market – signed – on board – 15½ x 23½in.
(Sotheby's) **$990** **£660**

TREVOR HADDON – Venetian Water Carriers – signed – oil on canvas – 54 x 74cm.
(Henry Spencer & Sons) **$990** **£660**

LOUIS HAGHE – The Music Lesson – signed and dated 1864 – watercolour over pencil, heightened with bodycolour – 10 x 12½in.
(Sotheby's) **$674** **£462**

LOUIS HAGHE – The Artist's Studio, Painting A Cavalier – signed and dated 1861 – watercolour and bodycolour – 26 x 35½in.
(Christie's) **$2,755** **£1,836**

ANDERSON HAGUE – A Barley Field – inscribed – on canvas – 27½ x 35½in.
(Sotheby's) **$738** **£506**

CLIFFORD HALL – Three Clowns – signed, dated 1946 and inscribed on the reverse – oil on canvas – 39½ x 30¼in.
(Sotheby's) **$931** **£638**

FRED HALL – Hens And Roosters –
signed – oil -- on panel – 16 x 12in.
(Sotheby's) **$1,155** **£770**

H. HALL – 'Fleur de Lys', A Bay Racehorse With Roberts Up – 20¾ x 26in.
(Christie's) **$3,240** **£2,160**

H. R. HALL – Returning To The Homestead – signed, inscribed on the reverse
– oil on canvas – 20 x 30in.
(Sotheby's) **$569** **£385**

HARRY HALL – Doncaster, A Chestnut
Racehorse In A Stable – signed and dated
1873 – 17 x 21in.
(Sotheby's) **$2,730** **£1,870**

DIRCK HALS – An Elegant Company –
on panel – 13 x 22¾in.
(Sotheby's) **$18,562** **£12,375**

FRANS HALS, Follower of – A Young
Man Smoking A Pipe – inscribed 1653
– 36¼ x 31in.
(Sotheby's) **$4,620** **£3,080**

KEELEY HALSWELLE – Lady By A Duck Pond With Country House And Church Beyond – signed and dated 1876 – on canvas – 22 x 30in.
(Sotheby's)   **$1,365**   **£935**

CHARLES HANCOCK – A Study Of A Foxhound In A Landscape – signed and dated 1827 – oil on panel – 9¼ x 11¾in.
(Sotheby's)   **$1,420**   **£990**

JAMES WHITELAW HAMILTON – A Fishing Village In Berwickshire – signed – 14 x 17½in.
(Christie's & Edmiston's)   **$450**   **£300**

WILLIAM LEE HANKEY – Entrance To The Gypsy Quarter, Granada, Spain – signed – oil on canvas – 24 x 32in.
(Christie's)   **$4,350**   **£2,900**

R. J. HAMMOND – Leading The Plough Horse – signed – 16 x 24in.
(Sotheby's)   **$825**   **£550**

WILLIAM LEE HANKEY – The Traveller – signed – watercolour over pencil – 11 x 14in.
(Sotheby's)   **$759**   **£506**

WILLIAM LEE HANKEY – Stepping
Stones – signed and dated '92 – water-
colour – 14 x 10in.
(Sotheby's)   **$3,051**   **£2,090**

WILLIAM LEE HANKEY – Mrs Lee
Hankey (Edith Mary Garner) – signed
also inscribed on a label – watercolour
over pencil, heightened with bodycolour – 13 x 9½in.
(Sotheby's)   **$2,516**   **£1,760**

HEINRICH HANSEN – Copenhagen –
signed with initials and dated '87 – 15¾
x 25½in.
(Christie's)   **$14,385**   **£9,720**

FREDERICK DANIEL HARDY –
Christmas Morning – signed and dated
1890 – on panel – 9 x 7¼in.
(Sotheby's)   **$924**   **£616**

FREDERICK DANIEL HARDY – Too
Hot – on panel – 16 x 14in.
(Sotheby's)   **$990**   **£660**

GEORGE HARDY – 'Take Your Choice' – signed and dated 1857, and signed and inscribed on a label on the reverse – on panel – 10¾ x 10in.
(Christie's) **$2,430** **£1,620**

GEORGE HARDY – Supping Broth – signed – on panel – 11½ x 10in.
(Sotheby's) **$990** **£660**

HEYWOOD HARDY – A November Morning – signed – oil on canvas – 20 x 30in.
(Sotheby's) **$9,900** **£6,600**

HEYWOOD HARDY – Off To The Meet – signed and dated 1905 – 24½ x 36in.
(Sotheby's) **$13,651** **£9,350**

HEYWOOD HARDY – 'Forgiven' – signed and dated 1887-8 – on panel – 29¾ x 42in.
(Christie's) **$14,385** **£9,720**

HEYWOOD HARDY – The Squire's Visit – signed – oil on board – 18 x 24in.
(Sotheby's) **$8,250** **£5,500**

HEYWOOD HARDY – The Morning Ride – signed – oil on canvas – 20 x 30in.
(Sotheby's) **$14,674** **£10,120**

JAMES HARDY, Follower of – Boy
Resting On Common With His Pony
And Dogs – on canvas – 12¼in. diam.
(Sotheby's) **$610** **£418**

JAMES HARDY, JNR. – The Produce Of
The Fields – signed and dated '60 – on
panel – 6 x 8in.
(Christie's) **$1,053** **£702**

THOMAS BUSH HARDY – The Grand
Canal, Venice, Fishing Boats By The
Salute – signed and inscribed – water-
colour – 17¼ x 27¼in.
(Christie's) **$3,240** **£2,160**

THOMAS BUSH HARDY – 'South
Shields' – signed, inscribed and dated
1896 – watercolour – 44 x 77cm.
*(Henry Spencer &
Sons)* **$496** **£340**

THOMAS BUSH HARDY – Portsmouth
Harbour – signed and inscribed – watercolour heightened with bodycolour and
with scratching out – 15¼ x 30¼in.
(Sotheby's) **$1,041** **£726**

ALEXIS ALEXEIEVICH HARLAMOFF
– Portrait Of A Young Girl – oil.
(Andrew Grant) **$10,800** **£7,200**

GEORGE HENRY HARLOW – Portrait
Of Charles Mayne Young, The Actor –
30 x 25¼in.
(Sotheby's)   **$1,650**   **£1,100**

HENRI JOSEPH HARPIGNIES – La Mare
a Herissons – signed and dated 1879 –
14¼ x 10¾in.
(Christie's)   **$8,100**   **£5,400**

WILLIAM MICHAEL HARNETT – Still
Life With Turnips And Beer Stein –
signed and dated '83 – oil on board –
7¼ x 5½in.
(Christie's)   **$68,200**   **£47,361**

J. C. HARRISON – Birds Of Prey –
signed – watercolour – 20 x 15in.
(Lawrence)   **$660**   **£440**

ALEXANDER HARRISON – Cliffs, Treport – signed – oil on canvas – 23¾ x 21¼in.
(Christie's) **$3,300 £2,222**

JAMES MACDOUGAL HART – The Hay Wagon On A Bridge – signed – oil on canvas – 13½ x 23½in.
(Robert W. Skinner Inc.) **$2,000 $1,335**

JOHN CYRIL HARRISON – An Osprey – signed – watercolour, heightened with bodycolour – 28 x 22in.
(Sotheby's) **$1,485 £990**

KEVEN PRO HART – Shacks – signed – oil on board – 14 x 19in.
(Woolley & Wallis) **$435 £300**

WILLIAM HART – 'Mountainous Land-scape' – signed and dated '67 – oil on board – 10in. diam.
(Stalker & Boos) **$2,300 £1,438**

JAMES MACDOUGAL HART – Going To Town – signed and dated 1874 – oil on canvas – 20¼ x 34¼in.
(Christie's) **$17,600 £11,891**

WILLIAM HART – Standing Heifer – signed – oil on canvas – 12 x 16in.
(Robert W. Skinner Inc.) **$400 £266**

HARTLEY

MARSDEN HARTLEY – Sunken
Treasure – oil on board – 18 x 23¾in.
(Christie's)   **$33,000 £22,916**

H. J. HARVEY – 'A Nude Study' –
signed – oil – 10½ x 9½in.
(Reeds Rains)   **$165   £110**

HAROLD HARVEY – The Close Of A
Summer's Day – signed and dated '09
– 50 x 40in.
(Sotheby's)   **$9,570   £6,380**

HAROLD HARVEY – 'Camelias' –
signed and dated 1915 – on canvas –
19½ x 17¼in.
(Sotheby's)   **$2,062 £1,375**

JOHN HASSALL – A Traveller – signed
and inscribed – watercolour – 14½ x
10½in.
(Sotheby's)   **$353   £242**

JOHN HASSELL – Views Of Egham And Englefield Green, Surrey – thirty-one, all signed, inscribed and dated 1822 or 1824 – pencil and watercolour; two tinted drawings 1821; three watercolours 1828 and 1830; and a sepia drawing – various sizes.
(Sotheby's) **$2,805 £1,870**

HENRI HAYDEN – Nature Morte a la Bouilloire – signed and dated '64 – oil on canvas – 24½ x 29½in.
(Christie's) **$1,540 £1,026**

EDWIN HAYES – Yarmouth, Fishing Smacks Entering Harbour – signed, inscribed and dated 1879 in pencil on an old label – oil on board – 6½ x 8in.
(Sotheby's) **$1,578 £1,100**

EDMUND HAVELL – Head And Shoulders Portrait Of A Young Woman – signed – pastel drawing – 18 x 14in.
(Lawrence) **$214 £143**

WILLIAM AND FREDERICK JAMES HAVELL – Covent Garden Market – watercolour over pencil heightened with bodycolour – 7¾ x 16¼in.
(Sotheby's) **$9,070 £6,050**

SYDNEY HAYES – In The Parlour – signed – 18 x 27in.
(Sotheby's) **$792 £528**

EDITH HAYLLAR – 'The First Of September' – signed and dated 1886(?) and inscribed on the reverse – 18¼ x 25¾in.
(Christie's)   **$9,590   £6,480**

JAMES HAYLLAR – Going To School – signed and dated 1870, inscribed on the reverse – oil on panel – 12 x 9in.
(Sotheby's)   **$8,772   £6,050**

JAMES HAYLLAR – 'May-Day' – signed, and signed and inscribed on the reverse – 40¼ x 60¼in.
(Christie's)   **$11,988   £8,100**

JAMES HAYLLAR – Going Punting – signed and dated 1898 – 18 x 24in.
(Christie's)   **$650   £432**

JESSICA HAYLLAR – Grandfather's Little Nurse – signed and dated 1893, inscribed on an old label to reverse – watercolour – 26½ x 20in.
(Sotheby's)   **$4,419   £3,080**

JOHN WILLIAM HAYNES – Motherhood – signed – oil on canvas – 49 x 39in.
(Sotheby's)   **$4,290   £2,860**

SIR GEORGE HAYTER, Follower of —
Portrait Of Lucy Katherine Deacon With
Her Daughter — oil on canvas — 43½ x
33in.
(Sotheby's)   **$947**   **£660**

ALFRED ROBERT HAYWARD — El
Charo — signed, dated '37 and inscribed
— oil on canvas — 36 x 34in.
(Sotheby's)   **$1,043**   **£715**

SIR GEORGE HAYTER, Circle of —
Portrait Of A Lady And Her Daughter —
49½ x 39½in.
(Sotheby's)   **$1,043**   **£715**

WILLIAM HEATH — Three Officers —
signed and indistinctly dated — watercolour over pencil heightened with bodycolour — 13¾ x 9¾in.
(Sotheby's)   **$312**   **£220**

JAN VAN DEN HECKE – A Still Life
With A Lobster And A Lute – signed –
46½ x 67in.
(Sotheby's) **$28,050 £18,700**

WILLEM CLAESZ. HEDA, Follower of
– A Still Life – oil on canvas – 27¼ x
24¼in.
(Sotheby's) **$4,336 £2,970**

ERICH HECKEL – Am Ufer – signed,
inscribed and dated '23 – watercolour
with black chalk on paper – 23 x 18¾in.
(Christie's) **$11,826 £8,100**

RALPH HEDLEY – The Parish Registrar
Of Births And Deaths – signed and
dated 1892 – 52 x 61in.
(Sotheby's) **$9,900 £6,600**

ERICH HECKEL – Zwei Madchen Am
Wasser – signed and dated 1910 – oil
on board – 21½ x 27½in.
(Christie's) **$190,512 £129,600**

JAN DAVIDSZ. DE HEEM, Follower of
– Still Life Of Seafood And Fruit –
oil on canvas – 21¾ x 30in.
(Sotheby's) **$4,496 £3,080**

THOMAS HEEREMANS – A Winter
Landscape With A Frozen River – signed
and dated 1680 – 19½ x 25½in.
(Sotheby's) **$8,250 £5,500**

THOMAS HEEREMANS – A View Of
The Herring-Packers' Tower In Amsterdam
– signed – 34 x 44in.
(Sotheby's) **$5,940 £3,960**

THEODORE HEINS – Portrait Of A
Young Boy Feeding His Pet Parrot –
signed and dated 1735 – 48 x 36in.
(Sotheby's) **$1,320 £880**

HENDRICK HEERSCHOP – The
Alchemist – signed – oil on panel –
21½ x 17¼in.
(Sotheby's) **$11,070 £7,480**

J. T. HEINZ – Portrait Of A Lady, In A
White Satin Dress With Blue Bodice And
Ribbons – 29 x 24½in.
(Christie's) **$2,268 £1,512**

JACOB HEINRICH HELBIGK – A Trompe l'Oeil Of A Print Against A Boarded Wall With Two Paintings, A Tea-Set And Books On A Shelf Beneath – signed – 31 x 25¾in.
(Christie's)   **$1,944   £1,296**

J. VAN HELKE – Amsterdam – signed -- oil on canvas – 15½ x 23½in.
(Sotheby's)   **$868   £605**

PAUL-CESAR HELLEU – Madame Helleu A La Robe Rayee – signed – 18¾ x 25½in.
(Sotheby's)   **$20,075   £13,750**

HOWARD HELMICK – The Parlour Boarder – signed and dated '74 – oil on canvas – 22 x 19¼in.
(Sotheby's)   **$1,023   £682**

MATTHEUS VAN HELMONT – A Guard Room – inscribed – on panel – 24½ x 32½in.
(Sotheby's)   **$52,800   £35,200**

FRANCIS HELPS – The Red Hat – signed, inscribed on the reverse – 46 x 34in.
(Sotheby's)   **$990   £660**

FRANCIS HELPS – On The Sofa –
signed – oil on canvas – 30 x 40in.
(Sotheby's) **$972** **£528**

JAN VAN HEMESSEN – The Virgin
And Child In A Landscape – on panel
– 34 x 26¾in.
(Sotheby's) **$14,850** **£9,900**

JAN VAN HEMESSEN – Judah And
Tamar In A Landscape – on panel – 40½
x 55in.
(Sotheby's) **$14,025** **£9,350**

WILLIAM HEMSLEY – The Toilet –
signed and inscribed on the reverse – on
panel – 9 x 6in.
(Sotheby's) **$1,072** **£715**

WILLIAM HEMSLEY – A Good Joke,
Two Children Teasing A Sleeping Boy –
signed and dated 1860 – oil on panel –
12 x 9½in.
*(Dreweatt Watson &
Barton)* **$2,278** **£1,550**

WILLIAM HEMSLEY – The Village Post-
man – signed – oil on canvas – 30 x 24in.
(Sotheby's) **$6,699** **£4,620**

EDWARD LAMSON HENRY – Late
Afternoon, Port Ben, Ulster Co., NY –
signed and dated '94 – oil on board –
8¼ x 10¼in.
(Christie's) **$22,000** **£15,277**

GEORGE HENRY – Teatime – signed
– gouache over traces of pencil – 14½
x 10¼in.
(Sotheby's) **$618** **£418**

WILLIAM JOHN HENNESSY – The
Dandelion Clock – signed, inscribed and
dated 1890 on the reverse – oil on canvas laid on board – 20 x 14in.
(Sotheby's) **$4,466** **£3,080**

GEORGE HENRY – Sunset on the
River – signed and dated – 12 x 20in.
(Christie's) **$750** **£500**

GEORGE HENRY – The Orchard –
signed and dated '95 – oil on canvas –
18¼ x 20½in.
(Sotheby's) **$1,499 £1,045**

ROBERT HERDMAN – At The Fountain, Italy – signed with monogram and
dated 1856 – 24¾ x 16in.
(Christie's) **$1,295 £864**

E. B. HERBERTE – Over The Fence –
16 x 30¼in.
(Sotheby's) **$642 £440**

AUGUSTE HERBIN – Nature Morte
Aux Onions – signed – oil on canvas –
15 x 18in.
(Christie's) **$1,576 £1,080**

SIR HUBERT VON HERKOMER – The
Guard's Cheer – signed – watercolour
heightened with bodycolour over a
photogravure print – 32 x 21in.
(Sotheby's) **$1,815 £1,210**

WILLEM VAN HERP — A Woman In
An Interior — signed — on panel — 12¾
x 17¼in.
(Sotheby's)   **$7,068   £4,620**

SIR HUBERT VON HERKOMER —
'And Culture Stills His Harmonies To
Heed The Inspiration Of The Untaught
Seed' — signed with monogram and
dated 1903 — watercolour heightened
with bodycolour — 20 x 14in.
(Sotheby's)   **$660   £440**

J. F. HERRING — A Groom Holding A
Carriage Horse, With Dogs, In A Loosebox
— 34¾ x 27½in.
(Christie's)   **$3,888   £2,592**

CHARLES HERMANS — Circe — signed
— 78¼ x 49in.
(Christie's)   **$23,976 £16,200**

JOHN FREDERICK HERRING,
Follower of — Watering The Horses —
bears signature — on canvas — 16½ x
21in.
(Sotheby's)   **$835   £572**

JOHN FREDERICK HERRING, JNR. –
Four Horses, Cattle And Chickens In A
Farm Yard – signed – 14 x 19in.
(Chrystals
Auctions) **$10,950 £7,500**

JOHN FREDERICK HERRING, JNR. –
Horses, Goats And Poultry In A Farm-
yard – signed – on panel – 7½ x 7½in.
(Christie's) **$2,413 £1,620**

JOHN FREDERICK HERRING, JNR. –
Two Horses In A Field With A Pond And
Ducks – signed – on board – 8 x 10in.
(Woolley &
Wallis) **$1,170 £780**

JOHN FREDERICK HERRING, JNR. –
Ducks And Rabbits – signed – 20 x 31in.
(Sotheby's) **$4,290 £2,860**

JOHN FREDERICK HERRING, JNR. –
A Farmyard – signed – oil on canvas –
28 x 35in.
(Sotheby's) **$7,975 £5,500**

JOHN FREDERICK HERRING, JNR. –
The Farmyard – signed and dated 1851
– 15 x 20in.
(Sotheby's) **$10,439 £7,150**

JOHN FREDERICK HERRING, JNR. –
Sheep And A Dog In A Landscape –
signed – on board – 6 x 8in.
(Christie's) **$1,375 £918**

HERRING

JOHN FREDERICK HERRING, SNR.,
Follower of – An Officer Of The 17th
Lancers Holding His Charger – on
canvas – 21 x 26in.
(Sotheby's) **$1,122 £748**

JOHN FREDERICK HERRING, SNR. –
Horses Feeding – signed and dated 1851
– 21½ x 29¾in.
(Sotheby's) **$31,350 £20,900**

JOHN FREDERICK HERRING, SNR. –
Mare And Foal – signed and dated 1854-6
– on panel – 9¾ x 12in.
(Sotheby's) **$4,125 £2,750**

JOHN FREDERICK HERRING, SNR.,
Attributed to – Little Wonder, A Bay
Racehorse With A Jockey Up, In A
Landscape – with signature, inscription
and the date 1840 – 14¼ x 18in.
(Christie's) **$4,827 £3,240**

JOHN FREDERICK HERRING, SNR.
– Donkeys – signed and dated 1852 –
on panel – 10 x 12in.
(Sotheby's) **$1,320 £880**

JOHN FREDERICK HERRING, SNR. –
Waiting Beside The Gate – signed and
dated 1846 – 21½ x 29½in.
(Sotheby's) **$37,800 £25,200**

JOHN FREDERICK HERRING, SNR. –
Jerry, A Black Racehorse, With Ben Smith
Up – signed and dated 1824 – 21 x
29¼in.
(Sotheby's)   **$67,650 £45,100**

ALDRO THOMPSON HIBBARD –
Vermont Church – signed – oil on
canvas laid on board – 18 x 23½in.
(Robert W. Skinner
Inc.)   **$1,100   £735**

GUSTAAF A. F. HEYLIGERS – A
Possible Purchase – indistinctly signed
– on canvas – 22¼ x 27¼in.
(Sotheby's)   **$4,125   £2,750**

ALDRO THOMPSON HIBBARD –
Frozen Brook – signed – oil on canvas
– 25 x 30in.
(Robert W. Skinner
Inc.)   **$3,500   £2,333**

SIR HANS HEYSEN – 'Valley In The
Flinders' – signed – watercolour – 32
x 39cm.
(Australian Art
Auctions)   **$4,021   £2,681**

ALDRO THOMPSON HIBBARD –
Valley Farmstead In Winter – signed –
oil on canvas – 15 x 30in.
(Robert W. Skinner
Inc.)   **$3,400   £2,266**

HICKS

GEORGE ELGAR HICKS – A Summer Rose – signed and dated 1910 – 24 x 20in.
(Christie's) **$730** **£486**

JOSEPH HIGHMORE – Portrait Of A Lady, In A Yellow And White Dress With A Blue Scarf, Holding A Floral Wreath – signed and dated 1737 – 35 x 27in.
(Christie's) **$3,888** **£2,592**

T. VON HIENEMAN – Dutch Canal Scene – signed – oil on canvas – 23½ x 18½in.
(Sotheby's) **$931** **£638**

JOSEPH HIGHMORE – Portrait Of Mrs Franklin, Daughter Of Dr. R. Middleton – oil on canvas – 50 x 40in.
(Sotheby's) **$1,980** **£1,320**

HOWARD L. HILDEBRANDT –
'Esmeralda' – signed – oil on canvas –
27 x 27in.
(Robert W. Skinner
Inc.) **$3,500 £2,335**

JAMES JOHN HILL – The Shepherd
Boy – signed and dated 1872 – 49 x
39in.
(Sotheby's) **$3,854 £2,640**

RICHARD H. HILDER – Near Cranbrook,
Kent – oil on canvas – 14 x 18in.
(Sotheby's) **$3,157 £2,200**

HARRY HILL – A Chestnut Hunter In
A Stable – signed and dated 1863 – on
canvas – 17 x 21in.
(Sotheby's) **$1,445 £990**

JAMES JOHN HILL – Young Motherhood
– signed and dated 1868 – 36 x 27in.
(Sotheby's) **$9,900 £6,600**

JUSTUS HILL – Playing With Dolly
– signed – oil on canvas – 12 x 8in.
(Sotheby's) **$1,402** **£935**

ROBIN HILL – Sea Eagle, Redbacked
– signed, inscribed and dated '64 –
watercolour, heightened with bodycolour – 29 x 20in.
(Sotheby's) **$429** **£286**

ROBERT ALEXANDER HILLINGFORD
– Napoleon's Peril At Brienne-le-Chateau
– signed and dated 1891 – 38¾ x 55½in.
(Christie's) **$35,164** **£23,760**

ROBERT ALEXANDER HILLINGFORD
– Come Upstairs – signed – oil on canvas
– 20 x 30in.
(Sotheby's) **$2,871** **£1,980**

ROBERT HILLS – A Farmyard With
Donkeys, Pigs And Poultry – signed and
dated 1809 – watercolour – 12 x 16¼in.
(Sotheby's) **$2,640** **£1,760**

ROBERT HILLS – Cattle Watering By A
Farm; and Cattle Grazing – watercolour
– 4 x 5½in.
(Sotheby's) **$1,015** **£715 Pair**

FREDERICK HINES – By The Duck
Pond – signed – watercolour heightened
with bodycolour – 21 x 14in.
(Sotheby's)　　　**$577**　**£385**

IVON HITCHENS – Spring Landscape
At Moatlands – signed, and signed again
and inscribed on the stretcher – oil on
canvas – 20 x 30in.
(Christie's)　　**$7,290**　**£4,860**

MEINDERT HOBBEMA, Circle of – A
Village Landscape With A Mill And
Fishermen – bears inscription – oil on
panel – 29½ x 43¼in.
(Sotheby's)　　**$5,621**　**£3,850**

WILLIAM HOARE, Attributed to –
Portrait Of John Meredith Of Templerany,
Co. Wicklow – 48 x 38¼in.
(Sotheby's)　　**$1,237**　**£825**

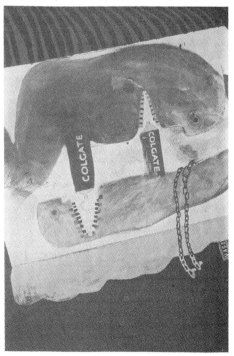

DAVID HOCKNEY – Cleaning Teeth;
Early Evening (10pm), W.11 – signed,
and inscribed and dated 1962 on the
reverse – oil on canvas – 72 x 48in.
(Christie's)　　**$22,075**　**£15,120**

269

DAVID HOCKNEY – Boy About To Take
A Shower – acrylic on canvas – 36 x 36in.
(Christie's) **$100,440 £66,960**

FERDINAND HODLER – Schreitende
Frau – signed and dated 1917 – oil on
canvas – 130 x 70cm.
*(Germann
Auktionshaus)* **$55,823 £38,235**

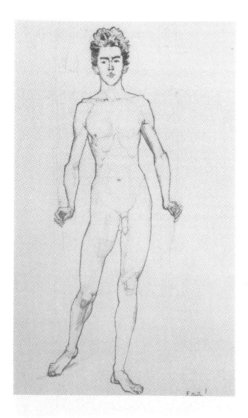

FERDINAND HODLER – Studie Zu
'Jungling Vom Weibe Bewundert' –
signed – pen and black ink over pencil
on squared paper – 17¼ x 10¾in.
(Christie's) **$3,888 £2,592**

FRANCIS EDWIN HODGE – Carnival
– signed, dated 1895 and inscribed on
the reverse – on canvas – 25¼ x 30¼in.
(Sotheby's) **$321 £220**

GEORGE HODGSON – Head Of A
Negro – signed – oil on panel – 10 x
7¾in.
(Sotheby's) **$759** **£550**

KARL HOFER – Sitzender Akt –
signed with monogram – watercolour
on paper – 20¼ x 16¼in.
(Christie's) **$2,207** **£1,512**

HANS HOFFMANN – A Hare Among
Plants, With A Robin, Lizards And
Insects – on panel – 24¾ x 31in.
(Sotheby's) **$610,500 £407,000**

**THOMAS CHRISTOPHER HOFLAND,
Attributed to** – A View Of Crossbasket
Castle, High Blantyre, Lanarkshire, The
Property Of Captain Thomas Peter –
21¾ x 29½in.
(Sotheby's) **$3,465** **£2,310**

**THOMAS CHRISTOPHER HOFLAND,
Follower of** – A Wooded River Landscape
With Rustics And A Fortune Teller In The
Foreground – 27½ x 35½in.
(Sotheby's) **$544** **£363**

271

HANS HOLBEIN, The Younger, Circle of – Portrait Of A Man In Black – oil on panel – 14½ x 12¼in.
(Sotheby's)   **$15,954 £10,780**

THOMAS W. HOLGATE – The Music Lesson – signed – oil on canvas – 22 x 30in.
(Sotheby's)   **$5,582   £3,850**

JAMES HOLLAND – Rouen From The River Seine – signed and indistinctly dated – watercolour over pencil heightened with bodycolour on grey paper – 11¾ x 17in.
(Sotheby's)   **$1,980   £1,320**

WINSLOW HOMER – Out On A Limb – signed – watercolour and pencil on paper – 6 x 8in.
(Christie's)   **$55,000   £38,194**

HONDECOETER – Peacock, Pigeons, Chickens And Chicks In A Landscape – 34 x 54in.
(Lawrence)   **$3,960   £2,640**

N. HONE – Portrait Of Miss Henrietta Lovelace, In A Blue And White Dress – on canvas on panel – 12 x 9½in.
(Christie's)   **$1,539   £1,026**

NATHANIEL HONE – Portrait Of James Kirkpatrick With His Sons James And George – oil on canvas – 68¾ x 83½in. *(Sotheby's)* **$42,900 £28,600**

GERRIT VAN HONTHORST, Studio of – A Concert – oil on canvas – 51¾ x 71½in. *(Sotheby's)* **$8,833 £6,050**

JAMES CLARKE HOOK – Catching A Mermaid – signed with monogram and dated '83 – 36 x 55in. *(Christie's)* **$7,192 £4,860**

JOHN HORACE HOOPER – Sunset Near Gomshall, Surrey – signed and inscribed on the reverse – on canvas – 40 x 60in. *(Sotheby's)* **$1,525 £1,045**

JOHN HORACE HOOPER – Sunset On The Arun – signed and inscribed – on canvas – 24¼ x 42in. *(Sotheby's)* **$1,155 £770**

ARTHUR HOPKINS – The Siren's Cave
– signed and dated 1907 – watercolour
heightened with white – 22¾ x 38in.
(Christie's) **$704** **£486**

ARTHUR HOPKINS – The New Rick
– signed and dated 1911 – watercolour
heightened with scratching out – 24 x
17in.
(Sotheby's) **$8,910** **£5,940**

FRANCES ANN HOPKINS – The Fruits
Of The Orchard – signed with initials –
watercolour over pencil heightened with
bodycolour – 12¾ x 17½in.
(Sotheby's) **$495** **£330**

E. HORARI – The Goose Girl – signed –
oil on canvas – 19¼ x 23½in.
(Sotheby's) **$315** **£220**

JAN JOSEF HOREMANS, Circle of –
Interior With A Music Party – indistinctly
signed – oil on canvas – 18½ x 22in.
(Sotheby's) **$4,558** **£3,080**

GEORGE W. HORLOR – Give A Poor
Dog A Bone – signed and dated 1856 –
oil on canvas – 17 x 21in.
(Sotheby's) **$3,256** **£2,200**

GEORGE W. HORLOR – Watchers Of
The Herd – signed and dated 1891 –
oil on canvas – 18 x 24in.
(Sotheby's) **$1,383** **£935**

JOSEPH HORLOR – Fisherfolk On The
Beach Below St. Michael's Mount –
signed – on canvas – 12¼ x 25¼in.
(Sotheby's) **$481** **£330**

THOMAS LYDE HORNBROOK –
English Frigates At Anchor In Corunna
Harbour – 17 x 24in.
(Sotheby's) **$3,300** **£2,200**

EDWARD ATKINSON HORNEL –
Gathering Primroses – signed and
dated 1918 – oil – 25 x 30in.
(Sotheby's) **$6,270** **£4,180**

EDWARD ATKINSON HORNEL –
Butterflies – signed and dated 1906 –
canvas on board – 26¼ x 47¾in.
(Christie's) **$16,500** **£11,000**

EDWARD ATKINSON HORNEL – The
Lily Pond – signed and dated '99 – 24
x 20in.
*(Christie's &
Edmiston's)* **$11,250** **£7,500**

EDWARD ATKINSON HORNEL – The
Bird's Nest – signed and dated 1919 –
20 x 24in.
*(Christie's &
Edmiston's)* **$5,700** **£3,800**

ERNEST ATKINSON HORNEL – 'A
Fairy Tale' – signed and dated 1911 –
on canvas – 39¾ x 29½in.
(Sotheby's) **$12,848 £8,800**

THOMAS HORNER, Circle of – A
Fantastic Landscape With A Valley
Appearing Through A Frame Of Trees
– oil on canvas – 13 x 15in.
(Sotheby's) **$742 £495**

JOHN CALLCOTT HORSLEY –
'The World Forgetting', Sunday Afternoon In Kensington Gardens, A.D. 1780
– signed – 34¼ x 48¼in.
(Christie's) **$11,264 £7,560**

ELMYR DE HORY – Portrait Of A Girl,
After Renoir – signed on the reverse –
oil on canvas – 29½ x 24½in.
(Sotheby's) **$990 £660**

ELMYR DE HORY – Nude, After
Kisling – signed – oil on canvas – 25½
x 19¾in.
(Sotheby's) **$4,290 £2,860**

JOHN ADAM P. HOUSTON – The Skipp-
ing Rope – signed and dated 1863, inscribed on the reverse – oil on canvas – 21½
x 14½in.
(Sotheby's) **$907 £605**

JOHN ADAM P. HOUSTON – The Pansy Seller – signed and dated 1866, inscribed on the reverse – oil – 25½ x 17in.
(Sotheby's) **$1,567** **£1,045**

WILLIAM HOWARD – A Dutch Town – signed – 30 x 50in.
(Sotheby's) **$2,475** **£1,650**

WILLIAM HOWARD – The White Hart Hotel, Sonning – signed – 29½ x 49¼in.
(Christie's) **$2,105** **£1,404**

PHILIPP HOYOLL – Very Wise Politicians – signed, inscribed on a label on the reverse – oil on canvas – 12 x 9½in.
(Sotheby's) **$1,402** **£935**

LOUIS HUBNER – A Monkey With Peaches, Plums And Other Fruit On A Ledge – signed – 28¼ x 35½in.
(Christie's) **$5,184** **£3,456**

ANNA HOPE HUDSON – The Violin Solo – oil on canvas – 24 x 20in.
(Christie's) **$4,860** **£3,240**

WILLIAM HUGGINS – Antelope And
Fawn – indistinctly signed, signed and
inscribed on the reverse – diameter 28in.
(Sotheby's)   **$990   £660**

WILLIAM HUGGINS – Study Of A Cow's
Head – signed with initials and dated 1853
– on canvas – diameter 8½in.
(Sotheby's)   **$560   £374**

ARTHUR HUGHES – The Rescue –
signed – 43 x 21in.
(Sotheby's)   **$24,750 £16,500**

ARTHUR HUGHES – The Beggar Maid
– signed – on panel – 14½ x 10¼in.
(Christie's)   **$1,458   £972**

JOHN JOSEPH HUGHES – A Country
House In A Valley – signed and dated
1865 – 42 x 54in.
(Sotheby's)   **$2,475   £1,650**

WILLIAM HUGHES – A Still Life Study
Of Mixed Fruit And A Silver Goblet On
A Table Top – signed and dated '83 –
oil on canvas – 25½ x 19½in.
(Sotheby's) **$1,736 £1,210**

FREDERICK WILLIAM HULME,
Follower of – Anglers Resting Beside A
River – oil on canvas – 29½ x 24¼in.
(Sotheby's) **$835 £572**

ABRAHAM HULK, SNR. – Beached
Fishing Boats At Low Tide – signed –
oil on canvas – 15 x 23¼in.
(Sotheby's) **$1,606 £1,100**

FRANS DE HULST – A River Landscape – on panel – 16¼ x 21in.
(Sotheby's) **$7,590 £5,060**

ABRAHAM HULK, SNR. – Shipping In
A Choppy Sea – signed – watercolour
– 5¾ x 9in.
(Sotheby's) **$693 £462**

EDITH HUME – The Model Boat –
signed – oil on canvas – 16 x 24in.
(Sotheby's) **$8,580 £5,720**

OZIAS HUMPHREY – Portrait Of George Stubbs – signed on the reverse and dated 1777 – black and white chalk on brown paper – 16½ x 14¾in.
(Sotheby's)   **$66,000   £44,000**

THOMAS H. HUNN – 'Windsor Castle From The Water Meadows' – watercolour – 17 x 25½in.
(Riddetts)   **$675   £450**

CHARLES HUNT – A Street Fight – signed and dated 1884 – 24 x 36in.
(Sotheby's)   **$13,200   £8,800**

CHARLES HUNT – The Young Soldier – signed and dated 1871 – 19½ x 23in.
(Christie's)   **$2,574   £1,728**

CHARLES HUNT – A Carriage Ride – signed and dated 1869 – 25 x 36in.
(Sotheby's)   **$6,270   £4,180**

CHARLES HUNT – The Young Soldier – signed with initials and dated '72 – 21 x 16in.
(Christie's)   **$1,295   £864**

CHARLES HUNT – The Original Minstrels – signed and dated 1873 – 24 x 36in.
(Sotheby's)   **$6,105   £4,070**

EDGAR HUNT – Geese And Donkeys In A Barn – signed and dated 1951 – oil on canvas board – 10½ x 14½in.
(Sotheby's)   **$5,366   £3,740**

EDGAR HUNT – Hen, Chicks And Tortoise – signed – on canvas board – 9½ x 7¾in.
(Lawrence)   **$3,395   £2,310**

EDGAR HUNT – Doves Feeding – signed and dated 1912 – 7 x 10in.
(Sotheby's)   **$3,300   £2,200**

EDGAR HUNT – A Barn Interior With Goats, Chickens And A Rabbit – signed and dated 1951 – oil on canvas – 10½ x 14½in.
(Sotheby's) $6,629   £4,620

EDGAR HUNT – Chickens And Rabbits – signed and dated 1917 – on canvas – 7¾ x 10¾in.
(Sotheby's) $4,950   £3,300

EDGAR HUNT – Ducks By A Pond – signed and dated 1924 – 14 x 12in.
(Christie's) $9,333   £6,264

EDGAR HUNT – Family Pride – signed and dated 1907 – 12 x 10in.
(Sotheby's) $5,139   £3,520

EDGAR HUNT – Best Of Friends – signed and dated 1916 – 23¾ x 36in.
(Christie's) $3,240   £2,160

EDGAR HUNT – Goats And Hens – signed and dated 1945 – on canvas board – 10¾ x 14½in.
(Lawrence) $6,548   £4,455

REUBEN HUNT – Dressing The Well –
signed and dated 1882 – oil on canvas –
30 x 50in.
(Sotheby's)　　**$3,190**　**£2,200**

WALTER HUNT – A Barn Interior With
Calves And Chickens – signed, dated
1897 and inscribed on the reverse – on
canvas – 12 x 16in.
(Sotheby's)　　**$6,270**　**£4,180**

WALTER HUNT – A Gipsy Girl With
Donkeys And Puppies – signed and
dated 1894 – on board – 10 x 17¼in.
(Sotheby's)　　**$5,610**　**£3,740**

WALTER HUNT – Divided Affection –
signed and dated '96 – 42½ x 30½in.
(Sotheby's)　　**$18,150**　**£12,100**

WALTER HUNT – Good Friends –
signed and dated 1903 – 19½ x 29½in.
(Christie's)　　**$20,115**　**£13,500**

WILLIAM HENRY HUNT – The Russian
Game Seller – signed – watercolour
heightened with white – 14¼ x 10in.
(Christie's)　　**$1,053**　**£702**

WILLIAM HENRY HUNT – A Young Girl Seated On A Chair – signed – watercolour over pencil – 10¾ x 7¼in. *(Sotheby's)*   **$907   £605**

WILLIAM HENRY HUNT – New Red Shoes – watercolour heightened with bodycolour with scratching out – 13 x 8¼in. *(Sotheby's)*   **$9,075   £6,050**

WILLIAM HENRY HUNT – The Attack; and The Defeat – signed and dated 1834 – watercolour heightened with bodycolour and gum arabic, with scratching out – 16½ x 11½in. *(Sotheby's)*   **$7,260 £4,840 Pair**

WILLIAM HOLMAN HUNT – A Young Shepherd – oil on canvas – 23½ x 18½in.
(Sotheby's) **$4,125 £2,750**

WILLIAM MORRIS HUNT – 'June Clouds' – oil on canvas – 30½ x 20½in.
(Robert W. Skinner Inc.) **$4,000 £2,665**

COLIN HUNTER – Summer Twilight – signed and dated 1884 – oil on canvas – 27 x 48in.
(Sotheby's) **$1,736 £1,210**

GEORGE LESLIE HUNTER – Still Life, Vase of Flowers And Fruit On A Table – signed – paper on panel – 14 x 11¾in.
(Woolley & Wallis) **$390 £260**

GEORGE LESLIE HUNTER – Still Life With A Compotier And A Blue Ginger Jar – signed – on board – 22 x 17½in.
(Christie's & Edmiston's) **$5,400 £3,600**

HURT

LOUIS B. HURT – Cattle In Scottish
Highlands – oil – 24 x 36in.
(Dacre, Son &
Hartley) **$1,950 £1,300**

LOUIS BOSWORTH HURT – Resting
A Herd, Glen Etive – signed and
dated 1882, inscribed on the reverse –
oil on canvas – 24 x 35in.
(Sotheby's) **$1,651 £1,155**

ROBERT GEMMELL HUTCHISON –
Lullaby – signed, inscribed on a label
on frame – oil on canvas – 24 x 17in.
(Sotheby's) **$11,233 £7,590**

GILES HUSSEY – Profile Portrait Of
Prince Charles Edward Stuart, The Young
Pretender – inscribed – pen with grey
and brown ink and wash, on laid paper
– oval 9¼ x 7¼in.
(Sotheby's) **$3,135 £2,090**

ROBERT GEMMELL HUTCHISON –
Tending Geraniums – signed – 16 x 12in.
(Sotheby's) **$6,270 £4,180**

ROBERT GEMMELL HUTCHISON –
Feeding The Chickens – signed – oil
on canvas – 13 x 16in.
(Sotheby's)   **$2,930   £1,980**

ROBERT GEMMELL HUTCHISON –
An Orchard Near Carluke – signed and
inscribed – 20 x 16¼in.
(Christie's)   **$2,850   £1,900**

ROBERT GEMMELL HUTCHISON –
Sailing Boats – signed – oil on canvas
– 12 x 16in.
(Sotheby's)   **$7,814   £5,280**

WILLIAM HENRY FLORIO HUTCHISON
– Buffalo Shooting From Elephants; and
Sand Grouse Shooting From Elephants –
one signed and dated 1837 – 24¼ x 29¼in.
(Sotheby's)   **$16,500   £11,000 Pair**

JAN VAN HUYSUM – A Still Life Of
Fruit And Flowers – signed – oil on
canvas – 16½ x 13¼in.
(Sotheby's)   **$166,056 £112,200**

IBBETSON

JULIUS CAESAR IBBETSON − Taking Cattle To Market − signed and dated 1793 − watercolour − 6¾ x 9in.
(Sotheby's) **$874** **£616**

RUDOLPH IHLEE − Gosses − signed and dated '21 − oil on canvas − 28 x 36in.
(Sotheby's) **$1,179** **£825**

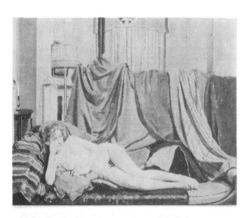

RUDOLPH IHLEE − Reclining Nude − signed and dated '20 − on panel − 15 x 18in.
(Sotheby's) **$759** **£506**

INNOCENZO DA IMOLA − Portrait Of A Young Woman − oil on panel − 23¾ x 17½in.
(Sotheby's) **$17,094** **£11,550**

RUDOLPH IHLEE − Breton Fisherfolk − signed and dated 1913 − oil on canvas − 28 x 36in.
(Sotheby's) **$597** **£418**

JOHN O'BRIEN INMAN − New York Landscape − signed and dated 1891 − oil on canvas − 18 x 29in.
(Robert W. Skinner Inc.) **$1,500** **£1,000**

MRS AUGUSTA INNES, nee Withers –
A Hen With Her Young – signed – watercolour heightened with white – 16¾ x
21in.
(Sotheby's)　　**$924**　　**£616**

MRS AUGUSTA INNES, nee Withers –
Red Legged Partridges With Their Brood
– signed and dated 1844 – watercolour
heightened with white – 17½ x 22¾in.
(Sotheby's)　　**$1,567**　**£1,045**

JOSEF ISRAELS – Mother And Child
At The Barn Door – signed – oil on
panel – 12½ x 8¾in.
(Sotheby's)　　**$947**　　**£660**

FREDERICK I'ONS – A Native Wood-
man With His Masters – oil on board –
12½ x 10½in.
(Sotheby's)　　**$297**　　**£198**

**NORTH ITALIAN SCHOOL, 16th
century** – Portrait Of A Man – oil on
panel – 15¼ x 12in.
(Sotheby's)　　**$1,302**　　**£880**

SAMUEL PHILLIPS JACKSON – Sty Head Tarn, Cumberland, Early Morning – signed and dated 1858 and inscribed on the reverse – watercolour – 22½ x 36in.
(Sotheby's) **$660** **£440**

ANTONIO JACOBSEN – Pilot Boat – signed, dated 1884 and inscribed – oil on canvas – 21¾ x 36in.
(Christie's) **$8,800** **£5,865**

WILLY JAECKEL, Attributed to – Der Denker – signed – gouache on vellum – 11 x 10¾in.
(Christie's) **$598** **£410**

DAVID JAMES – Devon Waves – oil.
(Andrew Grant) **$2,475** **£1,650**

DAVID JAMES – Atlantic Breakers – signed and dated 1891 – oil on canvas – 24 x 36in.
(Sotheby's) **$1,320** **£880**

DAVID JAMES – An Ebbing Tide, Coast Of Devon – signed and dated '91, inscribed on the reverse – oil on canvas – 24½ x 49½in.
(Sotheby's) **$6,765** **£4,510**

WILLIAM JAMES – A View Of The Thames Looking Towards London Bridge With The Royal Barge – oil on canvas – 29½ x 49¼in.
(Sotheby's) **$26,400** **£17,600**

WILLY JAMES – Paris, La Rue En Ete – signed – pastel – 33 x 41cm.
(Germann Auktionshaus) **$1,002** **£668**

MIDDLETON JAMESON – In The Fields – signed and dated 1883 – oil on canvas – 28 x 21in.
(Sotheby's) **$1,953** **£1,320**

JOHANNES JANSON – Pastoral Landscape With A Peasant Family, Their Sheep And Cattle In The Foreground – signed and dated 1777 – oil on panel – 15¾ x 13¾in.
(Sotheby's) **$2,649** **£1,815**

J. W. JANKOWSKY – 'The Grand Canal, Venice' – signed – oil on canvas – 20 x 16in.
(Morphets) **$790** **£525**

ABRAHAM JANSSENS – The Virgin And Child With The Infant Saint John – oil on canvas – 48½ x 38½in.
(Sotheby's) **$34,188** **£23,100**

HIERONYMUS JANSSENS, Follower of
– The Prodigal Son Removed From The
Brothel – oil on canvas – 31¾ x 39in.
(Sotheby's) **$1,124** **£770**

WILLIAM SAMUEL JAY – By A Mill
– signed and dated '71 – oil on canvas
– 25 x 40in.
(Sotheby's) **$865** **£605**

ALEXEJ JAWLENSKY – Junges Madchen Mit Grunen Augen – signed,
indistinctly inscribed on the reverse – oil
on board – 21¼ x 19½in.
(Christie's) **$259,200 £172,800**

ARTHUR JENKINS – On The Way To
Bath Races – signed and inscribed on the
reverse – oil on panel – 13½ x 17¼in.
(Sotheby's) **$1,262** **£880**

ALEXEJ JAWLENSKY – Natali –
signed – oil on board – 25½ x 19¼in.
(Christie's) **$238,140 £162,000**

D. C. JENKINS – Two Children Seated
Below Apple Blossom Trees – signed
and dated – on canvas – 26 x 21in.
(Morphets) **$480** **£320**

HARALD ADOF NIKOLAJ JERICHAU
– The Parthenon El Plaza With The
Temple Of Theseus, Athens – signed
with initials – watercolour over pencil
heightened with white and gum arabic
– 24¼ x 31in.
(Sotheby's)   **$1,184   £858**

AUGUSTUS JOHN – Coastal Scene –
signed on the reverse – oil on panel – 9½
x 13in.
(Christie's)   **$2,915   £1,944**

BALDOMERO GALOFRE Y JIMENEZ
– Bullocks At A Water Trough – signed
– oil on panel – 7 x 11in.
(Sotheby's)   **$2,871   £1,980**

AUGUSTUS JOHN – Portrait Of Robin
– oil on canvas – 21½ x 18in.
(Christie's)   **$12,635   £8,424**

AUGUSTUS JOHN – Dorelia Standing
– signed – watercolour and pencil –
21 x 10¾in.
(Christie's)   **$12,636   £8,424**

AUGUSTUS JOHN – Olive Trees In
A Mediterranean Landscape – signed –
oil on canvas – 15 x 22in.
(Christie's)   **$5,754**   **£3,888**

AUGUSTUS JOHN – Portrait Of The
Countess Of Kimberley – 25½ x 20in.
(Sotheby's)   **$3,630**   **£2,420**

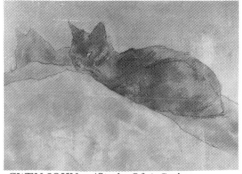

GWEN JOHN – 'Study Of A Cat' –
gouache – 6½ x 8¼in.
(Sotheby's)   **$2,569**   **£1,760**

AUGUSTUS JOHN – Head Studies Of
Ida – pen, black ink and pencil on light
beige paper – 10¾ x 8in.
(Christie's)   **$1,780**   **£1,188**

CORNELIUS JOHNSON – Portrait Of
Anne Campion – oil on canvas – 29½
x 24¼in.
(Sotheby's)   **$12,993**   **£8,250**

EASTMAN JOHNSON – The Picture
Book – signed and dated 1855 – pencil
on brown paper – 11½ x 13¼in.
(Christie's)   **$104,500 £72,569**

CORNELIUS JOHNSON – Portrait Of
A Gentleman – signed and dated 1633
– oil on panel – 31 x 24½in.
(Sotheby's)   **$14,025   £9,350**

CORNELIUS JOHNSON – Portrait Of
Sir John Heath – signed and dated 1632
– oil on panel – 29 x 22in.
(Sotheby's)   **$6,600   £4,400**

EASTMAN JOHNSON – Ragamuffin –
signed – oil on board – 11½ x 6¼in.
(Christie's)   **$39,600 £27,500**

EDWARD KILLINGWORTH JOHNSON – Catching The Pony – signed and dated 1879 – watercolour over pencil, heightened with bodycolour – 20 x 30in.
(Sotheby's) $13,651 £9,350

EDWARD KILLINGWORTH JOHNSON
– Collecting Roses – signed and dated
1874 – watercolour and bodycolour –
25 x 18in.
(Christie's) $10,962   £7,560

ALEXANDER JOHNSTON – The Letter
– signed – oil on canvas – 17 x 13in.
(Dreweatt Watson &
Barton) $1,470   £1,000

J. HUMPHREYS JOHNSTON – A Breton
Girl Threshing – on canvas – 39 x 31in.
(Sotheby's)   **$379   £253**

ADRIAN JONES – An Arab Stallion
– signed – oil on canvas – 20 x 16in.
(Sotheby's)   **$4,554   £3,300**

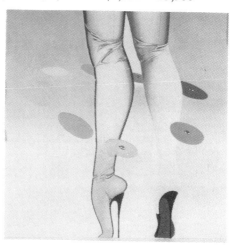

ALLEN JONES – Gallery Gasper –
signed, inscribed and dated 1966/67
– oil on canvas – 36 x 36in.
(Christie's)   **$9,460   £6,480**

WALTER JONAS – Frau In Rot –
signed – oil on canvas – 47 x 38cm.
*(Germann
    Auktionshaus)* **$1,458   £972**

CHARLES JONES – Autumn, Hamp-
shire Downs With Sheep – signed with
monogram – oil on canvas – 24 x 41¼in.
(Sotheby's)   **$1,650   £1,100**

CHARLES JONES – A Study Of Sheep
– signed with monogram and dated
1884 on the reverse – on canvas – 8 x
12in.
(Sotheby's) **$1,124** **£770**

CHARLES JONES – A Calf And Pigs
In A Barn – signed in monogram and
signed on the reverse – on board – 12
x 16in.
(Christie's) **$1,045** **£702**

FRANCES COATES JONES - Picking
Summer Flowers– signed - oil on canvas
laid down on masonite. 17½x 11in.
(Sotheby's) **$6,600** **£4,715**

J. C. JONES – A Mountainous Landscape
– signed and dated 1890 – 8 x 16½in.
(Lawrence) **$95** **£60**

CHARLES JONES – An Avenue With
Numerous Sheep – signed in monogram
and dated 1862 – 29¾ x 24¾in.
(Christie's) **$2,252** **£1,512**

PAUL JONES, Follower of – Cock
Pheasants And A Hen In The Distance –
oil on canvas – 13¾ x 18in.
(Sotheby's) **$1,252** **£858**

T. HAMPSON JONES – Haymaking –
signed and dated 1875 – watercolour –
11 x 19¼in.
(Sotheby's)   **$346**   **£231**

J. H. AND PAUL JONES – Breaking
Cover – signed – oil on canvas – 28 x
36in.
(Sotheby's)   **$5,610**   **£3,740**

WILLIAM JONES – Pheasant Shooting
– 13½ x 17½in.
(Sotheby's)   **$1,980**   **£1,320**

JAN MARTSEN DE JONGE – Cavalry
Engaging Infantry – signed and dated
1627 – on panel – 9¼ x 11½in.
(Christie's)   **$3,564**   **£2,376**

JOHAN BARTHOLD JONGKIND – Vue
Du Pont De Notre Dame De Paris Avec Le
Palais De Justice – signed and dated 1858
– 12¾ x 17¾in.
(Sotheby's)   **$28,050**   **£18,700**

JOHAN BARTHOLD JONGKIND – La
Seine A Charenton – signed and dated
'68 – oil on canvas – 9¾ x 13in.
(Sotheby's) **$18,150 £12,100**

**NICOLAS JACQUES JULLIARD,
Attributed to** – A Pastoral Scene – oil
on canvas – 24 x 19¼in.
(Sotheby's) **$2,087 £1,430**

SINGLETON JOWETT – 'An Argument'
– signed – oil – 15 x 11in.
(Reeds Rains) **$812 £560**

JULES JOYANT, Attributed to – A
View Of The Admiralty., St. Petersburg
– pen and brown ink and wash – 11¾
x 17in.
(Sotheby's) **$502 £330**

JEAN MARIE AUGUSTE JUGELET –
Vessels Entering A Port – signed – on
panel – 9 x 11in.
*(Sotheby Beresford
 Adams)* **$406 £242**

NICO W. JUNGMANN – Two Little
Dutch Girls – signed – watercolour –
15 x 11¾in.
(Sotheby's) **$835 £572**

NICO W. JUNGMANN – Dutch Girl – watercolour heightened with body-colour – 15¼ x 11½in.
(Sotheby's) **$289** **£198**

NICO W. JUNGMANN – Dutch Canal Scene – signed with monogram – watercolour – 15½ x 11¾in.
(Sotheby's) **$693** **£462**

ANDREAS JUUEL – Geels Bakke, Near Copenhagen – signed and dated 1851 – 14 x 19½in. *(Christie's)* **$10,045 £6,696**

KADAR

BELA KADAR – Trois Jeunes Filles –
signed – gouache – 23 x 16½in.
(Sotheby's)   **$1,485**   **£990**

BELA KADAR – Les Danceurs – charcoal – 11¾ x 10in.
(Sotheby's)   **$412**   **£275**

BELA KADAR – Sans Titre – signed –
gouache on paper – 31¾ x 22¾in.
(Christie's)   **$1,684**   **£1,080**

BELA KADAR – Seated Nude – signed
– brown crayon heightened with brown
watercolour over pencil on paper – 17½
x 11½in.
(Christie's)   **$2,596**   **£1,728**

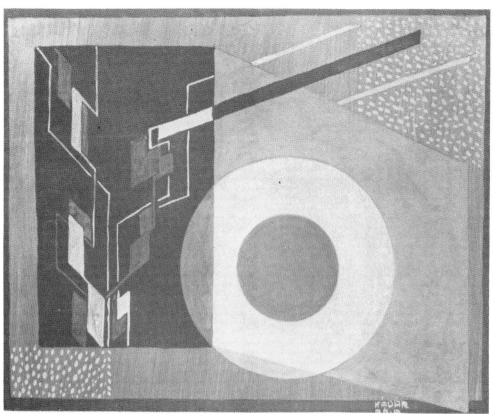

BELA KADAR – Red Circle – signed – watercolour over pencil – 9 x 11¼in.
(Christie's) $1,261   £864

WILLEM KALF, Manner of – A Barn Interior – oil on canvas – 8¾ x 12in.
(Sotheby's) $1,927   £1,320

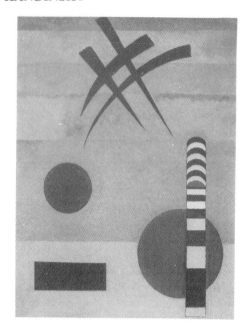

WASSILY KANDINSKY – Zeichen –
signed and dated '25, also signed and
dated on the reverse – oil on canvas –
26¾ x 19¼in.
(Sotheby's) $217,800 £145,200

ANGELICA KAUFFMAN – Portrait Of
Captain H. Taylor – oil on canvas – 30
x 22½in.
(Sotheby's)   **$7,425   £4,950**

JOHAN MARIE HENRI TEN KATE – The Absence Of The Painter –
signed – 25½ x 37in. *(Christie's)*   **$17,582 £11,880**

HERMANN KAUFFMANN – Caught –
signed and dated 1848 – on panel –
9 x 11in.
(Christie's)   **$11,188   £7,560**

ANGELICA KAUFFMAN – Cupid Dis-
covered By Cephisa; and The Clipping Of
Cupid's Wings – 23 x 15¾in.
(Sotheby's)   **$21,450   £14,300**

WILLIAM KAULA – Laurel And Birches
– oil on canvas – 29 x 24in.
(Christie's)   **$3,080   £2,053**

MARTIN KAVEL – Portrait Of A Lady
Wearing A Pink Band Round Her Blonde
Curly Hair, a Pink Dress With Velvet
Bodice – signed – oil – 98 x 70cm.
*(Henry Spencer &
    Sons)*   **$1,309   £850**

ANGELICA KAUFFMAN – The Holy
Family With An Angel – 10¾ x 9in.
(Sotheby's)   **$3,960   £2,640**

JAMES KAY — A Mediterranean Harbour — signed — on panel — 23 x 33in.
(Christie's) $3,796 £2,600

GEORGE KEATE — Bathing Machines At Margate — pen and grey ink and watercolour with touches of white heightening — 19¾ x 30in. *(Christie's)*
$3,888 £2,592

C. J. KEATS – A View In Rouen – signed and dated 1885 – 19 x 12½in.
(Lawrence) $77   £49

MICHAEL KEELING – Portrait Of Thomas Carlton Whitmore – signed on the reverse – oil on canvas – 50¾ x 40¾in.
(Sotheby's)   **$7,920**   **£5,280**

SIR GERALD KELLY – Consuela V, The Pink Shawl – signed and indistinctly dated – 22 x 18½in.
(Sotheby's)   **$2,045**   **£1,430**

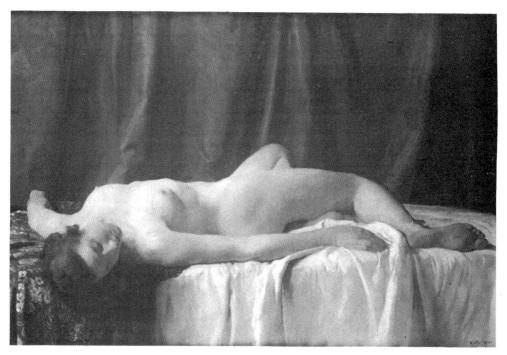

SIR GERALD KELLY – Siesta – signed and dated 1921 – oil on canvas – 37 x 62in. *(Christie's)*
$19,180 £12,960

ROBERT GEORGE TALBOT KELLY – Karnak – signed and dated 1912 –
watercolour – 15¼ x 21¼in. *(Christie's)*   **$1,782 £1,188**

ROBERT KEMM – Fisherfolk On The
Shore – signed – 20 x 24in.
(Sotheby's)   **$1,573   £1,078**

LUCY ELIZABETH KEMP-WELCH –
Children's Pony – signed – watercolour
heightened with white – 13 x 16in.
(Sotheby's)   **$4,950   £3,300**

SYDNEY KENDRICK – Reflections –
signed – 36 x 22in.
(Sotheby's)   **$2,263   £1,705**

SYDNEY KENDRICK – 'Yes Or No' – signed – 15½ x 23½in. *(Christie's)*
$885   £594

CECIL KENNEDY – Still Life, Anemonies In A Vase – signed – 20 x 16in. *(Woolley & Wallis)* $3,450   £2,300

CECIL KENNEDY – Summer Flowers In An Urn – signed – oil on canvas – 40 x 30in. *(Christie's)* $11,188   £7,560

CECIL KENNEDY – Camelias (Alba Simplex) And Spirea Aguta – signed – oil on canvas – 23½ x 19½in.
(Sotheby's)   **$7,550   £5,280**

CECIL KENNEDY – Mixed Flowers – signed – oil on canvas – 36 x 28in.
(Christie's)   **$12,960   £7,640**

CECIL KENNEDY – Spring Flowers – signed and inscribed on a label on the reverse – oil on canvas – 30 x 25in.
(Sotheby's)   **$4,336   £2,970**

ERIC KENNINGTON – The Arras Bapaume Road – signed – gouache over pencil, on buff paper – 19 x 13in.
(Sotheby's)   **$1,320   £880**

CARL KENZLER – A Forest In Winter – signed – 30¾ x 47in. *(Sotheby's)*
$429   £286

HARRY KERNOFF – After School –
signed and dated '25 – watercolour over
traces of pencil – 14 x 9½in.
(Sotheby's)   **$363**   **£242**

HENRY KERNOFF – Portrait Of Sean
O'Casey – signed – 15 x 11in.
(Sotheby's)   **$412**   **£275**

J. FRANKLIN KERSHAW – An Allegory
– signed and dated 1912, inscribed on
labels on the stretcher – 40 x 30in.
(Sotheby's)   **$1,402   £935**

**CARL LUDWIG FERDINAND
KERSTAN** – An Arab In Meditation –
signed with monogram – on panel –
22¼ x 19in.
(Christie's)   **$20,779   £14,040**

JAN VAN KESSEL – A Spaniel On A Cushion On An Artist's Table – signed with
initials – on panel – 9½ x 11½in. *(Christie's)*   **$4,942 £3,456**

JAN VAN KESSEL, The Elder – An
Assembly Of Birds Including Spoonbill
Cranes and Bitterns – signed and dated
1666 – on panel – 7½ x 10in.
(Sotheby's) **$11,220 £7,480**

JAN VAN KESSEL, The Younger –
Animals In A Landscape – on metal –
6¼ x 8¾in.
(Sotheby's) **$5,280 £3,520**

JAN VAN KESSEL, The Younger –
A Landscape With Monkeys Attacking
Penguins On The Coast Of Africa – on
metal – 7 x 9½in.
(Sotheby's) **$4,712 £3,080**

JAN VAN KESSEL, The Younger – A
Landscape With Dogs, A View Of Cologne
Beyond – on metal – 6¼ x 8½in.
(Sotheby's) **$8,415 £5,500**

JOHAN VAN KESSEL – A View Of The
Heiligewegs Poort, Amsterdam – signed
– 30 x 42¼in.
(Sotheby's) **$33,000 £22,000**

KEUNINCK

W. KEY – Portrait Of A Lady, In A
Black Dress And White Headdress – on
panel – 14½ x 11¼in.
(Christie's)   **$1,782**   **£1,188**

KERSTIAEN DE KEUNINCK, Circle of
– Apollo And Daphne – on panel –
18¼ x 14½in.
(Sotheby's)   **$1,485**   **£990**

JACOB-SIMON-HENDRIK KEVER –
Eltern Und Kinder Am Esstisch – signed
– oil on canvas – 60 x 51cm.
*(Germann
    Auktionshaus)* **$6,440**   **£4,411**

FERNAND KHNOPFF – A Portrait Of
Jules Philippson – signed and dated
1890 – on canvas laid down on panel –
25½ x 14½in.
(Sotheby's)   **$34,650** **£23,100**

CONRAD KIESEL – Portrait Of A
Young Girl – oil.
(Andrew Grant)   **$3,000   £2,000**

MICHEL KIKOINE – Autoportrait –
signed, and signed on the reverse – oil on
canvas – 9½ x 7½in.
(Christie's)   **$775   £518**

GEORGE GOODWIN KILBURNE, JNR. – Off Hunting – signed – watercolour
over traces of pencil – 10½ x 14in. *(Sotheby's)*   **$1,122   £748**

GEORGE GOODWIN KILBURNE – A
Cup Of Tea – signed – watercolour
heightened with white – 10¾ x 14¾in.
(Christie's)   **$1,540**   **£1,026**

GEORGE GOODWIN KILBURNE, JNR.
– The Groom's Dalliance – signed – oil
on board – 6 x 8½in.
(Sotheby's)   **$1,402**   **£935**

GEORGE GOODWIN KILBURNE – The
Sailor's Return – signed – watercolour,
heightened with bodycolour – 11½ x 9in.
(Sotheby's)   **$1,927**   **£1,320**

GEORGE GOODWIN KILBURNE –
The Rivals – signed – watercolour
over pencil with stopping out – 13¾ x
20¼in.
(Sotheby's)   **$1,567**   **£1,045**

GEORGE GOODWIN KILBURNE –
Light Refreshment – signed – watercolour over traces of pencil with scratching out – 13¼ x 17in.
(Sotheby's) **$3,465** **£2,310**

GEORGE GOODWIN KILBURNE –
Garden Spoil – signed and dated 1878
– pencil and watercolour – 34 x 24in.
(Christie's) **$9,082** **£6,264**

GEORGE GOODWIN KILBURNE –
Coming Down For Tea – signed and dated
– watercolour – 24 x 18in.
(Sotheby's) **$4,950** **£3,300**

GEORGE GOODWIN KILBURNE –
Standing Nude – signed – watercolour
– 10 x 6in.
(Sotheby's) **$1,155** **£770**

HAYNES KING – Mending The Nets
– signed – 18 x 14in.
(Christie's)　　　**$2,413**　**£1,620**

EDWARD KILLINGWORTH – Watching And Waiting – signed – watercolour,
heightened with white – 16½ x 9in.
(Sotheby's)　　　**$1,927**　**£1,320**

YEEND KING – The Stepping Stones –
signed – 10 x 14in.
(Taylors)　　　**$255**　　**£170**

HENRY JOHN YEEND KING – Looe
Village, Cornwall – signed, inscribed
and dated 1896 on the reverse – oil
on canvas – 18½ x 14in.
(Sotheby's)　　　**$660**　　**£462**

HENRY JOHN YEEND KING – Two Women Gardening Beside A Thatched Cottage, A River And Rolling Landscape Seen Beyond – signed – oil on canvas – 50 x 74cm. *(Henry Spencer & Sons)* **$4,433 £3,100**

HENRY JOHN YEEND KING – Beehives – signed – oil on canvas – 14 x 18in.
(Sotheby's) **$2,202 £1,540**

HENRY JOHN YEEND KING – Ladies In An English Garden – signed – oil on board – 16 x 20in.
(Sotheby's) **$4,950 £3,300**

HENRY JOHN YEEND KING – Summer Garden – signed – oil on canvas – 20 x 29in.
(Sotheby's) **$2,970 £1,980**

HENRY JOHN YEEND KING – 'Spring Time' – signed – on canvas – 17 x 23¾in.
(Sotheby's) **$2,145 £1,430**

HENRY JOHN YEEND KING – On A Foreshore – signed – on panel – 13½ x 18in.
(Sotheby's)   **$660**   **£440**

HENRY JOHN YEEND KING – Ducks By A Stream – signed – oil on board – 14 x 10in.
(Sotheby's)   **$471**   **£330**

HENRY JOHN YEEND KING – Cottage Gardeners – signed – 20 x 30in.
(Sotheby's)   **$5,610**   **£3,740**

HENRY JOHN KINNAIRD – A Cornfield Near Arundel – signed and inscribed – watercolour heightened with bodycolour – 10 x 14½in. *(Sotheby's)*
     $1,183 **£825**

HENRY JOHN KINNAIRD – Near Bury, Sussex – signed and inscribed – water-colour heightened with bodycolour – 10 x 14½in. *(Sotheby's)* **$1,183 £825**

HENRY JOHN KINNAIRD – Near Welwyn, Weyld – signed – oil on canvas – 17¼ x 31½in.
(Sotheby's) **$757 £528**

ERNST LUDWIG KIRCHNER – Hof Mit Sonnenstrahl – signed, and signed and inscribed on the reverse – 31½ x 27½in.
(Christie's) **$41,277 £28,080**

ERNST LUDWIG KIRCHNER – Zwei Akte – signed and dated '06 – coloured crayons on paper – 17¾ x 14in.
(Christie's) **$12,960 £8,640**

KIRCHNER

ERNST-LUDWIG KIRCHNER – Paar Im
Zimmer – watercolour and pen and ink
over pencil – 16¼ x 12¼in.
(Sotheby's) **$6,600 £4,400**

ERNST-LUDWIG KIRCHNER –
Stehender Akt – charcoal – 20½ x 13¼in.
(Sotheby's) **$5,773 £3,850**

ERNST-LUDWIG KIRCHNER –
Alpenlandschaft – signed and dated '24
– watercolour and pen and indian ink
over pencil – 14¼ x 19¼in.
(Sotheby's) **$11,165 £7,700**

JOSEPH KIRKPATRICK – A Market
Place, Kingston, Jamaica – signed, inscribed and dated 1903 – watercolour – 8
x 14½in.
(Sotheby's) **$449 £308**

MOISE KISLING – Portrait D'Un
Rabbin – signed and dated 1911 – oil
on canvas – 17¾ x 17¾in.
(Sotheby's) **$9,075 £6,050**

MOISE KISLING – Jeune Homme Au Veston Gris – signed – 25¼ x 20¾in. *(Sotheby's)* **$21,450 £14,300**

MOISE KISLING – Mere Et Fils – oil on canvas – 18 x 21½in. *(Christie's)* **$5,518 £3,780**

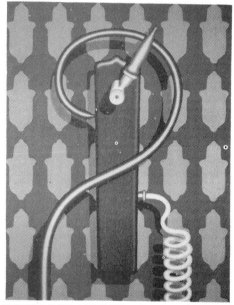

KONRAD KLAPHECK – Der Egozen-triker – signed, inscribed and dated 1964 on the reverse – oil on canvas – 43¼ x 33½in. *(Christie's)* **$12,960 £8,640**

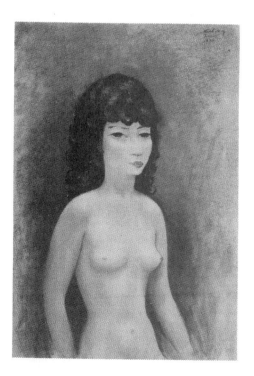

MOISE KISLING – Femme Nue Aux Cheveux Noires – signed and dated 1948 – oil on canvas – 21¾ x 15in. *(Christie's)* **$12,614 £8,640**

THEODOR KLEEHAAS – The Proposal – signed and dated 1887 – 29¾ x 49in. *(Christie's)* **$9,396 £6,264**

YVES KLEIN – I.K.B. – blue pigment
on canvas laid down on panel – 29½ x
22in.
(Sotheby's)   **$82,940   £57,200**

MAX KLINGER – Penelope, 1895 –
monogram and date – aquatint – 18
x 29.5cm.
(Christie's)   **$661   £450**

**JOHANNES CHRISTIAAN KARL
KLINKENBERG** – A Canal Scene In A
Dutch Town – signed – on panel – 16
x 22in.
(Christie's)   **$9,590   £6,480**

WILLIAM CALLCOTT KNELL –
Schooner Brig Running Before The Wind,
Off Broadstairs – signed – oil on canvas
– 32 x 52in.
(Sotheby's)   **$3,668   £2,530**

WILLIAM CALLCOTT KNELL –
Fishing Boats Off A Harbour Mouth –
signed – oil on canvas – 32 x 53in.
(Sotheby's)   **$4,147   £2,860**

SIR GODFREY KNELLER, Attributed
to – Portrait Of A Lady Wearing A
White Dress With Blue Trimming – oil
on canvas – 49½ x 39½in.
(Sotheby's)   **$1,365   £935**

KNELLER — Head And Shoulders Portrait Of Lady St. Barbe — 30 x 25in.
(Lawrence) **$759** **£506**

HAROLD KNIGHT — In The Studio — signed — oil on canvas — 24 x 20in.
(Christie's) **$3,516** **£2,376**

A. ROLAND KNIGHT — A Naval Engagement — signed, inscribed on the reverse — 16 x 24in.
(Sotheby's) **$627** **£418**

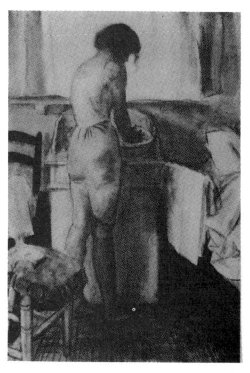

CLARA KNIGHT — 'The Old Cottage' — signed — watercolour — 10½ x 11½in.
(Reeds Rains) **$83** **£55**

DAME LAURA KNIGHT — The Washstand — signed — watercolour over traces of pencil — 25 x 17in.
(Sotheby's) **$1,573** **£1,100**

DAME LAURA KNIGHT – Untrodden Sand – signed – oil on board – 22 x 23¾in.
(Christie's)   **$9,590**   **£6,480**

WILLIAM HENRY KNIGHT – Their Youngest Child – signed and dated 1856 – oil on panel – 18 x 13in.
(Sotheby's)   **$2,392**   **£1,650**

DAVIDSON KNOWLES – A Professional Artist – signed and dated '95 – oil on canvas – 14 x 20in.
(Sotheby's)   **$2,392**   **£1,650**

GEORGE SHERIDAN KNOWLES – Faithful Friends – signed and dated 1903 – 32 x 23in.
(Sotheby's)   **$5,139**   **£3,520**

SUSAN RICKER KNOX – Chalute The Seminole – signed – oil on canvas – 24 x 20in.
(Robert W. Skinner Inc.)   **$400**   **£266**

WILLIAM KNOX – On The High Seas –
signed and dated 1947 – 24 x 36in.
(Sotheby's)   **$627**   **£418**

JAN KOBELL, After – Cows In A Landscape – oil.
(Andrew Grant)   **$450**   **£300**

GOTTLIEB VON KOCH – Pferdemarkt –
signed – tempera on board – 65 x 41cm.
(Germann
Auktionshaus)   **$865**   **£577**

HENDRIK BAREND KOEKKOEK –
Cattle And Drover In A Winter Landscape – signed – on canvas – 17¼ x
13½in.
(Sotheby's)   **$770**   **£528**

BAREND CORNELIS KOEKKOEK –
Peasants On A Path In A River Landscape
– signed and dated 1850 – on panel –
12¼ x 16in.
(Sotheby's)   **$18,150 £12,100**

ALEXANDER KOESTER – Morgenidylle
Am Ammersee – signed – oil on canvas –
46 x 76cm.
(Germann
Auktionshaus) **$27,910 £19,117**

KOKOSCHKA

OSKAR KOKOSCHKA – Venezia:
Santa Maria Della Salute – signed with
initials – oil on canvas – 33½ x 43¼in.
(Sotheby's)   **$267,300 £178,200**

OSKAR KOKOSCHKA – Die Tanzerin
– signed – red chalk on paper – 17 x
21½in.
(Christie's)   **$2,754   £1,836**

SEI KOYANAGUI – Perroquet – signed
– oil on canvas – 55 x 46cm.
*(Germann
    Auktionshaus)* **$1,276   £851**

PER KRAFT, The Elder, After – Portrait Of Charles XII Of Sweden – 48½ x
39½in.
(Sotheby's)   **$875   £572**

CHARLES LOUIS KRATKE – The
Dandy – signed and dated 1879 – oil
on panel – 12½ x 9½in.
(Sotheby's)   **$835   £572**

PINCHUS KREMEGNE – Nature Morte Au Poulet Et Brioche – signed – oil on canvas – 25½ x 32in.
(Christie's) **$2,915** **£1,944**

PEDER SEVERIN KROYER – Portrait Of The Artist, Head And Shoulders, At An Easel – 21½ x 17¾in.
(Christie's) **$8,791** **£5,940**

LEON KROLL – Dressing – signed – oil on canvas – 36 x 26¾in.
(Christie's) **$6,600** **£4,400**

LEON KROLL – Budding Romance – signed – oil on canvas – 36¼ x 48in.
(Christie's) **$14,300** **£8,535**

PEDER SEVERIN KROYER – A Portrait Of Marie, The Artist's Wife – signed and inscribed on a label – 24 x 16½in.
(Sotheby's) **$26,400** **£17,600**

ALFRED KUBIN – Die Schlange – pen and ink, grey wash and spritztechnik – image size 9 x 9¼in.
(Sotheby's) $14,850   £9,900

ALFRED KUBIN – Vampire – signed and dated '42 – watercolour, pen and ink and grey wash – 12 x 14½in.
(Sotheby's) $10,230   £6,820

ALFRED KUBIN – Mein Zweig – inscribed – pen and ink and ink wash heightened with watercolour on paper – 13¾ x 9¾in.
(Christie's) $7,776   £5,184

CHARLES EUPHRASIE KUWASSEG – Hauling The Boat Ashore – signed and dated 1867, also signed and dated on the reverse – oil on canvas – 12½ x 18in.
(Sotheby's) $3,030   £2,090

CHARLES EUPHRASIE KUWASSEG – Continental Coastal Town With Boats And Figures – signed and dated 1876 – 15 x 24in.
(Chrystals
    Auctions) $1,800   £1,200

CHARLES EUPHRASIE KUWASSEG, JNR. – On The Canal – signed and dated 1875 – 21½ x 17½in.
(Sotheby's) $4,290   £2,860

FELIX LABISSE – La Cote Des Maures
– signed, also signed and dated 1954 on
the reverse – oil on canvas – 23½ x 27½in.
(Sotheby's) **$4,620 £3,080**

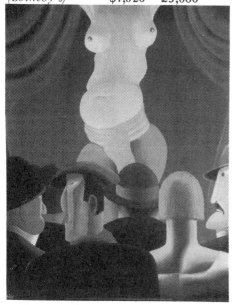

FELIX LABISSE – La Danse Du Ventre
– signed – oil on canvas – 35¾ x 28¼in.
(Sotheby's) **$15,675 £10,450**

CHARLES JOHN DE LACY – On The
Thames – signed and dated 1887 – oil
on canvas – 14 x 21in.
(Sotheby's) **$597 £418**

EDWARD LADELL – Grapes, A Peach,
Nuts, A Tazza Of Fruit And A Long-
Stemmed Glass On A Draped Table –
signed with monogram – 17 x 14in.
(Christie's) **$15,984 £10,800**

EDWARD LADELL – Fruit And Still
Life – signed with monogram – oil on
canvas – 13½ x 17½in.
(Sotheby's) **$13,200 £8,800**

EDWARD LADELL – Still Life Of Grapes,
Pears, A Bird's Nest And A Butterfly On A
Ledge – signed with monogram – 9½ x
11¾in.
(Christie's) **$5,670 £3,780**

ELLEN LADELL – Birds, A Bird's Nest, Blooms And Pears – signed – oil on canvas – 19 x 15in.
(Sotheby's) **$2,073** **£1,430**

REYNIER VAN DER LAECK – Bathers In A Southern Landscape – signed and dated 1643 – oil on panel – 15¼ x 18½in.
(Sotheby's) **$2,409** **£1,650**

TOMSON LAING – Kelp Gatherers – signed – 23 x 38in.
(Sotheby's) **$1,320** **£880**

TOMSON LAING – Highland Cattle By A Cottage – signed and dated 1900 – on canvas – 24½ x 20in.
(Sotheby's) **$346** **£231**

GERARD DE LAIRESSE – The Annunciation – oil on canvas – 58½ x 73in.
(Sotheby's) **$13,024** **£8,800**

GERARD DE LAIRESSE – The Circumcision – oil on canvas – 58½ x 73in.
(Sotheby's) **$16,280** **£11,000**

HENRY LAMB – Paradise Street, Poole
– signed and dated '23 – 20 x 25in.
(Sotheby's) **$7,920** **£5,280**

WILLIAM B. LAMOND – On The Shore
– signed – 14½ x 21in.
(Sotheby's) **$3,300** **£2,200**

AUGUSTUS OSBORNE LAMPLOUGH –
Arab Traders Outside A Mosque – signed
and dated 1908 – watercolour – 13¼ x
8¼in.
(Sotheby's) **$1,204** **£825**

AUGUSTUS OSBORNE LAMPLOUGH –
Feluccas On The Nile – signed – watercolour heightened with yellow – 25¼ x
38½in.
(Christie's) **$1,780** **£1,188**

GEORGE LANCE – 'Fruit' – signed and
dated 1853 – oil on canvas – 36 x 49in.
(Sotheby's) **$10,733** **£7,480**

GEORGE LANCE – A Still Life Study Of
Dead Game And Shellfish – signed and
dated 1837 – oil on panel – 13½ x 17¼in.
(Sotheby's) **$2,209** **£1,540**

GEORGE LANCE – Still Life With
Fruit On A Ledge – oil on board – 10
x 12in.
(Sotheby's) **$1,402** **£935**

LANDSEER

SIR EDWIN LANDSEER – Blea Tarn
Looking South To Wetherlam, Cumber-
land – on panel – 8 x 10in.
(Sotheby's)   **$42,900 £28,600**

SIR EDWIN LANDSEER – A Study For
The Monkey In 'The Cat's Paw' – on
panel – diameter 5in.
(Sotheby's)   **$2,475   £1,650**

SIR EDWIN LANDSEER – Waiting For
Master – on panel – 17 x 12¾in.
(Sotheby's)   **$4,950   £3,300**

SIR EDWIN HENRY LANDSEER –
Scene In Chillingham Park, Portrait Of
Lord Ossulton (also called Death Of The
Wild Bull) – 88 x 87¼in.
(Sotheby's)   **$280,500 £187,000**

SIR EDWIN HENRY LANDSEER –
Study Of A Stag – signed with initials
and dated 1845 – black, red and white
chalk – 13¾ x 19½in.
(Sotheby's)   **$4,290   £2,860**

SIR EDWIN HENRY LANDSEER –
Canine Friends, A Newfoundland And
An Irish Terrier Beside A Stream –
signed and dated 1822 – 24¾ x 30in.
(Sotheby's)   **$12,870   £8,580**

JOHANNES LANGENEGGER –
Alpfahrt Mit Wirtschaft – oil on paper
– 44.3 x 58cm.
(Germann
Auktionshaus) **$3,418** **£2,279**

SIR ERIK LANGKER – Blue Gums
Beside A River – signed – oil on board –
11½ x 14¾in.
(Sotheby's) **$591** **£374**

WALTER LANGLEY – A Quiet Read –
signed and dated '84 – watercolour – 9¾
x 6¾in.
(Sotheby's) **$2,525** **£1,760**

WALTER LANGLEY – The Greeting –
signed, and signed and inscribed on the
reverse – pencil and watercolour heightened with white – on board – 10½ x
1'3¼in.
(Christie's) **$1,539** **£1,026**

WALTER LANGLEY – Dusk – signed
– 30 x 22in.
(Sotheby's) **$3,630** **£2,420**

335

WALTER LANGLEY – Bread Winners –
signed and dated 1896, and inscribed on
the reverse – 46½ x 85¼in.
(Sotheby's)   **$18,150   £12,100**

ANDRE LANSKOY – Garcon Au
Cheval – signed – oil on canvas – 81.5
x 65cm.
*(Germann
    Auktionshaus)* **$2,245   £1,497**

WALTER LANGLEY – Constancy –
signed and dated 1884 – watercolour –
21¼ x 12¾in.
(Christie's)   **$5,184   £3,456**

GEORGE HENRY LAPORTE – A
Gentleman In A Horse-Drawn Trap –
signed with initials and dated 1836 – oil
on canvas – 19½ x 23½in.
(Sotheby's)   **$7,590   £5,060**

WALTER LANGLEY – Newlyn, Catching Up With The Cornish Telegraph –
signed – watercolour – 20 x 27½in.
(Christie's)   **$7,047   £4,860**

GEORGE HENRY LAPORTE, Follower
of – Breaking Cover; and Over The Ditch
– oil on canvas – 19¾ x 23½in.
(Sotheby's)   **$3,135   £2,090 Pair**

GEORGE HENRY LAPORTE – 'Grooming The Stallion' – indistinctly signed and dated 1826 – oil on canvas – 24 x 32¼in.
(Sotheby's)   **$883   £605**

GEORGES LAPORTE – Les Cordes A Linge – signed and dated '58 – oil on canvas – 23¼ x 31½in.
(Sotheby's)   **$1,650   £1,100**

GEORGINA LARA, Attributed to – Rural Scenes With Figures Outside An Inn – on canvas – 9¾ x 17½in.
(Sotheby's)   **$1,413   £968 Pair**

MIKHAIL LARIONOV – Nu A L'Interieur – signed – oil on panel – 5½ x 7¼in.
(Sotheby's)   **$2,640   £1,760**

NICOLAS DE LARGILLIERRE – Portrait Of A Lady Said To Be The Comtesse De Montreux – oil on canvas – 32 x 24in.
(Sotheby's)   **$17,094   £11,550**

NICOLAS DE LARGILLIERE, Attributed to – A Study Of Tulips And Peonies – 31 x 25in.
(Sotheby's)   **$16,170   £10,780**

337

LARKIN

WILLIAM LARKIN, Circle of – Portrait Of James Hay, First Earl Of Carlisle – oil on canvas – 77½ x 56¼in.
(Sotheby's) **$14,025 £9,350**

MARIE LAURENCIN – Tete De Femme or Dame Au Chapeau Et Ruban Rose – signed – oil on canvas – 18 x 15in.
(Christie's) **$40,996 £28,080**

MARIE LAURENCIN – Deux Filles Lisant – signed – watercolour over pencil – 11¼ x 9¼in.
(Sotheby's) **$12,375 £8,250**

MARIE LAURENCIN – Les Sirenes Et La Fille A La Mandoline – signed – oil on board – 13¾ x 9½in.
(Sotheby's) **$33,000 £22,000**

MARIE LAURENCIN – Trois Oiseaux Bleus – signed and dated 1933 – oil on canvas – 10¾ x 13¾in.
(Sotheby's) **$11,880 £7,920**

SIR JOHN LAVERY – Portrait Of Anne
Selby Burrell Ord, Fifth Lady Gwydyr –
signed and inscribed, also inscribed and
dated 1903 on the reverse – 78 x 42in.
(Sotheby's) **$1,888 £1,320**

SIR JOHN LAVERY – Admiral Sir
David Beatty In His Cabin Aboard H.M.S.
Queen Elizabeth – signed, and signed
again, inscribed and dated 1917 on the
reverse – oil on canvas – 25 x 30in.
(Christie's) **$9,395 £6,264**

SIR JOHN LAVERY – The Spanish Hat
Or Mrs Gerard Chowne – signed – oil on
canvas – 30¼ x 25in.
(Christie's) **$4,795 £3,240**

SIR JOHN LAVERY – Portrait Of Mrs
W. H. Radford Seated In An Armchair –
signed, also signed, inscribed and dated
1929 on the reverse – oil on canvas –
60 x 40in.
(Christie's) **$3,516 £2,376**

SIR JOHN LAVERY – The Tennis Party – signed, inscribed and dated 1885 – on board – 9½ x 23in. *(Sotheby's)* **$47,850 £31,900**

SIR JOHN LAVERY – Evening, The Coast Of Spain From Tangier – signed, inscribed and dated 1911-14 on the reverse – 25 x 30in. *(Sotheby's)* **$16,500 £11,000**

SIR THOMAS LAWRENCE – Portrait Of Admiral Sir Charles Paget – 29½ x 24½in. *(Sotheby's)* **$28,050 £18,700**

ANDREW LAW – A Street Party – signed – oil on canvas – 13½ x 17¾in. *(Sotheby's)* **$1,183 £.825**

JOHN LAWSON – The Pet Lamb – signed – watercolour – 7 x 5in. *(Sotheby's)* **$1,155 £770**

JOHN LAWSON – Pixie Games – watercolour over pencil, heightened with bodycolour – 2¾ x 4½in. *(Sotheby's)* **$722 £495 Pair**

BENJAMIN WILLIAMS LEADER – A Shepherd Boy And His Flock On A Country Lane – signed – on canvas – 24 x 20in.
(Sotheby's) **$4,125** **£2,750**

BENJAMIN WILLIAMS LEADER – Shere Church, Near Guildford, Surrey – signed and dated 1895 – on board – 13 x 10in.
(Sotheby's) **$3,051** **£2,090**

BENJAMIN WILLIAMS LEADER – The View From Burrows Cross – signed and dated 1919 – oil on canvas – 11½ x 17¼in.
(Sotheby's) **$835** **£572**

BENJAMIN WILLIAMS LEADER – Worcestershire Cottages – signed and dated 1894, also signed and inscribed on the stretcher – oil on canvas – 14 x 21in.
(Sotheby's) **$4,455** **£2,970**

BENJAMIN WILLIAMS LEADER – 'When Sun Is Set' – signed and dated 1900, and signed and inscribed on the reverse – 36 x 60in.
(Christie's) **$12,150** **£8,100**

BENJAMIN WILLIAMS LEADER – The Severn Below Worcester – signed and dated 1920 – oil on canvas – 12 x 18in.
(Sotheby's) **$1,980** **£1,320**

EDWARD LEAR – Campagna Di Roma, Via Pappia – signed with monogram, dated and inscribed – watercolour – 4 x 8in.
(Woolley & Wallis) **$2,682 £1,850**

CHARLES LEAVER – By A Country Gate – signed and dated 1875 – oil on canvas – 21 x 31in.
(Sotheby's) **$943 £660**

CHARLES LEAVER – Wargrave, Northamptonshire – signed and dated 1876, also inscribed on the reverse – 21 x 33in.
(Sotheby's) **$3,300 £2,200**

EDWARD LEAR, Circle of – A Folio Of Birds – 17 watercolours with pencil or sepia backgrounds – on wove paper, watermarked in the 1830's, 6 mounted in pairs – various sizes.
(Sotheby's) **$1,980 £1,320**

NOEL HARRY LEAVER – An Old Dutch Street – signed – watercolour heightened with white – 11¼ x 15½in.
(Christie's) **$783 £540**

NOEL HARRY LEAVER – Figures Near An Arch In An Italian Town – signed – watercolour over traces of pencil – 10¼ x 14¼in.
(Sotheby's) **$495 £330**

CHARLES LEAVER – A Snowy Farmyard – signed and indistinctly inscribed on the stretcher – 16 x 25in.
(Sotheby's) **$1,980 £1,320**

NOEL HARRY LEAVER – An Arab Street Scene – signed – watercolour – 10¾ x 14½in.
(Sotheby's) **$770 £528**

NOEL HARRY LEAVER – Lighthouse
And Pier, Scarborough – signed – water-
colour – 11 x 17¼in.
(Sotheby's) **$690** **£473**

NOEL HARRY LEAVER – An Arabian
City – signed – watercolour, heightened
with bodycolour – 14 x 21in.
(Sotheby's) **$2,970** **£1,980**

EDWARD CHALMERS LEAVITT –
Still Life With Berries, Grapes And
Peaches – signed and dated 1888 –
oil on canvas – 26 x 20in.
(Robert W. Skinner
Inc.) **$1,700** **£1,133**

HENRI LEBASQUE – Jeune Fille Sur
La Plage – signed – oil on canvas – 23½
x 28¾in.
(Christie's) **$28,382** **£19,440**

HENRI LEBASQUE – Jeune Femme
Endormie – signed – 19½ x 25½in.
(Sotheby's) **$12,045** **£8,250**

HENRI LEBASQUE – Femme Dans Le
Jardin – signed – 18¼ x 21½in.
(Sotheby's) **$12,848** **£8,800**

LAWRENCE LEBDUSKA – Still Life With Flowers And Fruit – signed and dated '56 – oil on canvas – 24 x 19¾in.
(Christie's)   **$220**   **£145**

PAUL EMILE LECOMTE – Sur Le Quai – signed – oil on canvas – 19¾ x 39¼in.
(Christie's)   **$1,375**   **£918**

JEANNE-PHILIBERTE LEDOUX, Attributed to – Le Reve – 25¾ x 31¾in.
(Sotheby's)   **$2,145**   **£1,430**

FREDERICK RICHARD LEE – The Ferry – signed and dated 1851 – oil on board – 13 x 21½in.
(Sotheby's)   **$4,125**   **£2,750**

FREDERICK RICHARD LEE – The Angler – signed and dated 1839 – on panel – 12 x 17in.
(Sotheby's)   **$3,693**   **£2,530**

JEFF LOUIS VAN LEEMPUTTEN – Chickens Feeding In An Extensive Landscape – signed and dated 1869 – oil on panel – 12¼ x 18in.
(Sotheby's)   **$1,092**   **£748**

JEFF LOUIS VAN LEEMPUTTEN – Chickens Feeding With Extensive Landscape Beyond – signed and dated 1869 – oil on panel – 12½ x 18in.
(Sotheby's)   **$1,365**   **£935**

GERRIT JAN LEEUWEN – Grapes, A
Peach And Other Fruit On A Ledge –
signed – on panel – 15 x 12½in.
(Christie's)   **$6,480   £4,320**

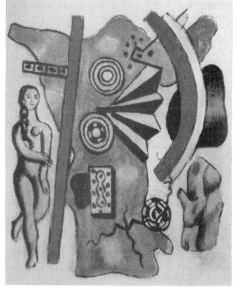

FERNAND LEGER – Composition A
La Danseuse – signed and dated on the
reverse – oil on canvas laid down on
board – 18¼ x 14¾in.
(Sotheby's)   **$31,350 £20,900**

FERNAND LEGER – Etude Pour La
Ville – brush and indian ink – 17¼ x
25¼in.
(Sotheby's)   **$12,760   £8,800**

FERNAND LEGER – Deux Femmes –
signed – canvas on board – 10 x 16in.
(Sotheby's)   **$27,720 £18,480**

FERNAND LEGER – Portrait de Madame
Leger – signed – brush and black ink
heightened with white on paper – 19¼ x
14in.
(Christie's)   **$19,440 £12,960**

FERNAND LEGER – Nature Morte
Aux Cartes – signed with initials and
dated '49 – gouache – 30¼ x 20¾in.
(Sotheby's)   **$27,115 £18,700**

FERNAND LEGER – Composition Avec Tete De Femme – lithograph in colour – 38 x 55.8cm.
(Germann Auktionshaus) **$729** **£486**

FERNAND LEGER – Le Buste – signed and dated '36 – gouache on paper – 16½ x 22½in.
(Christie's) **$12,960** **£8,640**

FERNAND LEGER – Le Garage – stamped with signature on the reverse – brush and indian ink and gouache on squared paper – 12 x 15½in.
(Sotheby's) **$12,375** **£8,250**

FERNAND LEGER – L'Ouvrier Accoude – signed with initials and dated '50 – pen and ink – 25¼ x 18¾in.
(Sotheby's) **$21,450 £14,300**

FERNAND LEGER – Les Deux Amoureux – signed and dated '52, also signed, dated and inscribed on the reverse – 25½ x 19¾in.
(Sotheby's) **$118,030 £81,400**

ALEXANDER LEGGATT – The Parting Glance – signed with monogram, inscribed and dated 1880 on the reverse – on board – 11 x 9½in.
(Sotheby's) **$660** **£440**

LOUIS LEGRAND – La Gosse –
pastel – 14½ x 10in.
(Sotheby's)   **$2,711   £1,870**

LOUIS LEGRAND – L'actrice – oil on
board – 81 x 54cm.
*(Germann
    Auktionshaus)* **$3,864   £2,647**

LOUIS LEGRAND – Devant Le Miroir
– signed – pastel – 48 x 62cm.
*(Germann
    Auktionshaus)* **$5,388   £3,592**

CHARLES LEICKERT – An Extensive
Rural View With Figures And Windmills
In The Distance – signed – oil on panel
– 6¼ x 9¼in.
(Sotheby's)   **$1,156   £792**

THOMAS LEIGH, Attributed to –
Portrait Of A Lady And A Gentleman
– 36½ x 44½in.
(Sotheby's)   **$1,650   £1,100**

LOUIS LEGRAND – Coquetterie –
pastel – 50 x 65cm.
*(Germann
    Auktionshaus)* **$5,152   £3,529**

EDMUND BLAIR LEIGHTON – A
Fond Farewell – signed with initials –
on panel – 13½ x 9¼in.
(Christie's) $2,896   £1,944

LEIGHTON, FREDERIC, Lord –
Old Damascus: Jews' Quarter or Gather-
ing Citrons – 51 x 41in.
(Christie's) $559,440 £378,000

LEIGHTON, FREDERIC, Lord – Music
– 103 x 60½in.
(Sotheby's) $51,150   £34,100

LEIGHTON, FREDERIC, Lord – Anita
– 12 x 8¼in.
(Sotheby's) $42,900   £28,600

RICHARD PRINCIPAL LEITCH – A
Continental Town Scene – signed and
dated 1880 – watercolour heightened
with gum arabic and bodycolour – 13
x 19½in.
(Sotheby's) **$412 £275**

LEIGHTON, FREDERIC, Lord –
Nausicaa – 57½ x 26½in.
(Christie's) **$340,200 £226,800**

LEIGHTON, FREDERIC, Lord – Study
Of A Bank – oil on canvas – 7¾ x 16¾in.
(Sotheby's) **$2,970 £1,980**

SIR PETER LELY, Studio of – Portrait
Of Henry Jermyn, Earl Of St. Albans –
oil on canvas – 90 x 52in.
(Sotheby's) **$12,375 £8,250**

ROBERT LEMAN – An Angler In A
Punt Near A Church – watercolour over
pencil – 7 x 10¾in.
(Sotheby's)   **$396**   **£264**

SIR PETER LELY – Portrait Of Francis
Crane Of Loughton, Half Length, In
Black Cloak With White Collar – 28¾ x
24in.
(Christie's)   **$2,430**   **£1,620**

FRANCOIS LEMOYNE – Hercules
And Omphale – oil on canvas – 54¾ x
38¼in.
(Sotheby's)   **$45,584**   **£30,800**

SIR PETER LELY, Studio of – Portrait
Of A Lady, Possibly Lady Dacre – oil
on canvas – 58¾ x 44in.
(Sotheby's)   **$3,135**   **£2,090**

LELY – Sir Philip Sydenham – 29 x
24in.
(Lawrence)   **$412**   **£275**

C. LEMPRIERE – Study Of A Crocodile
– signed and inscribed – pen, ink and
wash – 5 x 10¼in.
(Sotheby's)   **$445**   **£297**

BERNARD LENS III – Portrait Of Rubens With His Second Wife, Helena Fourment, And Child After Sir Peter Paul Rubens – signed and dated 1721, also inscribed – watercolour and body-colour – copy – 15¾ x 11¾in.
(Sotheby's) **$3,300 £2,200**

STANISLAS LEPINE – Vue Du Musee De Cluny – signed – oil on panel – 9¼ x 5¼in.
(Sotheby's) **$11,220 £7,480**

LOUIS LEPOITTEVIN – The Shepherd With His Flock – signed – 20¾ x 31¼in.
(Sotheby's) **$1,485 £990**

CHARLES LESLIE – Loch Achray, Perthshire; and In The Tayndrum Valley – both signed and dated 1884 – oil on canvas – 12 x 24in.
(Sotheby's) **$1,072 £715 Two**

JULES LESSORE – Norwich Cathedral – signed – watercolour – 26¼ x 20½in.
(Sotheby's) **$481 £330**

ADRIENNE LESTER – Playful Kittens
– signed – 19 x 29in.
(Sotheby's) **$2,805 £1,870**

J. B. LETHEM – 'Peeling Apples' – signed
– watercolour – 15 x 10½in.
(Sotheby's) **$561 £374**

RICHARD HAYLEY LEVER – Still
Life With Banjo – signed, also signed,
dated 1942 and inscribed on the reverse
– oil on masonite – 24 x 49¾in.
(Christie's) **$1,650 £1,100**

RICHARD HAYLEY LEVER – Still
Life With Satsuma Bowl And Blue
Vase – signed – oil on canvasboard
– 12 x 16in.
(Robert W. Skinner
Inc.) **$1,300 £865**

MAURICE LEVIS – Le Moulin De
Tison, Poitou – signed – on panel – 5½
x 8½in.
(Sotheby's) **$3,465 £2,310**

MOSES LEVY – Donne Dell Arem –
signed – oil on board – 18 x 12¾in.
(Sotheby's) **$670 £462**

FREDERICK GEORGE LEWIN — A
Folio Of Illustrations —eleven signed —
watercolour and one grey wash —
various sizes.
(Sotheby's)   **$907**   **£605**

STEPHEN LEWIN — The Antiquary —
signed and dated '84 — oil on canvas —
20 x 15½in.
(Sotheby's)   **$707**   **£495**

GEORGE ROBERT LEWIS — Reapers
Sharpening Their Scythes — signed —
pencil and watercolour — 8 x 12in.
(Christie's)   **$243**   **£162**

JOHN FREDERICK LEWIS — A Gondo-
lier, Venice — inscribed — 22¼ x 17¾in.
(Sotheby's)   **$12,375**   **£8,250**

JOHN FREDERICK LEWIS — A Shepherd With Mountain Goats — watercolour
over traces of pencil heightened with
bodycolour — 9¾ x 14¼in.
(Sotheby's)   **$5,280**   **£3,520**

LEWIS

PERCY WYNDHAM LEWIS – Red And
Black Olympus – signed and dated 1922
– watercolour, bodycolour, pen and
black ink – 10 x 17in.
(Christie's)   **$44,755   £30,240**

ANDRE LHOTE – Femme En Buste –
signed – 25½ x 21¼in.
(Sotheby's)   **$4,950   £3,300**

PERCY WYNDHAM LEWIS – Portrait
Of Malcolm Macdonald – signed and
dated 1945 – coloured chalk on grey
paper – 14¼ x 10½in.
(Sotheby's)   **$786   £550**

OTTO THEODORE LEYDE – Asleep
– signed and inscribed – 22 x 25in.
(Sotheby's)   **$2,640   £1,760**

ANDRE LHOTE – Jeune Fille Assise –
signed – pencil on paper – 13¼ x 7¾in.
(Christie's)   **$661   £453**

PIETRO LIBERI – An Allegory: June (Cancer) With Diana As Protector Of Virtue – 45½ x 59¾in.
(Sotheby's)   **$7,425   £4,950**

CHARLES SILLEM LIDDERDALE – Girl With A Pitcher – signed with monogram and dated '79 – 15 x 11in.
(Sotheby's)   **$660   £440**

CHARLES WILLEM LIDDERDALE – A Little Maid – signed with monogram – 21 x 17in.
(Sotheby's)   **$1,485   £990**

CHARLES SILLEM LIDDERDALE – 'A Gipsy Girl' – signed with monogram – on canvas – 23½ x 15¾in.
(Sotheby's)   **$1,204   £825**

CHARLES WILLEM LIDDERDALE – A Favourite Puppy – signed with monogram and dated '84 – oil on canvas – 27 x 17in.
(Sotheby's)   **$5,940   £3,960**

LIEBERMANN

THOMAS LINDSAY – The River Thames Beneath Somerset House Looking Towards St. Paul's Cathedral – signed – watercolour over traces of pencil heightened with white – 11½ x 18¼in.
(Sotheby's)   **$812   £572**

MAX LIEBERMANN – A Rider On The Shore – signed – 19¼ x 23½in.
(Christie's)   **$15,984   £10,800**

HENRY HARRIS LINES – A Worcestershire Village – signed – on panel – 8¾ x 12in.
(Sotheby's)   **$693   £462**

MAX LIEBERMANN – Wannseelandschaft – signed – on panel – 12½ x 15¾in.
(Christie's)   **$45,360   £30,240**

PERCY LINDSAY – 'Pastoral Scene, Pymble' – signed – oil on board – 42 x 58cm.
(Australian Art Auctions)   **$2,600   £1,730**

JOHN LINNELL, Follower of – A Girl With A Wheatsheaf – oil on canvas – 21 x 17in.
(Sotheby's)   **$786   £550**

WILLIAM LINNELL – Showing The
Way – signed and dated 1859 – oil on
canvas – 21 x 30in.
(Sotheby's)   **$1,084**   **£748**

EMILY LITTLE – Reflections – signed
– 31 x 44in.
(Sotheby's)   **$5,280**   **£3,520**

VIOLET LINTON – Baby Sitting – signed
– oil on canvas – 15½ x 21¾in.
(Sotheby's)   **$546**   **£374**

HENRY LIVERSEEGE – Best Of
Friends – signed – oil on panel – 9
x 11¾in.
(Sotheby's)   **$1,815**   **£1,210**

H. G. LLOYD – Diamond Lake, New
Zealand – signed, dated 1882 and
inscribed – watercolour over pencil
heightened with white – 15½ x 21¾in.
(Sotheby's)   **$313**   **£209**

WILHELM LIST – Die Malerei –
gouache and gold paint over traces of
pencil – 12 x 8¼in.
(Sotheby's)   **$6,600**   **£4,400**

T. IVESTER LLOYD – The Pack In
Winter – signed – 14 x 18in.
(Sotheby's)   **$1,567**   **£1,045**

THOMAS J. LLOYD – On The River –
signed and dated 1888 – watercolour,
heightened with white – 20 x 36in.
(Sotheby's)   **$5,280   £3,520**

WALTER STUART LLOYD – 'Canterbury' – signed, inscribed on the reverse
– watercolour – 19¼ x 29¾in.
(Sotheby's)   **$642   £440**

WALTER STUART LLOYD – Canterbury
– signed – watercolour heightened with
bodycolour – 7½ x 22¼in.
(Sotheby's)   **$915   £638**

WALTER STUART LLOYD – Sopley
On The Avon – signed and inscribed on
the reverse – watercolour – 12 x 23in.
(Sotheby's)   **$610   £407**

WALTER STUART LLOYD – The
Fisherman's Home – signed and inscribed on reverse – watercolour – 19½ x
29in.
(Sotheby's)   **$505   £352**

WALTER STUART LLOYD – An
Evening's Punting – signed – watercolour
– 7¾ x 13¾in.
(Sotheby's)   **$660   £440**

E. LODER of Bath – 'Magenta', A Chestnut Hunter In A Loosebox; and 'Kelpie',
A Piebald Hunter In A Loosebox – one
signed and inscribed – 17¾ x 23¾in.
(Christie's)   **$1,539   £1,026 Pair**

GEORGE EDWARD LODGE – Tarim
Pheasant – signed – gouache – 18½ x
23½in.
(Sotheby's)   **$4,620   £3,080**

GEORGE EDWARD LODGE – Raven In The Snow – signed – watercolour – 10 x 9¾in.
(Dreweatt Watson &
Barton) **$352** **£240**

GEORGE EDWARD LODGE – Pheasants – signed – watercolour heightened with bodycolour – 11 x 17in.
(Sotheby's) **$3,581** **£2,420**

THOMAS LOGGAN – The Pantiles, Tunbridge Wells, Kent – inscribed – gouache over traces of pencil and watercolour – 9½ x 14½in.
(Sotheby's) **$1,897** **£1,265**

GUSTAVE LOISEAU – Les Falaises de Fecamp – signed and dated 1910 – oil on canvas – 21½ x 31¾in.
(Christie's) **$18,820** **£11,880**

GUSTAVE LOISEAU – L'Eglise – signed and dated 1901 – 25¼ x 31¼in.
(Sotheby's) **$15,510** **£10,340**

JOHN ARTHUR LOMAX – After A Good Day, The Cousin's Visit – signed – oil on panel – 11½ x 17½in.
(Sotheby's) **$7,337** **£5,060**

AMELIA LONG, Lady Farnborough – Arundel Castle, The Seat Of The Duke Of Norfolk – signed, inscribed and dated 1843 on verso – watercolour over pencil – 10½ x 17¾in.
(Sotheby's) **$396** **£264**

EDWIN LONG – Ancient Cyprus –
signed with monogram and dated 1887,
inscribed on the stretcher – 50 x 34in.
(Sotheby's) **$7,920** **£5,280**

ANTONIO LONZA – The Acrobat's
Rest – signed – oil on panel – 9 x
14½in.
(Sotheby's) **$1,355** **£935**

LAURENCE STEPHEN LOWRY –
Lancashire Village – signed and dated
1920 – on board – 17 x 21½in.
(Sotheby's) **$22,275** **£14,850**

EDWIN LONG – Fanchette –
signed and dated 1872 – oil on canvas
– 49 x 31in.
(Sotheby's) **$990** **£660**

LAURENCE STEPHEN LOWRY – Gentleman Looking At Something – signed and
dated 1963 – oil on canvas – 24 x 20in.
(Christie's) **$11,988** **£8,100**

LAURENCE STEPHEN LOWRY –
Industrial Landscape – signed and dated
1944 – oil on panel – 21½ x 24in.
(Christie's) **$43,740 £29,160**

LAURENCE STEPHEN LOWRY – Canal
Scene Near Accrington – signed and
dated 1939 – oil on canvas – 17 x 21in.
(Christie's) **$12,150 £8,100**

LAURENCE STEPHEN LOWRY – Man
Lying At The Foot Of Stairs – signed and
dated 1961 – oil on canvas – 18 x 14in.
(Christie's) **$11,508 £7,776**

LAURENCE STEPHEN LOWRY –
Millworkers – signed and dated 1948
– oil on canvas – 16¼ x 20¼in.
(Christie's) **$20,779 £14,040**

LAURENCE STEPHEN LOWRY – Three
Happy Children – signed and dated 1960
– soft pencil – 13½ x 9½in.
(Christie's) **$1,620 £1,080**

LUARD

LOWES DALBIAC LUARD – The Circus Act – signed – gouache over black chalk – 18½ x 25½in.
(Sotheby's)   **$912**   **£638**

CHRISTOPH LUBIENIETZKY – Interior With A Doctor, Writing At A Table – signed and dated 1728 – oil on panel – 16¾ x 14in.
(Sotheby's)   **$8,140**   **£5,500**

CHRISTOPH LUBIENIETZKY – Eine Prise Schnupftabak – signed – oil on canvas – 57 x 48.5cm.
(Germann Auktionshaus)   **$3,433**   **£2,352**

ALBERT DURER LUCAS – Still Life Study Of Blackberries And A Moth – on ivory – 5 x 4in.
(Sotheby's)   **$321**   **£220**

HENRY F. LUCAS LUCAS – Pepper – signed and dated '92, and signed, inscribed and dated 1892 on the reverse – 19½ x 25½in.
(Sotheby's)   **$597**   **£418**

JOHN TEMPLETON LUCAS – A Poacher Apprehended – signed and dated 1874 – 28 x 36in.
(Sotheby's)   **$4,950**   **£3,300**

MAXIMILIEN LUCE – Sevres, Inondation De 1910 – signed and dated – 19¾ x 25½in.
(Sotheby's)   **$19,800 £13,200**

MAXIMILIEN LUCE – Portrait De Madame Luce – signed and dated 1905 – 37¼ x 29¼in.
(Sotheby's)   **$22,484 £15,400**

ARTHUR WARDLE AND HAL LUDLOW – Yours Faithfully – signed and dated '92 – on panel – 14 x 10in.
(Sotheby's)   **$1,485   £990**

MAXIMILIEN LUCE – La Couture Au Jardin – signed – 19¾ x 23¾in.
(Sotheby's)   **$35,332 £24,200**

HENRY STEPHEN LUDLOW – A Reverie – signed, inscribed on a label on the backboard – on board – 13½ x 10½in.
(Sotheby's)   **$660   £440**

ALBERT LUDOVICI, JNR. – Fisherfolk On A West Country Beach – signed and dated 1883 – oil on canvas – 30 x 50in. *(Sotheby's)*   **$6,380 £4,400**

WILLIAM LUKER – 'Surprised' – signed and dated 1878 in pencil on stretcher – on canvas – 16 x 24in.
(Sotheby's)   **$2,475 £1,650**

WILLIAM LUKER – A Shepherd Boy And A Flock Of Sheep In A Wooded Landscape – signed and dated 1871 – 36¼ x 60½in.
(Christie's)   **$3,057 £2,052**

GEORGE LUKS – Nursemaids, High Bridge Park – signed – oil on canvas. *(Sotheby's)*   **$220,000 £152,778**

HARRIET RANDALL LUMIS – Meadow Brook – signed – oil on canvas – 28¼ x 24in.
(Christie's)   **$2,420 £1,610**

FREDERIK CHRISTIAN LUND –
Fisherfolk By A Beached Sailing Vessel
– signed and dated 1883 – 18½ x 29½in.
(Christie's) **$9,910** **£6,696**

EGRON SILLIF LUNDGREN, Attributed
to – The Syrian Girl – inscribed – watercolour – 12 x 9¼in.
(Sotheby's) **$546** **£374**

THOMAS LUNY – A British Man Of
War At The Mouth Of The Dart –
signed and dated 1829 – 23½ x 33¼in.
(Sotheby's) **$13,200** **£8,800**

THOMAS LUNY – A Dutch Indiaman
And Other Shipping In Distress In The
Downs – signed – on panel – 10 x 16½in.
(Christie's) **$810** **£540**

THOMAS LUNY – Fisherfolk And Their
Vessels By A Shore At Sunset – signed –
14¾ x 19¾in.
(Sotheby's) **$803** **£550**

THOMAS LUNY – Despatched Under
Full Sail – 19¼ x 26½in.
(Sotheby's) **$4,455** **£2,970**

HENRY ANDREWS LUSCOMBE – A
Naval Review – signed and dated 1868
– on canvas – 37 x 51in.
(Sotheby's) **$4,978** **£3,410**

OTTO LUSSI – Stilleben Mit Roter
Vase – oil on canvas – 72 x 60cm.
*(Germann
      Auktionshaus)* **$1,167** **£778**

OTTO LUSSI – Figur Mit Facher, 1931
– signed – oil on canvas – 61 x 50cm.
*(Germann
      Auktionshaus)* **$1,630** **£1,117**

**THEOPHILE MARIE FRANCOIS
LYBAERT** – Le Divin Emperem Caligula
Pere Des Emperems Et Des Cesars; Un
Jour d'Adoration – signed, dated 1885
and inscribed – 47¼ x 25in.
(Sotheby's) **$3,960** **£2,640**

CORNEILLE DE LYON, Follower of –
Portrait Of A Young Man, In A Black
Jacket And Plumed Hat – on panel –
4¾ x 3¾in.
(Christie's) **$772** **£540**

WILLIAM McALPINE – An Estuary
Scene With Shipping – signed – on canvas
– 8 x 16in.
(Sotheby's)   **$396**   **£264**

WILLIAM McALPINE – Coming Into
Harbour – on paper – 7 x 12in.
(Sotheby's)   **$346**   **£242**

ROBERT WALKER MacBETH –
September – signed with monogram and
dated 1880 – oil on canvas – 22 x 17in.
(Sotheby's)   **$5,742** **£3,960**

ARTHUR DAVID McCORMICK – The
Place Of Campaign – signed and inscribed
on an old label on reverse – watercolour
– 14¼ x 21¼in.
(Sotheby's)   **$441**   **£308**

A. McDONALD – A Farmer, His Horse
And Cart On The Outskirts Of A Village
– signed and dated 1894 – watercolour
– 10 x 15¾in.
(Sotheby's)   **$610**   **£418**

J. MacDONALD – Caught – signed
and dated 1852 – oil on canvas – 28
x 36in.
(Sotheby's)   **$1,058**   **£715**

WILLIAM MACDUFF – Christmas
Visitors – signed and dated 1860 – 24 x
32½in.
(Christie's)   **$15,184   £10,260**

TOM McEWAN – A Book O'Ballads
– signed, signed and inscribed on the
reverse – oil – 20 x 15½in.
(Sotheby's)   **$1,237   £825**

AMBROSE McEVOY – Portrait Of A
Lady In Evening Dress – watercolour
over pencil – 21 x 14in.
(Sotheby's)   **$742   £495**

JESSIE M. McGEEHAN – The Little
Flower Girl, Holland – signed – oil –
19½ x 33in.
(Sotheby's)   **$2,640   £1,760**

TOM McEWAN – For Winter Wear –
signed – oil on canvas – 19½ x 24in.
(Sotheby's)   **$1,953   £1,320**

JESSIE M. McGEEHAN – A Gift For
Grandma – signed – oil – 16 x 20in.
(Sotheby's)   **$1,567   £1,045**

WILLIAM STEWART MacGEORGE –
Hide And Seek – signed – 20 x 23in.
(Sotheby's)   **$1,815   £1,210**

ROBERT McGREGOR – Shrimping
– signed – oil on canvas – 10 x 14in.
(Sotheby's)   **$2,116   £1,430**

ROBERT McGREGOR – The Pink
Blouse, A Portrait Of Helen McGregor,
The Artist's Daughter – signed with
initials – oil on board – 9½ x 7in.
(Sotheby's)   **$390   £264**

ROBERT McGREGOR – The Kelp Gatherers – signed – oil on canvas – 26 x
40½in. *(Sotheby's)*
                        $7,814   £5,280

McGREGOR

ROBERT McGREGOR – A Thorn In
The Foot – signed – 20 x 27in.
(Christie's) **$6,900** **£4,600**

WILLIAM YORKE MACGREGOR –
Amiens – signed – coloured chalk –
23½ x 19in.
(Sotheby's) **$276** **£187**

FANNY MacIAN – The Pet Of The
Tribe – signed and dated 1843 – oil on
canvas – 36 x 28in.
(Sotheby's) **$1,116** **£770**

JOHN MACKAY – The Duck Pond –
signed – watercolour – 6 x 8in.
(Sotheby's) **$1,973** **£1,375**

DAVID HALL McKEWAN – The Watermill – signed – watercolour over pencil
– 13¾ x 20¾in.
(Sotheby's) **$462** **£308**

DAY McKILLIP – The Window Seat –
signed – 20 x 16in.
(Sotheby's) **$412** **£275**

DUNCAN FRASER McLEA – Trawlers
Entering Harbour – signed and dated
1887 – on canvas – 20 x 30in.
(Sotheby's) **$264** **£176**

ELISEE MACLET – Bateaux A Toulon,
1919 – signed – oil on board – 46 x
61cm.
*(Germann
Auktionshaus)* **$5,581** **£3,823**

ALEXANDER MACLEAN – A Windy
Day – signed – on canvas – 24 x 61in.
(Sotheby's) **$660** **£440**

ELISEE MACLET – Le Lapin Agile
– signed – oil on canvas – 23½ x 28¾in.
(Sotheby's) **$2,475** **£1,650**

McNEIL MACLEAN – Koblentz And
Ehrenbreitstein – signed, inscribed
and dated 1837 – 34 x 56in.
(Sotheby's) **$14,025** **£9,350**

McNEIL MACLEAY – A Scottish Loch
– signed and dated 1867 – oil on canvas
– 17 x 29in.
(Sotheby's) **$1,546** **£1,045**

ELISEE MACLET – Le Lapin Agile –
signed – oil on board – 18 x 21½in.
(Sotheby's) **$1,072** **£715**

ROBERT RUSSELL MACNEE – Loading The Cart – signed and dated '23 – oil on canvas – 28 x 42in.
(Sotheby's) $3,256   £2,200

DANIEL MACLISE – Lear And Cordelia – signed and dated 1853 – oil – 60 x 45cm.
(Henry Spencer & Sons) $1,095   £750

SAMUEL McCLOY – Awaiting The Fisherman's Return – signed – watercolour – 10¼ x 14½in.
(Christie's) $1,487   £1,026

ROBERT RUSSELL MACNEE – A Hen In A Yard – signed and dated '90 – watercolour – 12 x 9½in.
(Sotheby's) $495   £330

SIR DANIEL MACNEE, Attributed to – The Death Of King Lear – watercolour – 10¾ x 8½in.
(Sotheby's) $208   £143

ROBERT RUSSELL MACNEE – The Farmyard; and Hayricks – signed and dated '16 and '18 – oil on canvas – 14 x 18in.
(Sotheby's) $2,116   £1,430 Pair

LT.-COL. THOMAS WILLIAM OGILVIE McNIVER – Entrance To The Church Of The Holy Sepulchre, Jerusalem – inscribed on a label on the reverse – watercolour over pencil – 21 x 25in.
(Sotheby's) **$1,138** **£825**

WILLIAM McTAGGART – A Day On The Seashore (Portrait Group of the Children of Mr Henry Gourlay) – signed and dated 1877 – 28¼ x 40in.
(Christie's) **$4,200** **£2,800**

MINO MACCARI – La Modella (circa 1948) – signed – pastel on card – 42.5 x 30cm.
(Christie's) **$1,083** **£737**

JOHN MacWHIRTER – A Lonely Birch – signed with monogram – oil on canvas – 48 x 32in.
(Sotheby's) **$4,558** **£3,080**

AUGUST MACKE – Tochter Des Dr. Jaggi – charcoal – 6¼ x 4¼in.
(Sotheby's) **$8,250** **£5,500**

JOHN CHARLES MAGGS – 'Outside
The Crown Inn' – signed and dated
1879 – 14 x 26in.
(Christie's)   **$2,430   £1,620**

JOHN CHARLES MAGGS – London
Mails at Cold Ashton; and Changing
Horses At Swann Inn – signed – oil
on canvas – 14 x 27in.
(Sotheby's)   **$3,067   £2,145 Pair**

RENE MAGRITTE – L'Homme Au
Chapeau – signed – blue crayon – 11¾
x 8½in.
(Sotheby's)   **$23,100   £15,400**

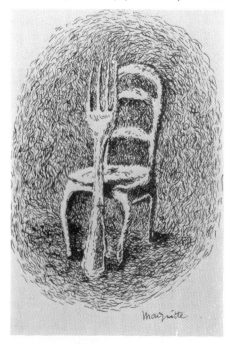

RENE MAGRITTE – Fourchette Et
Chaise – signed – pen and black ink on
paper – 11½ x 8¼in.
(Christie's)   **$5,832   £3,888**

RENE MAGRITTE – La Moralite De
Sommeil – signed – gouache – 13 x
9½in.
(Sotheby's)   **$36,685   £25,300**

RENE MAGRITTE – La Perspective Amoureuse – signed – pencil on paper – 16 x 10¼in.
(Christie's) **$30,780 £20,520**

JAMES MAHONEY – A Break For Lunch – signed and with monogram, indistinctly signed and dated 1868 – watercolour and bodycolour – 5 x 6¼in.
(Sotheby's) **$825 £550**

RAFFAELE MAINELLA – Boys Fishing In The Lagoon With Venice Beyond – signed – watercolour – 6¼ x 12¼in.
(Sotheby's) **$1,124 £770**

ERNEST LEE MAJOR – A Young French Girl – signed and dated 1888 – oil on canvas – 16 x 13in.
(Robert W. Skinner Inc.) **$1,400 £933**

ROY DE MAISTRE – The Deposition – signed – on board – 16 x 12in.
(Sotheby's) **$577 £385**

ERNEST LEE MAJOR – Profile Of A Young Woman From The Back – signed and dated 1892 – oil on canvas – 20 x 16in.
(Robert W. Skinner Inc.) **$1,500 £1,000**

ERNEST LEE MAJOR – Regal Lilies
– signed – oil on canvas – 34 x 28in.
*(Robert W. Skinner
Inc.)* $127   £85

ERNEST LEE MAJOR – Autumn
Still Life – signed – oil on canvas –
30 x 38in.
*(Robert W. Skinner
Inc.)* $1,500   £1,000

PHILIPPE MALIAVINE – Femme Nue
Assise – signed – oil on canvas – 81 x
65cm.
*(Germann
Auktionshaus)* $2,469   £1,646

ERNEST LEE MAJOR – Sleeping
Woman – signed and dated '88 – oil
on panel – 16 x 13in.
*(Robert W. Skinner
Inc.)* $650   £433

WILLIAM HENRY MANDER – A
Wooded River Landscape – signed and
dated 1901 – 19½ x 29¼in.
(Christie's) $1,609   £1,080

WILLIAM HENRY MANDER – At Llan Urst, Looking Towards Trefriar, Bettws-y-Coed, North Wales – signed and dated '87, also signed and inscribed on the reverse – oil on canvas – 22 x 38in.
(Sotheby's) $5,280 £3,520

MANE-KATZ – Portrait De Jeune Rabbin – signed – oil on canvas – 28¾ x 23½in.
(Sotheby's) $13,200 £8,800

HENRI MANGUIN – Nu Sous Les Arbres – signed – 21¼ x 25½in.
(Sotheby's) $44,550 £29,700

MANE-KATZ – Deux Freres Avec Une Chevre – signed – oil on canvas – 30¾ x 15in.
(Sotheby's) $24,750 £16,500

HENRI MANGUIN – Nu A Cavaliere Ou La Petite Bacchante – signed and dated 1906 – 32 x 39¼in.
(Sotheby's) $39,875 £27,500

HENRI MANGUIN – Annette Devant
La Porte – signed – oil on canvas –
28 x 22¾in.
(Sotheby's)   **$8,745**   **£5,830**

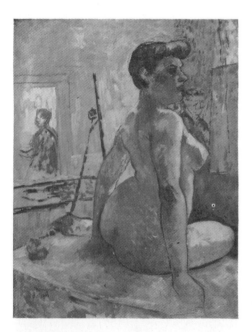

HENRI MANGUIN – Nu A L'Atelier Ou
La Croupe, Rue Courseault – signed and
dated 1903 – oil on canvas – 36¼ x
28¾in.
(Sotheby's)   **$69,300 £46,200**

HENRI MANGUIN – Colombier,
Neuchatel – signed – oil on canvas – 19½
x 21½in.
(Christie's)   **$4,698**   **£3,132**

JOSHUA HARGRAVE SAMS MANN –
The First Earrings – oil on canvas –
18 x 14in.
(Sotheby's)   **$2,233**   **£1,540**

CHARLES MARCHAND – A Venetian
View – signed and indistinctly dated
18' – 19¼ x 31½in.
(Sotheby's)   **$1,237**   **£825**

PINKY MARCIUS-SIMONS – A Lazy
Day – signed – oil on canvas – 32¼ x
21½in.
(Christie's)   **$3,300**   **£2,200**

MICHELE MARIESCHI, Follower of —
Venice, San Michele Al Isola — oil on
canvas — 18¾ x 26in.
(Sotheby's) $5,781 £3,960

GEORGE MARKS — A Tune To Himself
— signed and dated 1879 — watercolour,
heightened with bodycolour — 9 x 7in.
(Sotheby's) **$1,284** **£880**

HENRY STACEY MARKS — Thoughts
Of Christmas — signed and dated 1870 —
watercolour, heightened with bodycolour — 22 x 32in.
(Sotheby's) **$2,730** **£1,870**

HENRY STACY MARKS — A Pelican
And A Heron By A Wall — signed — 29½
x 30in.
(Christie's) **$2,590** **£1,728**

ALBERT MARLOW — St. Martin's
Church, Bullring, Birmingham — signed
and dated 1887 — oil on canvas — 36½
x 50in.
(Sotheby's) **$8,580** **£5,720**

PAUL MARNY — Port L'Abbe, Brittany
— signed and inscribed — watercolour —
24 x 41in.
(Sotheby's) **$528** **£352**

ALBERT MARQUET – Le Port De Saint-Jean-De-Luz – signed – 25½ x 32¼in.
(Sotheby's) **$85,800 £57,200**

ALBERT MARQUET – Bateaux Dans Le Port; Les Sables D'Olonne – signed – oil on canvas laid on panel – 13 x 16¼in.
(Christie's) **$41,277 £28,080**

ALBERT MARQUET – Paysage de Sidi-Bou-Said – signed – oil on canvas board – 13¼ x 16¼in.
(Christie's) **$15,390 £10,260**

ARTHUR H. MARSH – A Blustery Day – signed – watercolour with stopping out – 36 x 24in.
(Sotheby's) **$495 £330**

REGINALD MARSH – Merry-Go-Round – signed and dated '43 – oil on masonite – 36 x 24in.
(Christie's) **$38,500 £26,736**

REGINALD MARSH – Street Scenes:
Double Sided – watercolour, black wash
and gouache on paper – 22¼ x 30¾in.
(Christie's)   **$6,600   £4,400**

B. MARSHALL – A Bay Hunter Outside
A Stable – 18 x 23¾in.
(Christie's)   **$259   £140**

HERBERT MENZIES MARSHALL –
Angers – signed and dated 1906 –
watercolour – 8 x 12in.
(Sotheby's)   **$345   £231**

JOHN MARSHALL – Caught In A Storm
– signed – on canvas – 12 x 14in.
(Sotheby's)   **$726   £484**

**ROBERTO ANGELO KITTERMASTER
MARSHALL** – Sheep Grazing In A
Meadow – signed – watercolour with
scratching out – 13½ x 20½in.
(Sotheby's)   **$868   £605**

THOMAS FALCON MARSHALL –
Christmas Morning – signed with initials
and dated '65 – pencil and watercolour
heightened with white – 15¾ x 23½in.
(Christie's)   **$1,215   £810**

ELLIOTT H. MARTEN – The Downs Near
Lewes – signed – watercolour – 9¼ x
20¼in.
(Edgar Horne)   **$132   £88**

FRANC P. MARTIN – June, Iona –
signed – oil on panel – 22 x 48in.
(Sotheby's)   **$550   £385**

JOHN MARTIN – Edinburgh Castle –
signed with initials and dated 1855,
inscribed on the reverse – on board –
17 x 11½in.
(Sotheby's)   **$1,320   £880**

WILLIAM ALISON MARTIN – Amongst
The Trees – signed – on panel – 18 x
24in.
(Sotheby's) **$1,155** **£770**

EDITH MARTINEAU – Palmy Days –
signed and dated 1877 – watercolour
over pencil, heightened with bodycolour – 16 x 11in.
(Sotheby's) **$674** **£462**

GERTRUDE MARTINEAU – The Picture Book – signed and dated 1891 –
oil on canvas – 18 x 20in.
(Sotheby's) **$1,650** **£1,100**

FRANS MASEREEL – The Couple –
signed – brush and black ink on paper
– 10¼ x 7¾in.
(Christie's) **$346** **£237**

FRANK H. MASON – The Grand Canal,
Venice – signed – watercolour – 19¼ x
29¼in.
(Sotheby's) **$835** **£572**

FRANK HENRY MASON – Armed Trawlers From Hull And Grimsby, The Ameer,
Resono And Lord Roberts In Action,
1915 – signed – watercolour and bodycolour – 14 x 20½in.
(Sotheby's) **$990** **£660**

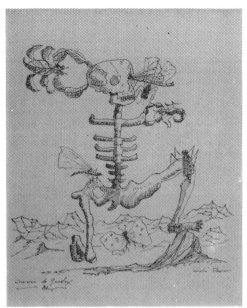

ANDRE MASSON – Sierra De Guadix –
signed and dated '34 – pen and ink – 17¾
x 16¼in.
(Sotheby's) **$1,650** **£1,100**

CHARLES PAULIN FRANCOIS MATET
– Portrait Of A Boy, Seated On A Cushion,
Holding A Horn – signed and dated 182(?)
– 38¾ x 31in.
(Christie's) **$4,860** **£3,240**

AGOSTINO MASSUCCI, Circle of – St.
Francis Of Assisi Blessing A Child – oil
on copper – 13 x 9½in.
(Sotheby's) **$733** **£495**

HENRI MATISSE – Jeune Femme
Lisant – signed – charcoal and estompe
– 14½ x 9½in.
(Sotheby's) **$27,225** **£18,150**

HENRI MATISSE – Tete De Femme –
signed – pencil drawing – 19.5 x 26cm.
*(Germann
     Auktionshaus)* **$7,300** **£5,000**

HENRI MATISSE – Femme Assise En
Robe Longue – signed and dated '39 –
charcoal – 18¾ x 14¼in.
(Sotheby's) **$46,255** **£31,900**

MATTA, Robert Echaurren – Les
Etournaux – inscribed – pen and black
ink on paper – 19 x 25in.
(Christie's) **$355** **£237**

JAN MATULKA – Bathers – signed –
conte crayon on buff paper – 14¾ x
20¾in.
(Christie's) **$1,980** **£1,320**

JAMES MAUBERT – Portrait Of
Henrietta, Duchess Of Bolton As St. Agnes
– signed and inscribed – 69½ x 60in.
(Sotheby's) **$10,230** **£6,820**

ALFRED HENRY MAURER – Head
Of A Woman – signed – oil on masonite
– 36 x 25½in.
(Christie's) **$20,900** **£14,513**

J. MAURER – A View In Ranelagh Gardens, With The Rotunda In The Centre And Ladies And Gentlemen Conversing – 25½ x 37½in.
(Christie's)   **$2,916**   **£1,944**

PAUL MAZE – Le Pont – signed, labelled on verso 1945 – oil – 10.5 x 18in. *(Woolley & Wallis)*   **$1,073**   **£740**

ARTHUR JOSEPH MEADOWS – The Bacino, From The Grand Canal, Venice – signed and dated 1895 – 29½ x 49¼in.
(Christie's)   **$4,860**   **£3,240**

ARTHUR DAMPIER MAY – Before The Bath – signed and dated 1905 – 31 x 15in.
(Sotheby's)   **$3,533**   **£2,420**

EDWIN L. MEADOWS – The Midday Break – signed and dated '81, indistinctly signed and inscribed on the reverse – oil on canvas – 16 x 14in.
(Sotheby's)   **$1,435**   **£990**

MEADOWS

JAMES MEADOWS, Attributed to –
Fishing Off The Coast – signed and dated
1856 – oil on canvas – 11½ x 19½in.
(Sotheby's)   **$1,365**   **£935**

JAMES EDWIN MEADOWS – View Of
A Cottage, With Figures, In The Foreground – signed and dated 1862 – on
canvas – 15½ x 13in.
(Sotheby's)   **$1,255**   **£836**

JAMES EDWIN MEADOWS – A
Country Lane – signed and dated 1878
– oil on canvas – 24 x 36in.
(Sotheby's)   **$4,125**   **£2,750**

JAMES EDWIN MEADOWS – Children
And Haywain In Wooded Landscape –
signed and dated 1873 – oil – 20 x
30in.
*(Dacre, Son &
Hartley)*   **$1,716**   **£1,200**

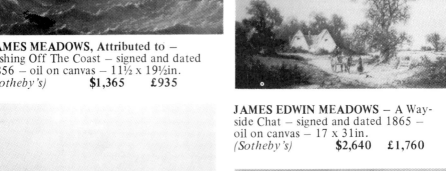

JAMES EDWIN MEADOWS – A Wayside Chat – signed and dated 1865 –
oil on canvas – 17 x 31in.
(Sotheby's)   **$2,640**   **£1,760**

WILLIAM MEADOWS – End Of Grand
Canal, Venice – signed and inscribed –
15½ x 23½in.
(Sotheby's)   **$560**   **£374**

JEAN CHARLES MEISSONIER – The
Musicians – signed and dated 1882 –
oil on canvas – 21¾ x 27¼in.
(Sotheby's)   **$6,380**   **£4,400**

WILHELM MELBYE – Shipping In A Storm – signed and dated – oil – 17 x 37in.
(Woolley & Wallis)   **$3,045 £2,100**

WILHELM MELBYE – Shipwreck In
Kynance Cove, Cornwall – signed and
dated 1865 – 39½ x 65¾in.
(Lawrence)   **$1,617   £1,100**

CAMPBELL A. MELLON – November
Sketch – signed – on panel – 9 x 11½in.
(Lawrence)   **$462   £308**

GARI MELCHERS – The Young Mother
– signed – oil on canvas – 24¾ x 21¼in.
(Christie's)   **$28,600 £19,861**

CAMPBELL MELLON – Valley Of Trent
– signed, inscribed and dated 1929 on the
reverse – on board – 20 x 24in.
(Sotheby's)   **$742   £495**

MELLOR

WILLIAM MELLOR – A Waterfall –
signed – oil on canvas – 36 x 27in.
(Sotheby's) **$1,402** **£935**

WILLIAM MELLOR – On The Ure,
Wensleydale – signed and inscribed on
reverse – oil on canvas – 24 x 36in.
(Morphets) **$1,812** **£1,250**

WILLIAM MELLOR – River Wharfe
And Bolton Woods In Autumn – signed
– oil – 29½ x 20in.
*(Dacre, Son &
Hartley)* **$540** **£360**

WILLIAM MELLOR – Wooded River
Scene With Cattle – signed – oil – 20 x
30in.
*(Dacre, Son &
Hartley)* **$2,025** **£1,350**

WILLIAM MELLOR – A Bridge Over A
Wooded Stream – signed – oil on canvas
– 36 x 28in.
(Sotheby's) **$558** **£385**

ARTHUR MELVILLE – The Street
Market, Granville – signed and dated
1878 – watercolour – 11 x 17½in.
(Sotheby's) **$1,302** **£880**

ANTON RAPHAEL MENGS, Attributed to – The Triumph Of Amphitrite – on gold ground panel – 19¾ x 21¾in.
(Christie's)   **$4,860   £3,240**

MIGUEL JACINTO MENENDEZ, Attributed to – A Study Of A Young Girl – red chalk – 171 x 149mm.
(Sotheby's)   **$693   £462**

SIGMUND MENKES – Nude With A Mandolin – signed – oil on canvas – 32 x 25½in.
(Robert W. Skinner Inc.)   **$1,100   £733**

ANTON RAPHAEL MENGS, Manner of – Portrait Of A Nobleman In A Painted Interior – 31½ x 25in.
(Sotheby's)   **$1,346   £880**

MORTIMER MENPES – Milk Sellers, Morocco – signed, inscribed on the reverse – on board – 8¼ x 10in.
(Sotheby's)   **$907   £605**

MENPES

MORTIMER MENPES – Two Japanese
Children In A Street – signed – on panel
– 10¼ x 7¾in.
(Sotheby's)   **$605**   **£352**

EDOUART MENTA – Maler Vor Seiner
Staffelei – signed with monogram and
dated 1901 – oil on canvas – 47.5 x
40.5cm.
*(Germann
Auktionshaus)*   **$2,097**   **£1,398**

MENTIAGNIE – A Tyrolean Lake Scene
– indistinctly signed – oil on canvas –
15 x 20in.
*(Sotheby, King &
Chasemore)*   **$969**   **£570**

**ADOLPH FRIEDRICH ERDMANN
MENZEL** – Portrait Of A Bearded Man,
Head And Shoulders – signed with initials and dated '55 – on paper laid on
canvas – 23 x 18¼in.
(Christie's)   **$60,740**   **£41,040**

MAX VON MENZ – A Meeting On The
Water – signed, dated 1857 and inscribed
– on canvas – 24½ x 33½in.
(Sotheby's)   **$2,557**   **£1,705**

PHILIP MERCIER, Attributed to – Portrait Of A Young Lady, In A Brown
Dress And White Cap, By A Fountain In
A Landscape – 20 x 13½in.
(Christie's)   **$4,536**   **£3,024**

JOSEPH MERCKELBAGH – Driving The Flock Home – signed and dated 1915 – oil on canvas – 15 x 11in.
(Sotheby's)　　**$803**　　**£550**

GEORG MERKEL – Young Girl Leaning On Hand – signed – coloured chalk drawing – 18 x 12in.
(Lawrence)　　**$485**　　**£330**

ANNA LEA MERRITT – The Black Bonnet – signed with monogram – oil on canvas – 20 x 16in.
(Sotheby's)　　**$1,402**　　**£935**

E. L. T. MESENS – La Fissure – signed and dated 1961 – collage – 11¼ x 11¼in.
(Christie's)　　**$394**　　**£270**

ANNA LEA MERRITT – Eve – signed and dated 1885 – oil on canvas – 30 x 42in.
(Sotheby's)　　**$14,355　£9,900**

GABRIEL METSU – A Young Woman Reading A Letter – traces of a signature – on panel – 10 x 8in.
(Sotheby's) **$44,550 £29,700**

JEAN METZINGER – Paysage Cubiste – indistinctly signed – oil on canvas – 28½ x 21¼in.
(Christie's) **$12,150 £8,100**

LOUIS MEYER – Fishing Boats At Sea – signed – on panel – 5¼ x 7in.
(Sotheby's) **$3,135 £2,090**

EDWARD FRANZ MEYERHEIM – 'Storytime' – signed and dated 1868 – on canvas – 20¼ x 24½in. *(Sotheby's)* **$12,210 £8,140**

902

HERMANN MEYERHEIM – A Busy
Estuary – signed – 26 x 37½in.
(Sotheby's) $7,590 £5,060

CHARLES MEYNIER – La Sagesse
Preservant L'Adolescence Des Traites
De L'Amour – signed – 95¼ x 81in.
(Sotheby's) $39,600 £26,400

THEOBALD MICHAU – A Market In A
River Landscape With Antwerp In The
Distance – signed – oil on panel – 22 x
28¼in.
(Sotheby's) $64,240 £44,000

A. MIDY – The Treasure Trove – signed
and indistinctly inscribed – watercolour
– 14 x 8½in.
(Sotheby's) $297 £198

**W. MIERIS, 17th/18th century Dutch
School** – The Game Seller – oil on
panel – 17 x 12in.
*(W. H. Lane &
Son)* $2,336 £1,600

393

MIERIS

WILLEM VAN MIERIS — The Poulterer's Shop — signed and dated 1727 — on panel — 15½ x 12¾in.
(Sotheby's) **$44,550 £29,700**

GIUSEPPE MIGNECO — Ritratto Di Contadino — signed — oil on canvas — 22 x 18¼in.
(Sotheby's) **$8,932 £6,160**

WILLEM VAN MIERIS, Follower of — A Sleeping Shepherdess Surprised By A Man — bears signature and dated 1718 — oil on panel — 7½ x 6¾in.
(Sotheby's) **$8,465 £5,720**

MILANESE SCHOOL, 16th century — Portrait Of A Young Man Said To Be Chancellor Alessandro Moroni — on panel — 6½ x 5in.
(Sotheby's) **$9,900 £6,600**

MILANESE SCHOOL, First Half Of The 16th Century – An Allegorical Subject – on panel – 16¼ x 21in.
(Sotheby's)   **$5,940   £3,960**

SIR JOHN EVERETT MILLAIS – Biblical Scene – oil.
(Andrew Grant)   **$3,150   £2,100**

THOMAS ROSE MILES – Steephill Cove, nr. Ventnor, Isle of Wight – signed and inscribed on reverse – oil on canvas – 30 x 50in.
(Sotheby's)   **$1,284   £880**

SIR JOHN EVERETT MILLAIS – The Proscribed Royalist, 1651 – signed and dated 1853 – 40½ x 29in.
(Christie's)   **$1,246,752 £842,400**

SIR JOHN EVERETT MILLAIS, Follower of – Children's Voices – with Millais monogram – 21¼ x 17½in.
(Christie's)   **$674   £453**

JAMES MILLER – View Towards Hanover Square From The South, London – signed, dated 1783 and inscribed – watercolour and gouache – 18½ x 22in.
(Sotheby's)   **$5,940   £3,960**

MILLER

R. RUSSELL MILLER – A Hunter And His Dog – signed – on canvas – 18 x 12in.
(Sotheby's)   **$346**   **£231**

VICTOR MARAIS MILTON – The Connoisseur – signed – on panel – 13¾ x 9¾in.
(Sotheby's)   **$1,155**   **£770**

WILLIAM RICKARBY MILLER – On The Passaic River, Patterson – signed and dated 1880, also signed and inscribed on the reverse – watercolour on paper on board – 12¼ x 9¼in.
(Christie's)   **$2,090**   **£1,393**

ANDRE MINAUX – Vase de Tournesols – signed – oil on canvas – 39¼ x 27½in.
(Christie's)   **$1,375**   **£918**

JOHN MINTON – Porthleven, Cornwall
– signed and dated 1945 – 29½ x 20in.
(Sotheby's)   **$8,580   £5,720**

ERNEST GABRIEL MITCHELL – Harvest
Moon – signed and dated 1899 – watercolour, heightened with scratching out –
14 x 20in.
(Sotheby's)   **$462   £308**

PHILIP MITCHELL – A Village In The
West Country – signed and dated 1861
– watercolour heightened with white –
15½ x 25½in.
(Sotheby's)   **$660   £440**

T. MITCHELL – 'The Ship Sherwood In
A Hurricane' -- signed – 77 x 120cm.
(Reeds Rains)   **$1,320   £880**

AMEDEO MODIGLIANI – La Rousse
Aux Yeux Bleus – signed – 21¾ x 18in.
(Sotheby's)   **$429,000 £286,000**

AMEDEO MODIGLIANI – Portrait De
Leopold Zborowski – signed – 15¾ x
12½in.
(Sotheby's)   **$143,550   £99,000**

MOGFORD

THOMAS MOGFORD of Exeter – A Chestnut Stallion With A Dog In A Landscape; and A Dark Bay Stallion In A Landscape – one signed – 25 x 30in.
(Lawrence) **$957** **£638 Pair**

JOHN HENRY MOLE – Tarbert Castle, Loch Fynne – signed and dated 1879 – watercolour – 25 x 39½in.
(Sotheby's) **$2,683** **£1,870**

PIER FRANCESCO MOLA – An Allegory, A Girl And An Old Man Pour A Libation For An Ass – oil on canvas – 47¼ x 36½in.
(Sotheby's) **$5,210** **£3,520**

JAN MIENSE MOLENAER, Attributed to – An Interior With Peasants Playing Cards – bears signature – on panel – 13¼ x 16½in.
(Sotheby's) **$2,475** **£1,650**

PIER FRANCESCO MOLA, Circle of – Susannah And The Elders – oil on canvas – 57 x 76in.
(Sotheby's) **$7,163** **£4,840**

KLAES MOLENAER – A Winter River Landscape – oil on panel – 12½ x 15in.
(Sotheby's) **$3,581** **£2,420**

KLAES MOLENAER – A Winter Landscape With Figures Near A Village –
signed – on panel – 15½ x 22in.
(Sotheby's) **$17,325 £11,550**

HENDRICK MOMMERS – A Southern
Landscape With Peasants On A Road –
indistinctly signed – oil on panel – 15¾
x 26in.
(Sotheby's) **$1,927 £1,320**

PIETER DE MOLIJN – A Dune Land-
scape With Peasants Kneeling Before A
Shrine – signed – on panel – 12¼ x 14in.
(Sotheby's) **$16,500 £11,000**

PETER MONAMY – A British Man Of
War With Other Vessels In Calm Waters
– 35 x 35½in.
(Sotheby's) **$3,960 £2,640**

EVERT MOLL – Canal Scenes – signed
– oil on canvas – 20¼ x 25½in.
(Sotheby's) **$2,342 £1,650 Pair**

PETER MONAMY – The Evening Gun: A
British Man Of War And Other Vessels Off-
Shore – indistinctly signed – 19 x 23½in.
(Sotheby's) **$2,475 £1,650**

399

MONAMY

PETER MONAMY – A Man-Of-War Anchored By Mont Orgeuil Tower, Jersey – signed – 7¾ x 11in.
(Sotheby's)   **$927**   **£605**

PETER MONAMY – A Dutch Cutter With Other Shipping Beyond – oil on canvas – 11½ x 12½in.
(Sotheby's)   **$1,485**   **£990**

PIET MONDRIAN – Composition With Red, Blue And Yellow – signed and dated '30 – oil on canvas – 20¼ x 20¼in.
(Christie's)   **$2,268,000 £1,512,000**

PIET MONDRIAN – Zeeland Girl – signed with monogram – oil on canvas – 24¾ x 19in.
(Christie's)   **$63,504 £43,200**

CLAUDE MONET – La Seine Pres De Giverny – 21¼ x 31¾in.
(Sotheby's)   **$115,500 £77,000**

LOUIS DE MONI – A Market Scene – oil on panel – 16½ x 13½in.
(Sotheby's)   **$6,424   £4,400**

DAVID MONIES – A Toast To The Young Bugler, Charlottenlund Wood – signed – 51½ x 69½in.
(Christie's)   **$19,180 £12,960**

ALFRED MONTAGUE – A Continental Town – signed – oil on canvas – 20 x 30in.
(Sotheby's)　　**$2,145**　**£1,430**

ALFRED MONTAGUE – Shipping In Squally Weather – signed and dated 1867 – oil on canvas – 11¼ x 19¼in.
(Sotheby's)　　**$2,640**　**£1,760**

PIERRE MONTEZIN – Femme Etendant Du Linge – signed – oil on canvas – 21¼ x 25½in.
(Sotheby's)　　**$15,675**　**£10,450**

ROBERT ENRAGHT MOONY – The Black Sally Bush – signed, once with monogram and dated 1923 – watercolour over pencil, heightened with bodycolour – 17½ x 23½in.
(Sotheby's)　　**$907**　**£605**

A. HARVEY MOORE – Stalls On The Rialto Bridge, Venice – signed – watercolour and bodycolour – 14¼ x 8½in.
(Christie's)　　**$939**　**£648**

CLAUDE T. S. MOORE – British Man O'War At Anchor Outside A Harbour – signed and dated (18)91, also signed and dated on verso – oil on canvas – 50 x 76cm.
(Henry Spencer & Sons)　　**$5,250**　**£3,500**

CLAUDE T. STANFIELD MOORE – Men Of War In The Medway, Chatham Heights – signed and dated '92 – oil on canvas – 20 x 30in.
(Sotheby's)　　**$1,897**　**£1,265**

JOHN MOORE of Ipswich – A Clipper
At Sea – signed and dated 1890 – oil
on canvas – 20 x 30in.
(Sotheby's)   **$2,367   £1,650**

JAN EVERT MOREL – A Still Life Of
Summer Flowers – signed – 20¾ x
16½in.
(Sotheby's)   **$28,875   £19,250**

ANTONIS MOR, Circle of – Infanta
Catalina Micaela – 16¼ x 24¼in.
(Sotheby's)   **$18,150   £12,100**

ALFRED MORGAN – One Of The People
– Gladstone In An Omnibus – signed and
dated 1885 – 31¼ x 42½in.
(Christie's)   **$103,896   £70,200**

R. MORETTI – The Cardinals' Conference
– signed and inscribed – 21½ x 33in.
(Sotheby's)   **$1,897   £1,265**

EVELYN DE MORGAN – The Search
Light – signed with initials – 25¼ x
44¼in.
(Christie's)   **$17,582   £11,880**

FREDERICK MORGAN – A Picnic In
The Hay – signed – oil on board – 22
x 29in.
(Sotheby's)   **$19,800 £13,200**

JOHN MORGAN – Tired Out – signed
– oil on canvas – 8 x 10in.
(Sotheby's)   **$4,620   £3,080**

JOHN MORGAN – The School Room
– signed and dated 1876 – 28 x 36in.
(Sotheby's)   **$12,045   £8,250**

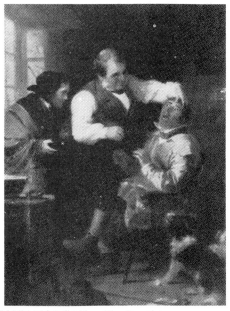

JOHN MORGAN – The Dentist –
signed – oil on canvas – 10 x 8in.
(Sotheby's)   **$1,485   £990**

JOHN MORGAN – Playmates –
signed – oil on canvas – 10 x 8in.
(Sotheby's)   **$2,640   £1,760**

JOHN MORGAN – Gee-Wo – signed –
24 x 36in.
(Sotheby's)   **$5,139   £3,520**

ERNST MORGENTHALER – Portrait
Prof. W. – signed with monogram and
dated 1946 – tempera on convas –
120.5 x 100cm.
*(Germann
    Auktionshaus)* **$1,458**   **£972**

BERTHE MORISOT – La Nourrice
Angele Allaitant Julie Manet – signed –
19¾ x 24in.
(Sotheby's)   **$51,392** **£35,200**

GEORGE MORLAND – The Slave Trade
– signed and dated 1787 (?) – 33 x 47½in.
(Sotheby's)   **$57,750** **£38,500**

GEORGE MORLAND – A Winter Landscape With Travellers On A Road –
signed with initials – 24½ x 29¼in.
(Sotheby's)   **$4,455** **£2,970**

GEORGE MORLAND – Beach Scene
With Fisherfolk Unloading The Catch –
oil – 18 x 24in.
*(Woolley &
    Wallis)*   **$2,610** **£1,800**

GEORGE MORLAND – The Shipwreck
– signed and dated 1796 – 24 x 29in.
(Sotheby's)   **$1,650** **£1,100**

GEORGE MORLAND – Shepherds In
A Landscape – signed – 13½ x 11½in.
(Lawrence) **$3,234 £2,200**

GEORGE MORLAND, Follower of – A
Gentleman, His Horse And Dog Beside A
Wood – oil on canvas – 24½ x 30in.
(Sotheby's) **$710 £528**

ROBERT MORLEY – Puppy Love –
signed and dated 1909 – oil on canvas –
36 x 28in.
(Sotheby's) **$1,294 £902**

HENRY ROBERT MORLAND – The
Letter Woman – 17½ x 14in.
(Sotheby's) **$1,650 £1,100**

SIR CEDRIC MORRIS – Winter Flowers
– signed – oil on canvas – 28 x 20in.
(Sotheby's) **$825 £550**

SIR CEDRIC MORRIS – Arcachon –
signed and dated '23 – oil on canvas –
23½ x 29in.
(Sotheby's)   **$707**   **£495**

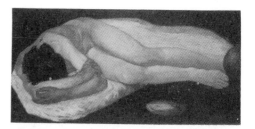

KOLOMAN MOSER – A Sleeping Nude
– signed – 20 x 40in.
(Sotheby's)   **$7,425**   **£4,950**

JOHN MORRIS – The Day's Bag –
signed – oil on canvas – 35½ x 27½in.
(Sotheby's)   **$1,846**   **£1,265**

MARY MOSER – A Vase Of Flowers –
signed and dated 1785(?) – watercolour
and bodycolour – 19½ x 14¼in.
(Sotheby's)   **$330**   **£220**

W. MORRIS – After A Good Day's Sport
– signed – 42 x 66in.
(Sotheby's)   **$3,795**   **£2,530**

GEORGE WILLIAM MOTE – By A River
– signed – 20 x 30in.
(Sotheby's)   **$1,237**   **£825**

WILLIAM SIDNEY MOUNT – The Trap
Sprung – signed and dated 1844, also
signed with initials and dated again on
the reverse – oil on panel – 12¾ x 17in.
(Christie's)   **$880,000 £611,111**

WILLIAM SIDNEY MOUNT – Bird-
Egging – signed and dated 1844 – oil
on panel – 12¾ x 17in.
(Christie's)   **$605,000 £420,138**

LEOPOLD CARL MULLER – A Negro
Head – oil on canvas – 29 x 19in.
(Sotheby's)   **$755   £528**

ARNOLD MOUNTFORT – Three Ladies In An Interior – signed and dated
1911 – 64 x 102in. *(Sotheby's)*   **$4,290 £2,860**

WILLIAM JAMES MULLER – A View
Of A Farmyard – signed – watercolour
heightened with white – 7¾ x 20¼in.
(Sotheby's)   **$990**   **£660**

WILLIAM MULREADY – Study Of Eve
Feeding A Dove With A Serpent Nearby
– inscribed in a later hand and dated 1869
– pencil and red chalk – 20 x 14½in.
(Sotheby's)   **$1,320**   **£880**

AUGUSTUS E. MULREADY, JNR. –
In Early Spring – signed and dated '04,
inscribed on the reverse – oil on canvas
– 12 x 9in.
(Sotheby's)   **$1,674**   **£1,155**

EDVARD MUNCH – Inger On The Beach
– signed – brush and ink and wash over
pencil – 8 x 11¼in.
(Sotheby's)   **$42,900**   **£28,600**

AUGUSTUS E. MULREADY, JNR. –
Happy While Sleeping – signed and
dated '83, inscribed on the reverse –
oil on canvas – 6¾ x 8½in.
(Sotheby's)   **$1,148**   **£792**

SIR ALFRED MUNNINGS – The River
Stour At Dedham – signed – oil on
canvas – 18 x 24in.
(Christie's)   **$19,180**   **£12,960**

SIR ALFRED MUNNINGS – The Start At Newmarket – signed – oil on canvas
– 25 x 30in. *(Christie's)* $351,648 £237,600

SIR ALFRED MUNNINGS – Norwich
Fair, A Stall At Bungay Races – signed
and dated 1909 – oil on canvas – 20 x
24¼in.
(Christie's) $103,896 £70,200

SIR ALFRED MUNNINGS – The Hunt
By The Sea – signed – oil on canvas –
22 x 18in.
(Christie's) $68,040 £45,360

SIR ALFRED MUNNINGS – O' Lady
Fair – signed, dated '06 and indistinctly
inscribed in pencil on the reverse –
pencil and sepia wash – 8¾ x 5¼in.
(Sotheby's) $963 £660

HUGH MUNRO – In A Galloway Rose Garden – signed – oil on canvas – 24 x 20in.
(Sotheby's)　　**$6,512**　**£4,400**

HJALMAR MUNSTERHJELM – A Lake Landscape With A Sailing Vessel – signed and dated '69 – 14½ x 22½in.
(Christie's)　　**$5,594**　**£3,780**

GABRIELE MUNTER – Metall-Blumen – signed and dated 1953 – oil on canvas – 21¾ x 15in.
(Christie's)　　**$11,826**　**£8,100**

SIR DAVID MURRAY – Waiting For A Bite – signed – watercolour – 11¾ x 18in.
(Christie's & Edmiston's)　**$1,050**　**£700**

THOMAS MURRAY – Portrait Of A Lady, Seated In A Garden Wearing A Yellow Dress – 48½ x 39in.
(Sotheby's)　　**$1,927**　**£1,320**

FRANS VAN DER MYN – Portrait Of A Lady Playing A Guitar, Seated In An Interior – signed and dated 1748 – 32½ x 25¾in.
(Christie's)　　**$4,324**　**£3,024**

CARLOS NADAL – Los Pirineos – signed and dated, and signed, inscribed and dated 1965 on the reverse – oil on canvas – 35½ x 28¼in.
(Christie's)   **$2,590**   **£1,728**

JOHN NASH – A Cornish Tin Mine – signed – watercolour over pencil, squared for transfer – 14½ x 19½in.
(Sotheby's)   **$786**   **£550**

CARLOS NADAL – Le Pont D'Uccle – signed and dated, also signed on the reverse – oil on canvas – 28¼ x 23¼in.
(Christie's)   **$1,576**   **£1,080**

JOSEPH NASH – In The Courtyard Of A Medieval Hall, Preparations For Hawking – signed and dated 1875 – pencil, watercolour and bodycolour on light brown paper – 13¼ x 19¼in.
(Christie's)   **$775**   **£518**

JOHN NASH – Landscape Near Hensborough – signed – watercolour over pencil – 16 x 21in.
(Sotheby's)   **$990**   **£660**

PAUL NASH – March Landscape (recto); and Still Life With Jug And Shelves (verso) – signed – oil on canvas – 20 x 26in.
(Christie's)   **$10,530**   **£7,020**

PAUL NASH – Swanage, Low Tide –
signed – watercolour and pencil – 15 x
22in.
(Christie's)   **$3,565   £2,376**

ALEXANDER NASMYTH – Classical
Landscape With Kinfauns Castle – 20
x 22in.
(Christie's &
Edmiston's)   **$2,700   £1,800**

PAUL NASH – March Woods, Whiteleaf,
Berkshire – oil on canvas – 30 x 19¾in.
(Christie's)   **$10,044   £6,696**

CHARLOTTE NASMYTH – View Of
Glencoe, Argyllshire – signed and dated
1852 – 18 x 24¼in.
(Christie's)   **$1,134   £756**

ALEXANDER NASMYTH – A Flour
Mill By A River – signed – oil on canvas
– 17 x 23in.
(Sotheby's)   **$11,550   £7,700**

PATRICK NASMYTH – A Farmstead –
signed and dated 1817 – on panel – 14 x
18¼in.
(Christie's)   **$1,944   £1,296**

JOHN CLAUDE NATTES – A View Of A House In Kensington – inscribed on the reverse – watercolour over pencil heightened with bodycolour – 10¾ x 15½in.
(Sotheby's) **$546** **£385**

JOHN CLAUDE NATTES – A Horseman Near The Steps To A Portico – signed and dated 1790 – watercolour over pencil – 10½ x 15in.
(Sotheby's) **$564** **£385**

ERNST WILHELM NAY – Die Blaue Stadt – signed and dated '46 – oil on panel – 24½ x 19in.
(Christie's) **$12,150** **£8,100**

NEAPOLITAN SCHOOL, Early 19th century – Camandoli Della Torre Del Preco – inscribed – gouache – 17½ x 26½in.
(Sotheby's) **$1,092** **£748**

NEAPOLITAN SCHOOL, 17th century – A Man Of War – 28¾ x 36½in.
(Sotheby's) **$1,072** **£715**

GEORGE LAURENCE NELSON – The Child's Supper – signed – oil on canvas – 40 x 32¼in.
(Christie's) **$7,700** **£5,347**

NETHERLANDISH

CONSTANTIJN NETSCHER – Portrait
Of A Family – 22 x 17in.
(Sotheby's)   **$13,530   £9,020**

**NETHERLANDISH SCHOOL, 16th
century** – The Virgin And Child –
oil on panel – 7 x 4¼in.
(Sotheby's)   **$3,533   £2,420**

CASPAR NETSCHER, Circle of – A
Little Girl Seated In A Park – oil on
canvas – 16 x 13in.
(Sotheby's)   **$6,905   £4,730**

NICOLAS DE NEUFCHATEL – Portrait
Of A Little Girl – oil on canvas – 25¼ x
18¾in.
(Sotheby's)   **$13,024   £8,800**

ALBERT NEUHUYS – An Interior Scene – signed and dated '78 – watercolour heightened with bodycolour – 13½ x 19¼in.
(Sotheby's)   **$2,604   £1,815**

ALPHONSE BRUNEL DE NEUVILLE – Spilt Ink – signed – oil on canvas – 21 x 24¾in.
(Sotheby's)   **$2,552   £1,760**

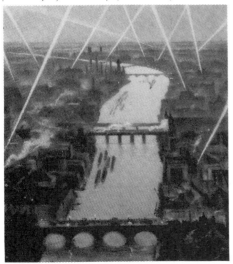

CHRISTOPHER RICHARD WYNNE NEVINSON – Among London Searchlights – oil on canvas – 24 x 18in.
(Christie's)   **$8,100   £5,400**

RICHARD HENRY NIBBS – Boats At Anchor – signed and inscribed – watercolour – 15 x 21¼in.
(Sotheby's)   **$345   £231**

RICHARD HENRY NIBBS – Low Tide, Shoreham Harbour – signed – watercolour – 25½ x 39in.
(Sotheby's)   **$495   £330**

ANDREW NICHOLL, Circle of – A Bank Of Flowers – watercolour heightened with bodycolour and gum arabic, with scratching out – 10 x 15in.
(Sotheby's)   **$412   £275**

ANDREW NICHOLL – The Great Sphinx With The Pyramid Of Khufu Beyond – signed – pen and brown ink and watercolour – 18½ x 28½in.
(Sotheby's)   **$726   £484**

BEN NICHOLSON – 1927 (Still Life) –
signed, dated 1927 and inscribed – oil on
canvas – 22 x 24in.
(Christie's)   **$16,200 £10,800**

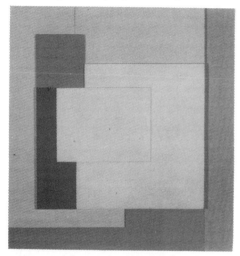

BEN NICHOLSON – 1940 (Painted
Relief) – signed, inscribed and dated
1940 on the reverse – oil on carved board
– 20½ x 19½in.
(Christie's)   **$42,120 £28,080**

FRANCIS NICHOLSON – Rievaulx
Abbey, Yorkshire – inscribed on the
reverse – watercolour over pencil – 11¾
x 15in.
(Sotheby's)   **$825 £550**

WINIFRED NICHOLSON – Heavy And
Light – 16¼ x 12¾in.
(Sotheby's)   **$363 £242**

ERSKINE NICOL – The Tenant – bears
a signature and dated 1890 – oil on canvas – 19 x 14in.
(Sotheby's)   **$1,445 £990**

ERSKINE NICOL – The Truant – signed
– 42 x 33in.
(Sotheby's) **$8,030 £5,500**

JOHN WATSON NICOL – A Good
Vintage – signed – 22 x 16¼in.
(Christie's) **$1,287 £864**

ERSKINE NICOL – Driving The Bargain
– signed and dated 1874 – oil – 30 x
25in.
Dacre, Son &
Hartley) **$1,950 £1,300**

EDMUND JOHN NIEMANN – Derbyshire River Landscape With A Village
In The Foreground – signed – on
canvas – 30 x 50in.
(Sotheby's) **$1,252 £858**

EDMUND JOHN NIEMANN, SNR. –
Blythburgh, Suffolk – signed and dated
'60 – 22 x 36in.
(Sotheby's) **$2,145 £1,430**

EDMUND JOHN NIEMANN, JNR. –
Hampstead Heath, Harrow In The Distance – signed – 16 x 26in.
(Sotheby's)   **$693**   **£468**

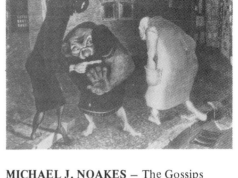

MICHAEL J. NOAKES – The Gossips
– signed and dated 1953 – tempera –
12 x 16½in.
(Lawrence)   **$330**   **£220**

BASIL NIGHTINGALE – A Lady On A
Horse – signed and dated 1907 – oil on
canvas – 28 x 36in.
(Sotheby's)   **$825**   **£550**

BASIL J. NIGHTINGALE – Taking A
Fence; and At Full Speed – one signed
and dated 1884 – watercolour over
pencil – 12 x 17½in.
(Sotheby's)   **$1,124**   **£770 Pair**

JOHN SARGENT NOBLE – The Otter
Hunt – signed and dated 1890 – oil
on canvas – 36 x 54in.
(Sotheby's)   **$2,767**   **£1,870**

NOEL LAURA NISBET – The Court
Of King Arthur – signed – pencil and
watercolour – 21 x 28½in.
(Christie's)   **$2,430**   **£1,620**

JOHN BATES NOEL – Among The Blue-
bells, Cowleigh Park – signed, dated 1908
and inscribed on the reverse – oil on canvas
– 18 x 24in.
(Sotheby's)   **$1,499**   **£1,045**

GIUSEPPE NOGARI, Follower of – Portrait Of A Lady With A Pug – 17 x 13¼in.
(Sotheby's) **$841** **£550**

EMILE NOLDE – Lilien Un Eisenhut – signed – watercolour on paper – 17¾ x 13½in.
(Christie's) **$53,611** **£36,720**

SIR SIDNEY NOLAN – Ayers Rock – signed – on board – 19½ x 15in.
(Sotheby's) **$2,640** **£1,760**

EMIL NOLDE – Bauer Mit Einer Sense – signed – brush and ink and watercolour – 19¼ x 14in.
(Sotheby's) **$16,500** **£11,000**

EMIL NOLDE – Sudseeinselbewohner – signed – watercolour and brush and ink – 18 x 13in.
(Sotheby's) **$62,205** **£42,900**

JAMES NORTHCOTE — Bonaparte On A White Horse — signed and dated 1801 — 107 x 94in.
(Sotheby's) **$15,675 £10,450**

JAMES NORTHCOTE, Circle of — The King Of The Jungle — 29½ x 35½in.
(Sotheby's) **$742 £495**

NORTHERN FRENCH SCHOOL — A Woman Seated At A Fruit And Vegetable Stall — dated 1607 — 39¼ x 49½in.
(Sotheby's) **$42,900 £28,600**

NORTHERN ITALIAN SCHOOL, Mid 18th century — Tancred And Erminia — 43¼ x 56in.
(Sotheby's) **$2,692 £1,760**

NORTHERN NETHERLANDISH SCHOOL, Late 15th century — The Annunciation — oil on panel — 31½ x 11¾in.
(Sotheby's) **$11,396 £7,700**

BENJAMIN CARN NORTON – A Study Of A Hunter And Terrier Dog, With Leckhampton Hill And Cotswold Landscape Beyond – signed and dated 1866 – on canvas – 19½ x 26¼in.
(Sotheby's)   **$4,620   £3,080**

BENJAMIN CARN NORTON – Meynell, A Hunter – signed and dated 1889 – 24 x 30in.
(Sotheby's)   **$2,409   £1,650**

WILLIAM EDWARD NORTON – A Parisian Street Scene – signed – on panel – 8¼ x 6in.
(Sotheby's)   **$1,732   £1,155**

DAVID EMILE JOSEPH DE NOTER – A Maid In A Kitchen – signed and dated '61 – on panel – 30½ x 25¼in.
(Christie's)   **$22,377   £15,120**

OTTO NOWAK – Flowers For The Table – signed – oil on panel – 16 x 13in.
(Robert W. Skinner Inc.)   **$650   £433**

FERNANDO NUNEZ – Seaweed Gatherers – signed – oil on canvas – 24½ x 36in.
(Robert W. Skinner Inc.)   **$1,250   £833**

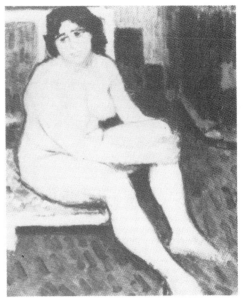

RODERIC O'CONOR – Nu Brun Assis
– signed and dated '13 – 25½ x 21½in.
(Sotheby's) **$5,940** **£3,960**

OCTAVIUS OAKLEY – The Flower Girl
– watercolour – 19¼ x 13½in.
(Sotheby's) **$594** **£396**

JOHN WRIGHT OAKES – A Country
House Overlooking A River With Fishermen In A Rowing Boat By A Bridge –
on board – 14¾ x 13½in.
(Christie's) **$610** **£410**

FRANS WILHELM ODELMARK – A
Street In Cairo – signed and inscribed
– oil on canvas – 35 x 24½in.
(Sotheby's) **$3,987** **£2,750**

FRANS DAVID OERDER – Stilleben –
signed – oil on board – 68 x 78cm.
*(Germann
Auktionshaus)* **$4,723   £3,235**

WILLIAM OLIVER – In The Orchard –
signed and dated 1884 – oil on canvas
– 24 x 18in.
(Sotheby's)   **$990   £660**

JULIUS OLSSON – A Fine Summer
Morning – signed – on canvas – 24 x
30¼in.
(Sotheby's)   **$363   £242**

ISAAC OLIVER, Circle of – Portrait
Of Lewes Bagot – on panel – 22 x
16½in.
(Sotheby's)   **$10,890   £7,260**

WILLIAM OLIVER – 'Vanity' – signed
– oil on board – 4½ x 11¾in.
(Sotheby's)   **$1,525   £1,045**

WILLIAM OLIVER – On The Terrace –
signed – 40 x 15in.
(Sotheby's)   **$1,650   £1,100**

GEORGE BERNARD O'NEILL – I'm
For The King – signed and dated 1903
– 24 x 29½in.
(Sotheby's)   **$3,854   £2,640**

O'NEILL

JAKOB VAN OPSTAL, The Younger, Attributed to – An Allegory Of Peace – 36½ x 51½in.
(Sotheby's)   **$3,630**   **£2,420**

GEORGE BERNARD O'NEILL – The Admirers – signed – oil on panel – 10 x 7½in.
(Sotheby's)   **$3,630**   **£2,420**

BERNAERT VAN ORLEY, Circle of – The Adoration Of The Magi – oil on panel – 40¼ x 38¼in.
(Sotheby's)   **$26,048**   **£17,600**

HENRY NELSON O'NEILL – The Cavalier's Courtship – signed and dated 1870 – 18 x 14in.
(Sotheby's)   **$594**   **£396**

V. ORMSBY – Washing Day – 19 x 25in.
(Sotheby's)   **$742**   **£495**

SIR WILLIAM ORPEN – The Beggar
Girl – signed – oil on canvas – 30 x
22in.
(Christie's) **$7,290 £4,860**

ADRIAEN VAN OSTADE, Follower of
– A Family In A Barn – oil on panel –
11 x 12½in.
(Sotheby's) **$1,252 £858**

ROLAND OUDOT – Evasion: L'Atelier
Au Violon Et A L'Astrolabe – signed –
oil on canvas – 45½ x 31¾in.
(Christie's) **$12,614 £8,640**

**GEORGIUS JACOBUS JOHANNES
VAN OS** – A Still Life Of A Dead Heron,
A Cockerel, A Partridge, Grapes, A Melon
And Flowers On A Ledge – signed and
dated 1840 – on panel – 39 x 31½in.
(Christie's) **$9,590 £6,480**

SAMUEL OWEN – Men O' War Off The
Coast – signed – watercolour – 4¾ x
8½in.
(Sotheby's) **$1,650 £1,100**

FERDINAND PACHER – Angenehmer
Besuch – signature and date 1875 – 35
x 49¼in.
(Christie's)   **$8,791**   **£5,940**

GEORGE PAICE – Regent And Paradox;
and Friar And Palafox – signed, inscribed
and one dated '05 – oil on board – 9 x
11½in.
(Sotheby's)   **$990**   **£660 Pair**

MARIE DANFORTH PAGE – Anna
Coleman Ladd – signed and dated
1913 – oil on canvas – 40 x 26½in.
(Robert W. Skinner
   Inc.)   **$4,000**   **£2,665**

GEORGE PAICE – The Belvoir Hounds
From Sir Bache Cunard's Kennels –
signed and dated '86, and inscribed,
signed and dated on the reverse – 13¾
x 18in.
(Christie's)   **$724**   **£486**

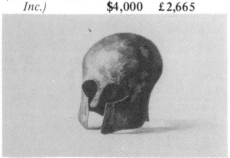

WILLIAM PAGE, Attributed to – A
Greek Helmet – inscribed – watercolour
over pencil – 10½ x 14½in.
(Sotheby's)   **$516**   **£374**

J. PALHAGY – Workers Returning From
The Field – signed – oil on canvas – 19¼
x 15in.
(Sotheby's)   **$315**   **£220**

J. PALHAGY – Harvesting – signed – oil on canvas – 15½ x 19½in.
(Sotheby's)   **$505**   **£352**

FILIPPO PALIZZI – Study Of A Dog – signed and dated 1878 on the reverse – oil on canvas – 8 x 7½in.
(Sotheby's)   **$289**   **£198**

HARRY SUTTON PALMER – Hastings – signed – watercolour over traces of pencil, heightened with scratching out – 13½ x 19½in.
(Sotheby's)   **$3,630**   **£2,530**

HARRY SUTTON PALMER – Water Lane, Nr. Ockham, Surrey – signed – water-colour – 24½ x 17½in.
(Sotheby's)   **$1,584**   **£1,056**

HARRY SUTTON PALMER – View Near Midhurst – signed and inscribed in pencil on reverse – watercolour – 14 x 21in.
(Sotheby's)   **$868**   **£605**

HARRY SUTTON PALMER – Near Steyning – signed in pencil – watercolour – 13½ x 20½in.
(Sotheby's)   **$1,136**   **£792**

LYNWOOD PALMER – A Bay Race-horse With A Groom In A Landscape – signed – 19½ x 25½in.
(Christie's) **$1,206** **£810**

LYNWOOD PALMER – Lord Annaly M.F.H. of the Pytchley – on canvas – 54½ x 49½in.
(Sotheby's) **$2,392** **£1,595**

GIOVANNI PAOLO PANINI, Studio of – Figures Among Roman Ruins – oil on canvas – 35 x 35in.
(Sotheby's) **$6,424** **£4,400**

JUAN DE PAREJA – St. Paul The Hermit And Saint Mary Magdalene – signed – oil on canvas – 32 x 40in.
(Sotheby's) **$2,930** **£1,980**

JOHN ARTHUR PARK – Herring Time, St. Ives – signed and inscribed on the reverse – on canvas – 28 x 36in.
(Sotheby's) **$990** **£660**

JOHN ARTHUR PARK – The Entrance Of A Harbour – signed – on canvas – 28 x 36in.
(Sotheby's) **$495** **£330**

HENRY H. PARKER – Backwater On The Wye, Surrey – signed – watercolour – 21¼ x 14¼in.
(Sotheby's) **$429** **£286**

HENRY H. PARKER – A Berkshire Homestead – signed, also signed and inscribed on the reverse – oil on canvas – 30 x 25in.
(Sotheby's)   **$3,300   £2,200**

HENRY H. PARKER – At Abinger, Surrey – signed, signed and inscribed on the verso – oil – 12 x 18in.
(Woolley & Wallis)   **$1,102   £760**

HENRY H. PARKER – A Surrey Cornfield, Dorking – signed, also signed and inscribed on the reverse – oil on canvas – 20 x 30in.
(Sotheby's)   **$3,135   £2,090**

HENRY H. PARKER – In Glenfinlas, Perthshire – signed – 10 x 14in.
(Lawrence)   **$420   £286**

ARTHUR WILDE PARSONS – Fernpit Ferry, Crantock – signed and inscribed on the reverse – oil on canvas – 15 x 23½in.
(Sotheby's)   **$417   £286**

ELLEN PARTRIDGE – View In The Severn Valley Above Bewdley – signed, inscribed on the reverse – 24 x 36in.
(Sotheby's)   **$2,475   £1,650**

PAUL PASCAL – An Encampment Near An Oasis, Sunset, and Watering Sheep At An Oasis – signed – bodycolour – 4¼ x 6¼in.
(Sotheby's)   **$726   £572 Pair**

ULRIKA PASCH, Attributed to —
Queen Louise Of Denmark — oil on
canvas — 29 x 24¼in.
(Sotheby's)   **$2,248   £1,540**

JULES PASCIN — Fernande — stamped
with signature — 31½ x 25¼in.
(Sotheby's)   **$28,050   £18,700**

LORENZO PASINELLI — The Rape Of Helen Of Troy — oil on canvas — 44¾
x 59½in. *(Sotheby's)*   **$8,140   £5,500**

DANIEL PASMORE – The Fair Pedlar –
signed and dated 1873 – 24½ x 29in.
(Christie's) **$2,105** **£1,404**

FRANK PATON – 'Kate' – signed and
dated 1885 – on canvas – 20 x 24in.
(Sotheby's) **$1,023** **£682**

**JOHN F. PASMORE AND CLARENCE
HENRY ROE** – Sheep In A Highland
Landscape – inscribed in pencil – 24
x 36in.
(Sotheby's) **$561** **£374**

SIR JOSEPH NOEL PATON, After Lippi
– The Madonna And Child – signed with
initials – 34 x 23in.
(Christie's) **$2,430** **£1,620**

JAMES PATERSON – St. Andrew's
Harbour – signed – watercolour – 21
x 14in.
(Sotheby's) **$390** **£264**

JAMES McINTOSH PATRICK – The
Bridge, Loch Spout, Rossie Priory, Angus
– signed – watercolour – 21½ x 29½in.
*(Christie's &
Edmiston's)* **$825** **£550**

JOHN PAUL — Lady On A Horse With
Parkland And Riders Beyond — signed
and indistinctly dated 18-4 — on canvas
— 24¼ x 29½in.
(Sotheby's)   **$2,649   £1,815**

JOHN PAUL — A View Of Greenwich
Hospital — oil on canvas — 38¼ x 42in.
(Sotheby's)   **$7,920   £5,280**

PHILIPPE PAVY — An Eastern Girl —
signed and dated 1881 — on canvas —
6¼ x 4½in.
(Sotheby's)   **$759   £506**

EUGENE PAVY — Arabs In A Courtyard —
signed and dated 1890 — on panel — 18 x
22in.
(Christie's)   **$12,960   £8,640**

PHILIPPE PAVY — 'A Close Shave' —
signed and dated '888, and signed, inscribed
and dated 1889 on the reverse — on panel —
15½ x 10½in.
(Christie's)   **$13,770   £9,180**

EDGAR ALWIN PAYNE – 'The Harbour, Doarnenez, France' – signed – oil on canvas – 10 x 24in.
(Robert W. Skinner Inc.) $3,300 £2,200

HARRY PAYNE – Officer Of The West Kent Yeomanry On Horseback – signed and dated 1907 – on canvas – 19½ x 26½in.
(Sotheby's) $825 £550

ROBERT PEAKE, Circle of – Portrait Of Henry Wriothesley, Third Earl Of Southampton – 76½ x 42½in.
(Sotheby's) $46,200 £30,800

WILLIAM PAYNE – Market Day – grey ink and watercolour heightened with white – 5 x 7in.
(Sotheby's) $593 £418

CHARLES PEARS – Daybreak After A Storm – signed and inscribed – oil on canvas – 19½ x 29½in.
(Sotheby's) $835 £572

P. PEARSE – A Rustic Boy With A
Basket, After Abraham Bloemaert –
signed and dated 1692 – pen and brown
ink, grey wash – copy – 6¾ x 4½in.
(Christie's) **$129** **£86**

MAX-HERMANN PECHSTEIN – Kleine
Brucke Uber Muhlengraben – signed –
watercolour and gouache – 18½ x 22in.
(Sotheby's) **$14,355** **£9,900**

MAX-HERMANN PECHSTEIN – Kleine
Brucke Uber Muhle Graben – signed and
dated 1933 – watercolour and brush and
ink over pencil – 23¼ x 27in.
(Sotheby's) **$11,220** **£7,480**

GIOVANNI PEDRINI, Attributed to,
Called Giampietrino – The Madonna
And Child – 20 x 15½in.
(Sotheby's) **$10,230** **£6,820**

JAMES PEEL – Punting, On A Country
Stream – oil on canvas – 16 x 24in.
(Sotheby's) **$1,815** **£1,210**

JAN PEETERS – Pioneers Left On A
Rocky Beach, A Fleet Offshore –
indistinctly signed with monogram – 13½
x 20½in.
(Christie's) **$4,050** **£2,700**

THOMAS KENT PELHAM – Spanish Lovers In Conversation – signed – oil – 35¼ x 27¼in.
(Anderson & Garland)   **$735**   **£490**

NARCISSE VIRGILE DIAZ DA LA PENA – A Young Child With Her Dog – on panel – 13¾ x 10½in.
(Sotheby's)   **$3,300**   **£2,200**

GEORG PENCZ, Manner of – Portrait Of A Lady – 31 x 22½in.
(Sotheby's)   **$1,043**   **£682**

CHARLES OLIVER DE PENNE – French Stag Hounds Drinking From A River – signed – watercolour – 11½ x 18in.
(Sotheby's)   **$1,124**   **£770**

EDWARD PENNY, Follower of – The King's Shilling – oil on canvas – 24½ x 29½in.
(Sotheby's)   **$1,732**   **£1,155**

EDWARD PENNY, Attributed to — Portrait Of A Lady In A Blue And White Dress And Hat — 29½ x 24½in.
(Christie's)   **$12,960**   **£8,640**

SIDNEY RICHARD PERCY — Loch Tay — signed and dated 1881 — oil on canvas — 32 x 24in.
(Sotheby's)   **$3,630**   **£2,420**

SAMUEL JOHN PEPLOE — A Street In The South Of France — signed — oil on board, laid on panel — 16 x 13in.
(Sotheby's)   **$6,186**   **£4,180**

SIDNEY RICHARD PERCY — In The Highlands — signed and dated 1867 — 24 x 38in.
(Sotheby's)   **$7,920**   **£5,280**

LILLA CABOT PERRY — Young Dancers — signed and dated '95 — oil on canvas — 31¾ x 25¾in.
(Robert W. Skinner Inc.)   **$3,100**   **£2,066**

RAFFY LE PERSAN – La Petite
Bergere – signed – oil on canvas – 17½
x 12½in.
(Sotheby's)   **$594**   **£396**

A. PESNE – Portrait Of A Girl, Wearing
A Blue Dress With Lace, Playing With A
Dove Tied To A Ribbon – 59 x 38½in.
(Christie's)   **$21,060   £14,040**

PERUGINO, Follower of – The Entombment – canvas on panel – 14½ x 15¾in.
(Christie's)   **$2,592   £1,728**

ANTON PESCHKE – Landschaft –
signed and dated 1923 – oil on paper –
12 x 18¾in.
(Sotheby's)   **$578   £385**

JOHN PETTIE – A Boy In Van Dyck
Costume – signed – 12¾ x 9¼in.
(Christie's)   **$1,609   £1,080**

WILLIAM PRESTON PHELPS – A Farm Scene – oil on canvas – 23½ x 36in.
(Robert W. Skinner Inc.) $750   £500

CONSTANCE PHILLOTT – Nine Peas! – signed and dated 1892 – pencil and watercolour heightened with white – 13 x 20¼in.
(Christie's) $1,722   £1,188

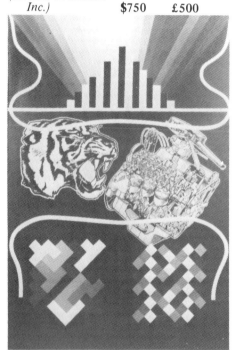

PETER PHILIPS – Tigerama Two – signed, inscribed and dated 1968 – oil and silkscreen on canvas – 62½ x 43in.
(Christie's) $2,365   £1,620

CONSTANCE PHILLOTT – Broken Toys – signed and dated 1894, and inscribed on the reverse – watercolour and bodycolour – 12¼ x 14¾in.
(Christie's) $972   £648

JOHN PHILLIP – Persian Dancers – oil – 11 x 16in.
(Reeds Rains) $1,377   £950

JAMES GEORGE PHILP – Silvery Sunshine In Mount's Bay, Cornwall – signed and inscribed on a label on the reverse – watercolour – 13¾ x 24¼in.
(Sotheby's) $445   £297

FRANCIS PICABIA – Les Cygnes Noirs
Sur Fond Bleu – signed – 34½ x 45in.
(Sotheby's)   **$14,850   £9,900**

LOUIS PICARD – Gare de Banlieue –
signed – 37½ x 56¼in.
(Christie's)   **$42,120   £28,080**

PABLO PICASSO – O.T., 5 Mai 1968 II
– signed – etching – 45.4 x 54.3cm.
*(Germann
    Auktionshaus)* **$2,469   £1,646**
PABLO PICASSO – O.T. 13 Avril 1968
III – signed – etching – 45.4 x 56.3cm.
*(Germann
    Auktionshaus)* **$2,278   £1,519**
PABLO PICASSO – Femme Accroupie
– signed – watercolour and pen and
brown ink – 3¾ x 5¼in.
(Sotheby's)   **$6,699   £4,620**

PABLO PICASSO – Femme Au Miroir
– signed – pen and ink – 5¾ x 4¾in.
(Sotheby's)   **$9,075   £6,050**

PABLO PICASSO – Femme Au Serpent
– signed – pen and ink and blue crayon
– 5¼ x 3¼in.
(Sotheby's)   **$8,250   £5,500**

ANDREA PICCINELLI, Called Andrea
Del Brescianino – The Virgin And Child,
The Infant Baptist And A Deacon Saint
– on panel – 27in. diam.
(Sotheby's)   **$10,230**   **£6,820**

ANDREA PICCINELLI, Called
Brescianino – The Virgin And Child
With St. Joseph And St. Anne – oil on
panel – 34 x 25½in.
(Sotheby's)   **$7,227**   **£4,950**

HAROLD H. PIFFARD – 'Here's To You'
– signed – canvas on board – 24 x 20in.
(Sotheby's)   **$792**   **£528**

WILLIAM HENRY PIKE – Children By
A Ford – signed and dated 1877 – oil
on canvas – 40 x 60in.
(Sotheby's)   **$2,552**   **£1,760**

SIR GEORGE PIRIE – Cows In A Barn
– signed – on canvas – 25 x 30in.
(Sotheby's)   **$610**   **£407**

CAMILLE PISSARRO – Paysanne
Accroupie – signed – pastel on grey paper
– 10¼ x 8¼in.
(Christie's)   **$21,060**   **£14,040**

CAMILLE PISSARRO – Le Port Du Havre – oil on canvas – 21½ x 25½in.
(Christie's) **$194,400 £129,600**

CAMILLE PISSARRO – Baigneuse Mettant Ses Bas – stamped with initials – watercolour and soft pencil on paper – 5½ x 7in.
(Christie's) **$4,860 £3,240**

CAMILLE PISSARRO – Jardin D'Automne, Eragny – 25½ x 31¾in.
(Sotheby's) **$277,200 £184,800**

CAMILLE PISSARRO – Bergere A Montfoucault – signed and dated 1875 – oil on canvas – 25½ x 34¼in.
(Sotheby's) **$136,950 £91,300**

CAMILLE PISSARRO – Femme Tenant Un Bol – watercolour and charcoal over pencil – 11 x 8¼in.
(Sotheby's) **$10,367 £7,150**

CAMILLE PISSARRO – Paysanne Et Enfant, Eragny – signed and dated '93 – 25½ x 21¼in.
(Sotheby's) **$183,425 £126,500**

PISSARRO

LUCIEN PISSARRO – View Of Milton
– signed with monogram and dated 1917
– watercolour, pen and black ink – 7½ x
10¾in.
(Christie's) **$1,944** **£1,296**

ANDRE PLANSON – Chasseurs a
Crouttes-Sur-Marne – signed and dated
'60 – oil on canvas – 35 x 45½in.
(Christie's) **$8,425** **£5,616**

JOHN PITMAN – Portrait Of A Bay
Horse In A Stable – signed and dated
1838 – 24½ x 29½in.
(Lawrence) **$759** **£506**

NICHOLAS POCOCK – The 'Apollo',
Private Ship-of-War – signed and dated
1781 – pen and wash – 16¾ x 22½in.
(Dreweatt Watson &
Barton) **$764** **£520**

GIOVANNI BATTISTA PITTONI – An
Allegory Of Winter And Summer – oil
on canvas – 59½ x 44in.
(Sotheby's) **$78,144** **£52,800**

THE DA PONTE, Circle of – Portrait
Of A Man – oil on panel – 16 x 13½in.
(Sotheby's) **$586** **£396**

PAUL FALCONER POOLE – At The Spring – signed with initials and dated 1869, inscribed on the reverse – oil on board – 20 x 16½in.
(Sotheby's) **$1,155** **£770**

PORDENONE, Follower of – Head Of A Bearded Man – bears inscription – red chalk – 312 x 239mm.
(Sotheby's) **$627** **£418**

GERARD PORTIELJE – A Good Vintage – signed and inscribed – on panel – 15½ x 12½in.
(Christie's) **$15,390 £10,260**

GERARD PORTIELJE – A Fine Vintage – signed and inscribed – 20 x 25in.
(Christie's) **$20,779 £14,040**

GERARD PORTIELJE – The Document – signed – on panel – 5½ x 7¼in.
(Sotheby's) **$990 £660**

PORTIELJE

GERARD PORTIELJE – In Disgrace –
signed and dated 1888(?) – on panel –
15½ x 12½in.
(Christie's) $9,720   £6,480

LASLETT JOHN POTT – Disinherited
– signed – 70 x 50in.
(Sotheby's) $3,960   £2,640

BERNARD POTHAST – A Mother And
Her Children – signed – oil on canvas –
30 x 25¼in.
(Sotheby's) $8,772   £6,050

C. WYTE POTTER – The Potato Harvest, Cumberland – signed, inscribed
and dated '03 on reverse – oil on canvas
– 28 x 36in.
(Sotheby's) $915   £638

C. M. POWELL – Speculative Seascape –
oil.
(Andrew Grant) $4,500   £3,000

SIR EDWARD JOHN POYNTER – Lady
Elizabeth Eastlake – signed with mono-
gram and dated 1864 – 16½ x 13in.
(Sotheby's) **$3,630 £2,420**

SIR EDWARD JOHN POYNTER –
Feeding The Sacred Ibis In The Halls Of
Karnac – signed with monogram and
dated 1871 – 36½ x 27¼in.
(Christie's) **$27,172 £18,360**

ATTILIO PRATELLA – Italian Washerwomen – signed – on panel – 8¼ x
13½in.
(Sotheby's) **$3,135 £2,090**

VALENTINE PRAX – Nature Morte –
signed – oil on canvas – 82 x 91cm.
*(Germann
    Auktionshaus)* **$3,592 £2,395**

CARLO PREDA, Attributed to – The
Beheading Of St John The Baptist –
inscribed on the reverse – on copper –
12 x 10in.
(Sotheby's) **$577 £325**

ALFRED PRIEST – Two Setters By A
Wood – signed and dated 1844 – 27½ x
35½in.
(Sotheby's) **$3,135** **£2,090**

BERTRAM PRIESTMAN – A Surrey
Bridge – signed and dated '30, and signed,
dated and inscribed on the reverse – 17 x
21in.
(Christie's) **$970** **£648**

W. J. PRINGLE – A Snowball Fight –
indistinctly signed and dated 1851 – oil
on canvas – 24 x 30in.
(Sotheby's) **$1,595** **£1,100**

W. J. PRINGLE – The Favourite Gun
Dog – signed and dated 1833 – 14 x
18in.
(Sotheby's) **$902** **£594**

JOHANNES HUIBERT PRINS – A River
Landscape – signed – on metal – 9¾ x
13¾in.
(Sotheby's) **$3,029** **£1,980**

VALENTINE CAMERON PRINSEP –
A Portrait Of A Damsel With Flowers In
Her Hair, Holding A Basket Of Fruit –
signed – oil on canvas – 35½ x 27½in.
*(Geering &
Colyer)* **$2,325** **£1,550**

WILLIAM PRINSEP – Government House And The Maidan, Calcutta – signed with monogram and indistinctly dated – 12 x 35½in.
(Sotheby's) **$9,900 £6,600**

VALENTINE CAMERON PRINSEP – Benedict And Beatrice – signed and inscribed on an old label on the reverse – 42 x 31¾in.
(Christie's) **$4,183 £2,808**

EDWARD PRITCHETT – The Mouth Of The Grand Canal, Venice – 18 x 26in.
(Christie's) **$1,460 £972**

EDWARD PRITCHETT – The Steps Of Santa Maria Della Salute – signed – 12 x 16in. *(Sotheby's)*
$1,320 £880

ROBERT TAYLOR PRITCHETT – An
Album Containing Sketches Of The Isle
Of Wight And Other Views – signed,
inscribed and dated 1848 – mostly pen-
cil sketches, some with watercolour.
(Sotheby's) $674   £462

ERNEST PROCTER – An Olympus –
signed – oil on canvas – 67 x 47in.
(Christie's) $2,270   £1,512

ERNEST PROCTER – Floodlighting At
The Royal Academy – signed and dated
1934 – on board – 34½ x 48in.
(Sotheby's) $2,552   £1,760

ERNEST PROCTOR – 'The Old Newlyn
Slipway' – oil on canvas – 18 x 14in.
*(W. H. Lane &
Son)* $1,287   £740

DOD PROCTER – A Lady On A Chaise Longue – signed and indistinctly dated
– 46 x 70in.) *(Sotheby's)* $28,050 £18,700

ERNEST PROCTER – The Judgement Of Paris – signed and dated '26 – on board – 24 x 22in.
(Sotheby's)   **$3,300   £2,200**

GEORGE FREDERICK PROSSER – Harrow On The Hill From Uxbridge Common – signed and inscribed – watercolour over pencil heightened with white – 9¾ x 13½in.
(Sotheby's)   **$792   £528**

JAMES PROUDFOOT – Wet Day, Liphook, Sussex – signed and dated 1939 – on board – 19¼ x 23½in.
(Sotheby's)   **$176   £121**

ADAM EDWIN PROCTOR – Picking Marsh Marigolds – signed and dated 1906 – oil on canvas – 17¼ x 11½in.
(Sotheby's)   **$770   £528**

JOHN SKINNER PROUT – Steep Street, Bristol – signed – watercolour heightened with white – 12¾ x 8¼in.
(Christie's)   **$500   £345**

SAMUEL PROUT – Domodossola, North
Italy – signed – pen and brown ink and
watercolour over pencil – 9 x 13in.
(Sotheby's) **$1,980 £1,320**

SAMUEL PROUT – A Continental Town
Square – signed – pen and brown ink
and watercolour heightened with white –
17¾ x 12¾in.
(Christie's) **$2,268 £1,512**

ALFRED PROVIS – Feeding The Pets
– signed and dated 1876 – on canvas –
12 x 16in.
(Sotheby's) **$1,567 £1,045**

ALFRED PROVIS – A Breton Interior – signed and dated 1854 – oil on canvas –
10½ x 14in. *(Sotheby's)* **$1,276 £880**

J. A. PULLER – First Attempt On The Fiddle – signed – oil on mahogany – 10 x 8in.
(Andrew Grant)   **$787**   **£525**

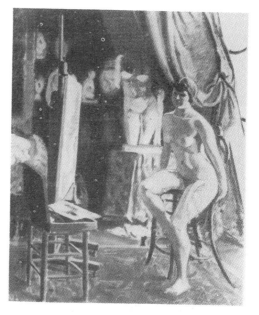

JEAN PUY – Nu Dans Un Interieur – signed and dated 1915 – oil on canvas – 39 x 34in.
(Christie's)   **$6,165**   **£4,104**

HOVSEP PUSHMAN – The Wife Of The Skeykh (Sheik) – signed – oil on canvasboard on panel – 34½ x 24¾in.
(Christie's)   **$4,950**   **£3,300**

HOWARD PYLE – The Battle Of Monmouth – signed – oil on board en grisaille – 23 x 15½in.
(Christie's)   **$12,100**   **£8,065**

CARLO QUAGLIA – Foro Romano – oil – 50 x 70cm. *(Christie's)*
$1,044 £696

ALFRED ROBERT QUINTON – The Backwater And Quarry Woods, Great
Marlow – signed – watercolour with scratching out – 16 x 24in. *(Sotheby's)*
$957 £638

ARTHUR RACKHAM – The Pied Piper And The Children – signed – pen and black ink and watercolour – 8½ x 5¼in. *(Christie's)*   **$10,179   £7,020**

JEAN FRANCOIS RAFFAELLI – A Street In Asnieres – signed – on panel – 23½ x 19¾in.
(Christie's)   **$10,530   £7,020**
THEODORE JACQUES RALLI – On Shipboard – signed, and indistinctly inscribed on the reverse – on board – 6¾ x 11½in.
(Christie's)   **$4,795   £3,240**

SIR HENRY RAEBURN – Portrait Of William Swanson of Leithhead Standing Full Length In A Landscape – 50 x 40in.
*(Christie's &
    Edmiston's)*   **$17,250   £11,500**

T. RAMSDEN – Childhood Sweethearts In An Orchard – signed – oil – 49 x 35in.
*(Anderson &
    Garland)*   **$1,725   £1,150**

453

ALFRED RANKLEY – The School Room
– signed with monogram and dated '53 –
27½ x 35½in.
(Christie's)   **$10,530   £7,020**

HEINRICH RASCH – The Sardine Catch
– signed and inscribed – 14¾ x 25½in.
(Sotheby's)   **$1,815   £1,210**

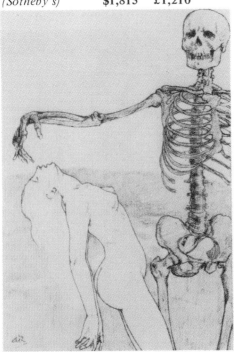

ARMAND RASSENFOSSE – La Mort
– signed and inscribed – pencil, pen
and ink on tracing paper – 7¾ x 5½in.
(Christie's)   **$1,892   £1,296**

ARMAND RASSENFOSSE – Le
Flacon – signed and inscribed – pen and
ink and coloured crayons on paper – 5¼
x 6¾in.
(Christie's)   **$2,328   £1,296**

JOHAN NEPOMUK RAUSCH – A Family
Group In The Garden Of A Country House
– signed and dated 1840 – 28 x 40in.
(Christie's)   **$13,770   £9,180**

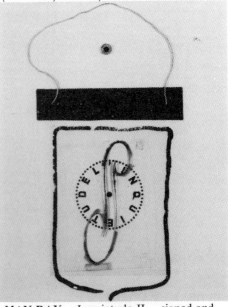

MAN RAY – Inquietude II – signed and
dated 1920 – mixed media collage on
paper – 25½ x 19¾in.
(Sotheby's)   **$3,190   £2,200**

MAN RAY -- Nude – signed and dated
1912 – charcoal – 21¾ x 13¾in.
(Sotheby's)   **$4,125   £2,750**

LOUISE J. RAYNER – A Street Scene
With Tradesmen And Children In The
Foreground – signed and indistinctly
inscribed on the reverse – watercolour
– 14 x 10¼in.
(Sotheby's)   **$1,445   £990**

LOUISE RAYNER – Watergate Street,
Chester – signed – watercolour, height-
ened with bodycolour – 17 x 22in.
(Sotheby's)   **$8,030   £5,500**

CATHERINE READ – Caroline, Samuel
Greame And Catherine Marsh – 27½ x
35in.
(Christie's)   **$6,156   £4,104**

RICHARD REDGRAVE – Starting For
The Christening – signed – 26¾ x 39¼in.
(Christie's)   **$7,192   £4,860**

ODILON REDON – La Barque
Mystique – signed – pastel – 20½ x
25½in.
(Christie's)   **$174,636 £118,800**

REDON

ODILON REDON – Rose Dans Un
Vase – signed – 13 x 11in.
(Sotheby's)   **$47,850   £33,000**

C. REEVES – Children's Pursuits –
signed and dated 1887, inscribed indistinctly on the reverse – 20 x 15in.
(Sotheby's)   **$1,815   £1,210**

ETHEL REED – Young Girl With Poppies
– signed – watercolour, bodycolour and
coloured chalks – 13½ x 17½in.
(Sotheby's)   **$858   £572**

C. REEVES – The Swing – signed and
dated 1887 – 16 x 20in.
(Sotheby's)   **$1,815   £1,210**

JOSEPH CHARLES REED – Harvesters
In A Cornfield Near A Church – signed
and dated '64 – watercolour with bodycolour – 12½ x 19in.
(Sotheby's)   **$2,475   £1,650**

C. REEVES – A Surprise – signed and
dated 1887 – 16 x 19½in.
(Sotheby's)   **$2,145   £1,430**

GEORGE OGILVY REID – The Wheelwright – signed and dated 1882 – on board – 15¾ x 12¾in.
(Sotheby's)   **$495**   **£330**

JULIUS CHRISTIAN REHDER – Bavarian Boy – signed – oil on canvas – 39 x 29in.
(Sotheby's)   **$1,231**   **£858**

FLORA MACDONALD REID – Gossips – signed and inscribed – oil on canvas – 6 x 8in.
(Sotheby's)   **$631**   **£440**

SIR GEORGE REID – Lord Breadalbane And Garry – signed with monogram – oil on canvas board – 18 x 10in.
(Sotheby's)   **$2,767**   **£1,870**

GEORGE OGILVY REID – A Discussion – signed and dated 1893 – oil on canvas – 50½ x 33in.
(Sotheby, King & Chasemore)   **$520**   **£297**

JOHN ROBERTSON REID – A Village Street – signed and dated '78 – oil on canvas – 21 x 14in.
(Sotheby's)   **$1,072**   **£715**

JOHN ROBERTSON REID – Young
Anglers – signed – oil on canvas –
14 x 21in.
(Sotheby's) **$814** **£550**

RICHARD RAMSAY REINAGLE – A
Boy In Yellow Breeches – signed and
dated 1812 – pencil and watercolour –
10¾ x 8½in.
(Sotheby's) **$505** **£352**

NANO REID – Head Of A Young Man
– signed – 22 x 19in.
(Sotheby's) **$990** **£660**

MARTIN ANDREAS REISSNER – The
Forest Queen In Winter – signed and
dated 1857 – oil on canvas – 30 x
40¼in.
(Christie's) **$126,500** **£84,335**

STEPHEN REID – 'Shall I compare thee
to a Summer's Day? Thou are more lovely
and more temperate' – signed, inscribed
and dated 1907 – pen and black ink and
watercolour – 7¾ x 11¼in.
(Christie's) **$1,096** **£756**

PIERRE AUGUSTE RENOIR – Nature
Morte Aux Deux Pommes – signed – 5¼ x
6¾in.
(Sotheby's) **$23,100** **£15,400**

PIERRE AUGUSTE RENOIR – Nu
Couche A Mi-Corps Ou La Dormeuse –
signed – oil on canvas – 18¼ x 21¾in.
(Sotheby's) **$363,000 £242,000**

PIERRE AUGUSTE RENOIR – Jeune
Fille En Chemise – signed – 13 x 9½in.
(Sotheby's) **$118,030 £81,400**

PIERRE AUGUSTE RENOIR – La Pointe
de Beg-Meil, Bretagne – signed – oil on
canvas – 18¼ x 21½in.
(Christie's) **$243,000 £162,000**

PIERRE AUGUSTE RENOIR – Deux
Femmes Dans Un Jardin – signed with
initials – 13 x 15¾in.
(Sotheby's) **$231,000 £154,000**

PIERRE AUGUSTE RENOIR – Couple
Lisant – signed – 12¾ x 9¾in.
(Sotheby's) **$622,050 £429,000**

PIERRE AUGUSTE RENOIR – Nu
Assis Sur Un Drap Blanc – signed – 8 x
7½in.
(Sotheby's)   **$24,090 £16,500**

HENRY MEYNELL RHEAM – A Lady
Guitarist – signed and dated 1902 –
watercolour heightened with bodycolour
– 28 x 18in.
(Sotheby's)   **$825   £550**

SIR JOSHUA REYNOLDS – Mrs.
Knapp – oil on canvas – 30 x 25in.
*(Robert W. Skinner
    Inc.)*   **$4,000   £2,666**

HENRY MEYNELL RHEAM – The
Flower Stall – signed – watercolour –
20½ x 30½in.
(Christie's)   **$2,105   £1,404**

**JUSEPE DE RIBERA, Called Lo
Spagnoletto** – The Martyrdom Of Saint
Bartholomew – signed and dated 1634 –
40½ x 44in.
(Sotheby's)   **$990,000 £660,000**

MARCO RICCI, Follower of — Figures On A Road By A Villa — gouache — 191 x 246mm.
(Sotheby's) **$330** **£220**

MARCO RICCI — View Of A Hill Town With Figures In The Foreground — tempera — 307 x 447mm.
(Sotheby's) **$7,920** **£5,280**

THOMAS MILES RICHARDSON, SNR, Attributed to — Crofters — watercolour — 23 x 35in.
(Sotheby's) **$976** **£660**

THOMAS MILES RICHARDSON, JNR. — View Of Luveno, Lago Maggiore — signed and dated 1824 — watercolour — 15½ x 23½in.
(Sotheby's) **$1,567** **£1,045**

AGNES M. RICHMOND — Portrait Of A Young Woman Seated By A Window — signed and dated 1925 — oil on canvas — 30 x 24in.
(Robert W. Skinner Inc.) **$950** **£633**

GEORGE RICHMOND — Portraits Of George Follett And Hardinge Gifford Follett, sons of Sir William Follett — both signed and dated 1856 and 1857 respectively — watercolour heightened with white on buff paper — 16 x 12¼in. and smaller.
(Christie's) **$1,377** **£918 Two**

HERBERT DAVIS RICHTER – A Sunlit Drawing Room – signed – oil on canvas – 24¾ x 29½in.
(Sotheby's) **$462** **£308**

PHILIP RICKMAN – Long-Tailed Duck (Male And Female) – signed – watercolour and bodycolour on light blue paper laid on card – 12¼ x 17¾in.
(Christie's) **$297** **£205**

PHILIP RICKMAN – Ptarmigan In The Snow – signed – watercolour heightened with bodycolour – 17½ x 22½in.
(Sotheby's) **$732** **£495**

PHILIP RICKMAN – Spring, Frenchmen, Red-Legged Partridge – signed and dated 1967 – watercolour and bodycolour on light-green paper – 19 x 15¼in.
(Christie's) **$970** **£648**

MICHELE DE RIDOLFO – The Virgin And Child With The Infant Saint John – on panel – 38¾ x 30½in.
(Sotheby's) **$17,325 £11,550**

REMBRANDT VAN RIJN, Circle of – Portrait Of A Lady With A Ruff – dated 1644 – oil on panel – 25¼ x 20in.
(Sotheby's) **$6,512 £4,400**

AIDEN LASSELL RIPLEY – Grouse – signed and dated 1934 – gouache and watercolour – 25 x 19in.
(Robert W. Skinner Inc.) **$1,600 £1,066**

S. RISEGARI – Child Holding Chicken – signed – 27½ x 17in.
(Lawrence) **$355 £242**

AIDEN LASSELL RIPLEY – Tyrolean Girl – signed, inscribed and dated 1925 – watercolour – 18 x 14in.
(Robert W. Skinner Inc.) **$650 £433**

JOHN RITCHIE – 'The Proclamation' – signed, and signed and inscribed on a label – 24 x 36in.
(Christie's) **$1,126 £756**

WILLIAM RITSCHEL – Surf On The Rocks – signed – watercolour on paper – 3½ x 5½in.
(Butterfield's) **$200 £119**

LEOPOLD RIVERS – The Old Mill, Winchelsea – signed – watercolour – 17½ x 29¼in.
(Sotheby's)   **$599**   **£418**

JOHANN ANTON RITZART – La Chanoiness Gimnick – inscribed on the reverse – 21¾ x 16in.
(Sotheby's)   **$1,485**   **£990**

BRITON RIVIERE – Persepolis – signed and dated 1878 – on canvas – 30½ x 55in.
(Sotheby's)   **$2,475**   **£1,650**

LEOPOLD RIVERS – Near Hornsey Church – inscribed on a label – on canvas – 11½ x 9½in.
(Sotheby's)   **$674**   **£462 Pair**

BRITON RIVIERE – A Fairy Tale – signed and dated 1872, and inscribed on an old label on the reverse – 43 x 40in.
(Christie's)   **$885**   **£594**

BRITON RIVIERE – Devotion – signed with monogram and dated 1908 – oil on canvas – 20 x 19in.
(Sotheby's) **$3,190 £2,200**

HUBERT ROBERT – Figures On Steps Beneath A Roman Bridge – oil on canvas – 54½ x 39in.
(Sotheby's) **$32,560 £22,000**

DAVID ROBERTS – Abbey Ruins – signed and dated 1831 – watercolour over traces of pencil heightened with bodycolour – 10 x 14in.
(Sotheby's) **$1,732 £1,155**

DAVID ROBERTS – View Of Bonchurch – signed, inscribed and dated 1856 – 28¼ x 37in.
(Christie's) **$1,931 £1,296**

DAVID ROBERTS, Circle of – River Scene In France – oil on canvas – 13½ x 17in.
(Sotheby's) **$957 £638**

EDWIN ROBERTS – Grist To The Mill – signed, inscribed on the reverse – oil on canvas – 14 x 12in.
(Sotheby's) **$742 £495**

WILLIAM ROBERTS – Died Of Wounds
– signed and dated 1919 – watercolour,
bodycolour, pen and black ink – 17½ x
20¾in.
(Christie's)   **$27,972   £18,900**

EDWIN ROBERTS – 'The Opera Box' –
signed and inscribed on the reverse – on
canvas – 13¾ x 11½in.
(Sotheby's)   **$1,237   £825**

GEORGE ROBERTSON – Landscape
With Horses; and Landscape With Cattle
– both signed and dated 1776 – pencil
heightened with red and white chalk –
9½ x 13¼in.
(Sotheby's)   **$1,320   £880 Pair**

WILLIAM ROBERTS – I Contadini –
signed and inscribed – watercolour and
pencil – 18¾ x 12¼in.
(Christie's)   **$2,916   £1,944**

J. ROBERTSON – Portrait Of Mr J.
Baylis On 'Birthday' With His Dog 'Rush'
– signed and dated 1850, inscribed on
the reverse – 20 x 27in.
(Sotheby's)   **$990   £660**

CHARLES ROBERTSON – A Story-Teller, Morocco – signed with monogram
and dated 1883 – watercolour heightened with white – 23½ x 50¾in.
(Christie's) $22,680   £15,120

THOMAS ROBINS, The Elder – A View
Of Hailes Abbey, Gloucestershire –
gouache over traces of pencil on vellum –
10½ x 14¾in.
(Sotheby's) $3,630   £2,420

JOHN ROBERTSON – Portrait Of A
Lady – signed and dated 1861 – oil on
canvas – 54 x 40in.
(Sotheby's) $707   £495

TOM ROBERTSON – Moonrise, Loch
Crinan – inscribed on label to reverse –
oil on canvas – 21 x 29in.
(Sotheby's) $473   £330

THOMAS SEWELL ROBINS – A Fishing Smack In A Stiff Breeze Near A Jetty
– signed with initials and dated '61 –
watercolour with scratching out and
bodycolour – 12½ x 19in.
(Sotheby's) $1,023   £682

THOMAS SEWELL ROBINS – Coastal
Scene With Fisherfolk And Beached
Vessels And A Quay In The Background
– signed and dated – watercolour – 10
x 16in.
(Morphets) **$489** **£340**

JORGEN ROED – In The Stable –
signed and dated 1852 – 24½ x 19¼in.
(Christie's) **$6,393** **£4,320**

HERMEN RODE OF LUBECK – Saint
Peter, recto; A Fragment From The
Road To Calvary, verso – oil on panel
– 42½ x 14in.
(Sotheby's) **$16,280** **£11,000**

CONRAET ROEPEL – A Still Life Of
Flowers In A Basket – signed and dated
1726 – 28 x 22½in.
(Sotheby's) **$39,600** **£26,400**

SEVERIN ROESEN – Still Life With
Fruit And Champagne – signed – oil on
canvas – 30 x 40in.
(Christie's)   **$33,000 £22,916**

ROELANDT ROGHMANN – A Winter
Landscape – on panel – 9¾ x 12in.
(Sotheby's)   **$2,062 £1,375**

**PIETER GERRITSZ. VAN
ROESTRAETEN, Attributed to** – A
Nautilus Cup, A Pilgrim Flask, A Watch
And Peaches On A Pewter Plate On A
Draped Ledge – 20½ x 26½in.
(Christie's)   **$4,324 £3,024**

HENRY LEONIDAS ROLFE – Perch
Feeding, The Dinner Hour – signed
and dated 1872 – 24 x 36in.
(Christie's)   **$2,091 £1,404**

PHILIP HUTCHINGS ROGERS – A View
Of Salzburg, With Washerwomen In The
Foreground – signed and dated 1842 –
40¼ x 60in.
(Christie's)   **$14,385 £9,720**

ALFRED ROLOFF – A Herd Of Horses
– signed – oil on canvas – 29 x 39in.
(Sotheby's)   **$2,073 £1,430**

G. ROMNEY – Portrait Of A Gentleman
Said To Be William Creyke, Half Length,
In A Blue Coat – 30 x 25in.
(Christie's) **$1,296** £864

HENRIETTE RONNER – Jack In The Box
– signed – 8½ x 11in.
(Christie's) **$4,860** £3,240

HENRIETTE RONNER-KNIPP – Cats
At Play – signed and dated 1897 – 48
x 37in.
(Christie's) **$30,369** £20,520

C. RONET – Three Gossips – signed –
oil – 21 x 17in.
(Dacre, Son &
Hartley) **$2,180** £1,525

EVA ROOS – An Impromptu Ball –
signed and dated 1899, and signed and
inscribed on a label – 31½ x 25in.
(Christie's) **$9,720** £6,480

ALBERT ROOSENBOOM – Blind Man's
Buff – signed – on canvas – 9½ x 7½in.
(Sotheby's) **$1,092** **£748**

OTTONE ROSAI – Stradale Toscanese –
signed and dated '42 – on board – 23¼
x 19¼in.
(Sotheby's) **$9,075** **£6,050**

OTTONE ROSAI – Preti, 1939 – oil on
canvas – 50 x 40cm.
(Christie's) **$7,830** **£5,327**

G. ROSATI – 'A Hard Bargain' – signed
– watercolour – 14 x 21in.
(Reeds Rains) **$3,750** **£2,500**

GIULIO ROSATI – Carpet Merchants
Chatting – signed – watercolour – 13¾
x 20¼in.
(Sotheby's) **$8,580** **£5,720**

JAMES ROSENQUIST – Spikey Thermometer – signed, inscribed and dated 1973 on the reverse – oil on canvas – 47 x 86in.
(Christie's)   **$4,888   £3,348**

SIR JOHN ROSS, After – The Isabella Rescuing Sir John Ross's Explorers, August 1833 – watercolour with scratching out – 6½ x 8¼in.
(Sotheby's)   **$759   £550**

JAMES ROSS – A Hawking Party – 30 x 48in.
(Sotheby's)   **$23,100 £15,400**

ALEXANDER M. ROSSI – A Morning Bathe – signed – oil on canvas – 36 x 28in.
(Sotheby's)   **$5,104   £3,520**

DANTE GABRIEL ROSSETTI – Blanzifiore, or Snowdrops – signed with monogram and dated 1873 – 16 x 12½in.
(Sotheby's)   **$66,000 £44,000**

ALEXANDER M. ROSSI – Children Fishing From A Breakwater – signed – 28 x 36in.
(Sotheby's)   **$4,015   £2,750**

CHARLES ROSSITER – Shake Hands With Doggy – signed – oil on canvas – 9½ x 7½in.
(Sotheby's) **$1,155 £770**

PIETRO ROTARI, Attributed to – A Young Woman Sleeping – oil on canvas – 17¾ x 13¾in.
(Sotheby's) **$1,465 £990**

JOHANN ROTTENHAMMER, Attributed to – A Courting Couple – oil on panel – 6¾ x 5¼in.
(Sotheby's) **$3,693 £2,530**

MOZART ROTTMANN – Arabs Rescuing A Wounded Youth – signed – oil on canvas – 38½ x 50in.
(Sotheby's) **$3,339 £2,420**

ALEXANDRE ROUBTZOFF – Tunisian Women Preparing Food – signed and dated 1917 – oil on canvas – 45 x 62in.
(Sotheby's) **$7,177 £4,950**

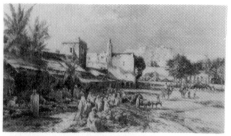

ROBERT WILLIAM ARTHUR ROUSE –
Arab Market, Algiers – signed and
inscribed – 16 x 24¾in.
(Sotheby's) **$957** **£638**

JEAN JACQUES ROUSSEAU – Matinie
Sur La Riviere De Canton – signed and
inscribed – on canvas – 10 x 17½in.
(Sotheby's) **$958** **£638**

CHARLES ROWBOTHAM – Near
Bellagio On Lake Como – signed and
dated – 14½ x 21in.
(Morphets) **$510** **£340**

T. L. ROWBOTHAM – Italian Coastal
Village Scene, With Fishing Boats And
Figures In Foreground And Castle In
Distance – signed and dated – heightened
in white – 7 x 19in.
(Morphets) **$300** **£200**

**THOMAS CHARLES LEESON
ROWBOTHAM** – On The Italian
Coast, Figures At A Wayside Shrine –
signed and dated 1874 – watercolour
heightened with white – 16¾ x 29¾in.
(Christie's) **$1,215** **£810**

THOMAS ROWLANDSON – A Pensioner
And Attendants – signature – pencil, pen
and ink and watercolour – 10¾ x 8½in.
(Christie's) **$1,944** **£1,296**

THOMAS ROWLANDSON – The Pros-
pect Before Us – inscribed and dated
1791 – watercolour – 12¼ x 18½in.
(Sotheby's) **$11,880** **£7,920**

THOMAS ROWLANDSON – The Monkey Man – inscribed – pencil, pen and brown ink and watercolour – 10¾ x 8¾in.
(Christie's) **$1,458** **£972**

THOMAS ROWLANDSON – Charity From The Kitchen Maid – signed and dated 18' – watercolour over pencil – 10½ x 8in.
(Sotheby's) **$1,320** **£880**

THOMAS ROWLANDSON – A Soldier Refreshing – signed and dated 1920 – pen and brown ink and watercolour – 11 x 8¾in.
(Sotheby's) **$859** **£605**

THOMAS ROWLANDSON – The Suitor – pen and red-grey ink and watercolour – 6 x 9in.
(Sotheby's) **$907** **£605**

THOMAS ROWLANDSON – Hungarian And Highland Broadsword Exercise – inscribed – pen and grey-brown ink and watercolour – 8¼ x 11in.
(Sotheby's) **$1,402** **£935**

THOMAS ROWLANDSON – Ship Building At Ringmore On The River Avon In Devon; and Shipping In A Harbour – pen and grey ink – one 6½ x 11in., the other 6½ x 8½in.
(Sotheby's) **$957** **£638 Two**

THOMAS ROWLANDSON — The Horn-Pipe — pen and grey ink and water-colour — 13¾ x 12¾in.
(Christie's)   **$3,240   £2,160**

HERBERT ROYLE — On The Wharfe, Bolton Abbey — signed — oil — 20 x 24in.
(Dacre, Son & Hartley)   **$750   £500**

HERBERT ROYLE — Dales Landscape With Haymakers — signed — 20 x 30in.
(Dacre, Son & Hartley)   **$893   £625**

SIR PETER PAUL RUBENS, Studio of — Saint Mary Magdalen — oil on paper laid down on panel — 24¾ x 19¾in.
(Christie's)   **$2.316   £1,620**

PETER PAUL RUBENS, Studio of — The Entombment — 82½ x 59¾in.
(Sotheby's)   **$18,975   £12,650**

HORACE VAN RUITH – Fruit Picking
– signed – 40 x 64in.
(Sotheby's)   **$660**   **£440**

GEORGE HERBERT RUSHTON – The
Old Fisherman, St. Abbs, Berwickshire –
signed and indistinctly inscribed on the
reverse – watercolour – 19¾ x 28½in.
(Sotheby's)   **$706**   **£484**

C. J. RUSSELL – Mother And Child In A
Hopfield – signed and dated 1899 – on
canvas – 36 x 28in.
(Sotheby's)   **$957**   **£638**

CHARLES RUSSELL – A Fisherman –
signed and dated '85(?) – oil on canvas –
20 x 16in.
(Sotheby's)   **$280**   **£187**

JOHN RUSSELL – Girl With A Basket
Of Eggs – signed and dated 1781 – pastel
– 24 x 18in.
(Sotheby's)   **$1,980**   **£1,320**

JOHN RUSSELL – The Day's Catch
– signed and dated 1872 – 19½ x 31in.
(Sotheby's) $2,475   £1,650

JOHN RUSSELL – Portrait Of Mrs.
Grant Of Gnoll Castle, Glamorganshire,
With Her Daughter Maria Louisa – signed
– pastel – 39 x 30½in.
(Christie's) $7,776   £5,184

SALOMON VAN RUYSDAEL – A River
Landscape With Riders On A Ferry –
signed and dated 1649 – on panel –
(Sotheby's) $495,000 £330,000

SALOMON VAN RUYSDAEL – Fishermen In Boats By A Wooded River Bank –
traces of a signature – on panel – 11½ x
16¾in.
(Sotheby's) $26,400 £17,600

FRANS RYCKHALS – Jacob With The
Flock Of Laban – signed in monogram
and dated 164(2?) – 49 x 83in.
(Sotheby's) $16,500 £11,000

HENRY RYLAND – Pre-Raphaelite
Coastal Scene – signed – watercolour –
52 x 82cm.
*(Henry Spencer &
    Sons)* $2,336   £1,600

HENRY RYLAND – The Nymph's
Toilette – signed and dated 1906 – water-
colour over pencil – 21 x 14½in.
(Sotheby's) $762   £495

THEO VAN RYSSELBERGHE – L'Ile
Du Levant, Vu Du Cap Benat – signed
with monogram – 17¾ x 25½in.
(Sotheby's) **$79,750 £55,000**

HENRY RYLAND – At The Temple
Door – signed – watercolour – 10 x
6½in.
(Sotheby's) **$660 £440**

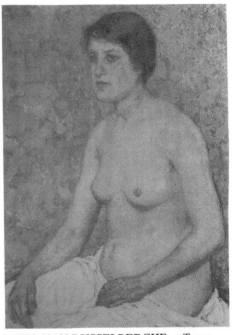

THEO VAN RYSSELBERGHE – Torse
De Jeune Femme – signed with mono-
gram and dated 1916 – 31½ x 23½in.
(Sotheby's) **$9,314 £6,380**

THEO VAN RYSSELBERGHE – Femme
Au Miroir – signed with monogram and
dated '07 – 31 x 35½in.
(Sotheby's) **$19,800 £13,200**

THEO VAN RYSSELBERGHE – Soleil
Couchant a Ambleteuse, Pas-de-Calais –
signed and dated '99 – oil on canvas –
26 x 32½in.
(Christie's) **$45,360 £30,240**

CORNELIS SAFTLEVEN – The Prodigal Son – on panel – 17¼ x 23½in.
(Christie's)   **$2,430**   **£1,620**

HERMAN SAFTLEVEN – A River Landscape With Boats In A Cove – bears signature and date 1676 – on panel – 10½ x 15in.
(Sotheby's)   **$12,870**   **£8,580**

PHILIPPE SADEE – Waiting For The Boats, A Mother And Children Looking Out To Sea – signed and dated '81 – oil – 27 x 21in.
(Neales)   **$3,900**   **£2,600**

PAOLO SALA – Cattle And Drover – signed – on canvas – 29½ x 40in.
(Sotheby's)   **$1,650**   **£1,100**

PEDRO SAENZ Y SAENZ – At The Opera – signed – oil on canvas – 40½ x 25in.
(Sotheby's)   **$1,595**   **£1,100**

ROBERT SALMON – 'Loch Fyne: Scottish Scenery' – initialled, and signed and dated 1832 on the reverse – oil on panel – 8 x 10in.
(Robert W. Skinner Inc.)   **$4,000**   **£2,665**

ROBERT SALMON – An Armed Merchantman In Two Positions Under Sail Off Liverpool – signed – oil on canvas – 26½ x 42¾in.
(Sotheby's)   **$92,400   £61,600**

PAUL SANDBY – The Welsh Bridge At Shrewsbury – bodycolour on paper on panel – 18¾ x 24½in.
(Christie's)   **$8,100   £5,400**

GEORGE SAMUEL – Dunster Castle, Somersetshire – 26 x 38¼in.
(Sotheby's)   **$5,775   £3,850**

PAUL SANDBY – View Of Newark Castle And Church – gouache – 15½ x 21½in.
(Sotheby's)   **$15,675   £10,450**

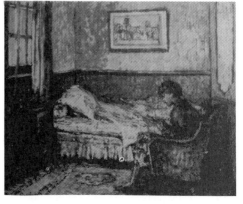

PAUL SANDBY – Travellers On A Road Approaching A Village – watercolour over pencil – 11 x 10¼in.
(Sotheby's)   **$2,392   £1,595**

ETHEL SANDS – The Alcove, Chateau D'Auppegard – signed – 20 x 24in.
(Sotheby's)   **$1,402   £935**

ANTHONY FREDERICK AUGUSTUS
SANDYS – Portrait Of Jane Lewis.
Seated In An Interior – signed, inscribed
and dated 1864 – on panel – 26 x 22in.
(Christie's)　　**$12,960　£8,640**

ANTHONY FREDERICK AUGUSTUS
SANDYS – Violet Louisa Ponsonby –
signed and dated 1887 – coloured
chalks on grey paper – 28 x 20in.
(Sotheby's)　　**$3,630　£2,420**

ANTHONY FREDERICK AUGUSTUS
SANDYS – Alcestis: Portrait Of Lady
Donaldson – signed, inscribed and dated
1877 – black, white, red and green chalk
heightened with white bodycolour, on
pale blue-green paper – on panel – 28½
x 21½in.
(Christie's)　　**$8,100　£5,400**

ANTHONY FREDERICK AUGUSTUS
SANDYS – Portraits Of Conrad Herbert
Flower And Violet Flower – signed and
dated 1885 – pencil and coloured chalks
– 27 x 20in.
(Sotheby's)　　**$5,775　£3,850**

ALESSANDRO SANI – Interior With A Priest Who Has Pricked His Thumb Mending His Shoe, A Woman Surveying The Damage – signed – oil – 15 x 18in. *(Woolley & Wallis)* **$2,175 £1,500**

JAMES SANT – The Pets – signed with monogram – on board – 18 x 12in. *(Sotheby's)* **$2,569 £1,760**

WILLIAM SANSON – Hagar And Ishmael – signed and dated 1842, and inscribed on the reverse – oil on board – 19¼ x 26½in. *(Sotheby's)* **$722 £495**

JAMES SANT – Portrait Of A Lady Holding Her Daughter, In An Interior – signed, dated 1851 and inscribed – 50 x 40in. *(Christie's)* **$885 £594**

JAMES SANT – It Is The Lark! The Herald Of The Moon – 85 x 48in. *(Sotheby's)* **$3,135 £2,090**

RUBENS SANTORO – 'Leaving The Mosque' – signed – on panel – 9½ x 7½in.
(Sotheby's)   **$7,095   £4,730**

JOHN SINGER SARGENT – Portrait Of Nicolo D'Inverno – oil on canvas – 24 x 18¼in.
(Christie's)   **$22,000   £15,277**

JOHN SINGER SARGENT – Palazzo Cavalli, Venice – signed and inscribed – watercolour over pencil, heightened with bodycolour – 14 x 20in.
(Sotheby's)   **$140,250   £93,500**

JOHN SINGER SARGENT – Mrs. George Disney Maquay (Nina Cooley) – signed and inscribed – black chalk – 23 x 19in.
(Sotheby's)   **$2,640   £1,760**

GIULIO ARISTIDE SARTORIO – Fregene, 1929 – signed and dated – pastel on card – 60 x 58cm.
(Christie's)   **$5,347   £3,688**

FRANCIS SARTORIUS – A Dark Bay
Racehorse With Jockey Up In A Landscape
– 17 x 23½in.
(Sotheby's)   **$2,990   £1,760**

JOHN FRANCIS SARTORIUS,
Attributed to – A Favourite King Charles
Spaniel – canvas on board – 12¼ x 18in.
(Sotheby's)   **$1,815   £1,210**

JOHN NOTT SARTORIUS – A Chestnut
Hunter And Groom Of The Pack Of Stag
Hounds Kept By Thomas Lermitte Esq.,
In Surrey – signed and dated 1782 –
24½ x 29¾in.
(Sotheby's)   **$11,550   £7,700**

ROBERT RICHARD SCANLON – Screw-
driver Dealer – signed with monogram –
pen and brown ink and watercolour heightened with white – 10¾ x 15½in.
(Christie's)   **$2,916   £1,944**

FREDERICK W. SCARBOROUGH –
Unloading Off Wapping, London –
signed and inscribed – watercolour –
9¼ x 13¼in.
(Sotheby's)   **$647   £451**

H. SCHAFER – Street Scene, Fecamp,
Normandy – oil on panel – 13 x 10in.
*(Warren &
    Wignall)*   **$525   £350**

HENRY SCHAFER – Abbeville, Normandy – signed with monogram and dated 1889, also inscribed on the reverse – oil on panel – 16 x 11½in.
(Sotheby's) **$676** **£473**

GODFRIED SCHALCKEN – Salome – 44¾ x 32¾in.
(Sotheby's) **$56,100** **£37,400**

GODFRIED SCHALCKEN – Portrait Of A Boy In A Gold-Embroidered Robe – signed – on panel – 11½ x 9in.
(Sotheby's) **$18,975** **£12,650**

HUGO SCHEIBER – Mann Vor Einen Haus – gouache and charcoal – 27 x 20¾in.
(Sotheby's) **$1,116** **£770**

ANDREAS SCHELFHOUT – Skaters In
A Frozen River Landscape – signed –
oil on canvas – 14¾ x 19½in.
(Sotheby's) **$7,656 £5,280**

AGNES SCHENK – Honeysuckle –
signed with monogram – oil on
canvas – 24 x 17in.
(Sotheby's) **$786 £550**

C. SCHENNEN – Soldiers Being Ferried
Across A River – indistinctly signed and
dated 1837 – oil on canvas – 12 x 14in.
(Sotheby's) **$1,499 £1,045**

JOHANN JACOB SCHEUCHZER – Two
Sheets Of Studies Of Shells – brown ink
and grey wash and numbered – 303 x
187mm.
(Sotheby's) **$291 £198**

EGON SCHIELE – Akt Mit Weissen
Tuch – signed and dated 1912 – water-
colour over pencil – 19¼ x 12¾in.
(Sotheby's) **$140,250 £93,500**

487

EGON SCHIELE – Bildnis Dr. Rieger –
signed, inscribed and dated 1917 –
watercolour, gouache and pencil – 17½
x 11¼in.
(Sotheby's)   **$115,500   £77,000**

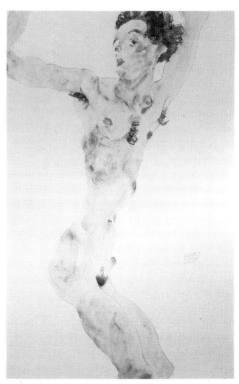

EGON SCHIELE – Selbst Bildnis –
signed and dated 1911 – watercolour over
pencil – 19½ x 12½in.
(Sotheby's)   **$181,500 £121,000**

EGON SCHIELE – Knieender Akt –
signed and dated 1915 – watercolour
and gouache over pencil – 13 x 19½in.
(Sotheby's)   **$151,525 £104,500**

FELIX SCHLESINGER – Tea For Granny
– signed – on panel – 23½ x 18in.
(Christie's)   **$8,100   £5,400**

KARL SCHMIDT-ROTTLUFF – Haus Mit Rotem Dach – signed – indian ink and pastel – 39 x 43cm.
(Germann Auktionshaus) **$6,869** **£4,705**

MATHYS SCHOEBAERDTS – A River Landscape With A Windmill – on copper – 12 x 16¾in.
(Sotheby's) **$21,450** **£14,300**

ADOLF SCHREYER – Arab Horsemen In A Landscape – signed – on panel -- 13 x 18in.
(Christie's) **$14,580** **£9,720**

ADOLF SCHREYER – The Sortie – signed – 25½ x 37½in.
(Christie's) **$15,390** **£10,260**

JOANNES F. SCHUTZ – Shipping In A Calm Sea – signed and dated 1879 – 27 x 41in.
(Sotheby's) **$1,237** **£825**

CHARLES HENRY SCHWANFELDER, Style of – A Favourite Dog At Horstead House Near Norwich – 25 x 30in.
(Sotheby's) **$3,300** **£2,200**

GIUSEPPE SCOPPAPA – Vedute di Napoli dal Carmine – signed – gouache – 16¼ x 25in.
(Geering & Colyer) **$1,200** **£800**

THE HON. LADY CAROLINE SCOTT – View Of Utrecht From The River – watercolour – 9½ x 16¼in.
(Sotheby's) **$297** **£198**

HENRY SCOTT – Clipper Ship 'Jessie Readman' – signed, inscribed on the reverse – oil on canvas – 40 x 48in.
(Christie's) **$4,212 £2,808**

SIR PETER SCOTT – Emperors In The Sun – signed and dated 1937 – oil on canvas – 15 x 18in.
(Christie's) **$1,135 £756**

JOHN H. SCOTT – 'Sion In The Rhone Valley' – watercolour – 27 x 40in.
(Reeds Rains) **$604 £420**

SAMUEL SCOTT, Follower of – A Vessel Aflame On The Thames At London Bridge With Fire Fighters Attempting To Quell The Fire – oil on canvas – 25 x 30in.
(Sotheby's) **$3,630 £2,420**

PETER MARKHAM SCOTT – 'Common Scoters', Ducks In Flight – indistinctly signed – oil on canvas – 24 x 24in.
(Sotheby's) **$513 £352**

SAMUEL SCOTT – Forrest's Action With De Kersaint, 21st October 1757 – 29½ x 47½in.
(Sotheby's) **$19,800 £13,200**

EDWARD SEAGO – Thames Barges
Swinging With The Tide – signed – oil
on board – 15¾ x 23¾in.
(Christie's)   **$7,290**   **£4,860**

EDWARD SEAGO – Cascais – signed –
watercolour over pencil – 11 x 15in.
(Sotheby's)   **$1,072**   **£715**

EDWARD SEAGO – A Chestnut
Stallion With Groom – signed – 25 x
30in.
(Sotheby's)   **$8,250**   **£5,500**

EDWARD SEAGO – Pin Mill – signed
– oil on board – 26 x 36in.
(Christie's)   **$24,300**   **£16,200**

HENRI VAN SEBEN – A Youth Fishing,
Leaning Against A Tree A Young Girl
Watching – signed and dated – on panel
– 10½ x 8½in.
(Woolley &
Wallis)   **$690**   **£460**

THOMAS SEEL – Cockatoo – oil –
24 x 18¼in.
(Capes Dunn &
Co.)   **$449**   **£310**

ANDRE DUNOYER DE SEGONZAC –
Sur La Terrasse, St. Tropez – signed –
watercolour and pen and ink on paper
– 22¼ x 29¾in.
(Christie's) **$28,382 £19,440**

DANIEL SEITER – 'Sine Cerere Et
Baccho Friget Venus' – oil on canvas –
46 x 66½in.
(Sotheby's) **$11,070 £7,480**

VINCENT SELLAER – Leda And The
Swan – oil on panel – 43 x 34½in.
(Sotheby's) **$6,837 £4,620**

RAFAEL PEREZ SENET – The Grand
Canal, Venice – signed – 18 x 31½in.
(Christie's) **$8,791 £5,940**

GEORG SEITZ – Summer Flowers In A
Vase With Fruit On A Ledge – signed –
18 x 14½in.
(Christie's) **$10,389 £7,020**

MARK SENIOR – A Farmyard In Summer – signed and dated 1905 – oil on
canvas – 14 x 16in.
(Sotheby's) **$1,365 £935**

JOHN THOMAS SERRES – An English
Man Of War At Anchor In Naples Harbour
– signed and dated 1823 – 23¼ x 35¼in.
(Sotheby's)   **$23,100   £15,400**

GEORGE HARCOURT SEPHTON –
El Tango – signed and dated 1911,
and signed and dated on the reverse
– 35 x 23in.
(Christie's)   **$965   £648**

ANTONIO TRAVI DA SESTRI, Follower
of – A Capriccio Landscape With Roman
Ruins – 39 x 51½in.
(Sotheby's)   **$1,606   £1,100**

**ZINAIDA EVGENEVNA
SEREBRIAKOVA** – Portrait Of Irene
Baronova – signed and dated 1933 –
pastel – 23¾ x 17½in.
(Sotheby's)   **$330   £220**

FRANS VAN SEVERDONCK – Sheep
Beside A Pond – signed and dated 1899
– oil on canvas – 7½ x 5in.
(Sotheby's)   **$1,276   £880**

FRANCOIS VAN SEVERDONCK –
White Horse And Sheep In A Landscape
– signed and dated 1880, also signed
and inscribed on the reverse – oil on
panel – 7 x 10in.
(Robert W. Skinner
Inc.)   **$1,500   £1,000**

JAMES SEYMOUR – A Chestnut Racehorse With Jockey Up – oil on canvas –
11¾ x 13½in.
(Sotheby's)   **$28,050   £18,700**

JAMES SEYMOUR – John Warington,
Esq., Of Morden In Surrey On His Dark
Bay Hunter Accompanied By A Hound In
Open Country – signed and dated 1746 –
28¼ x 27½in.
(Sotheby's)   **$57,750   £38,500**

WILLIAM SOMERVILLE SHANKS –
Still Life – signed – oil on board –
20 x 24in.
(Sotheby's)   **$2,145   £1,430**

JAMES SEYMOUR – Grey Horse Being
Held By Groom With Hound At His Feet
– signed with initials and dated 1751 –
35 x 47in.
(Lawrence)   **$15,675   £10,450**

FRANK HENRY SHAPLEIGH – 'The
Old Jenkins House At Scituate, Mass.' –
signed and dated 1891, also signed on
the reverse – oil on canvas – 10 x 16in.
(Robert W. Skinner
Inc.)   **$1,400   £933**

JOSEPH HENRY SHARP – Standing-Deer-Taos – signed, inscribed on the reverse – oil on canvas – 16¼ x 12¼in.
(Christie's) **$24,200 £16,805**

WILLIAM SHAYER, SNR., Attributed to – A Roadside Chat – bears a signature – on canvas – 40 x 33in.
(Sotheby's) **$3,854 £2,640**

WILLIAM SHAYER, SNR. – A Gypsy Encampment – 20 x 24in.
(Sotheby's) **$5,775 £3,850**

WILLIAM SHAYER, SNR. – The Fisherman's Cottage – signed – on panel – 10 x 8in.
(Sotheby's) **$907 £605**

WILLIAM SHAYER, Follower of – Boy And His Pony – bears a monogram – on canvas – 11 x 17½in.
(Sotheby's) **$803 £550**

WILLIAM JOSEPH SHAYER – The Shooting Pony – signed and dated 1848(?), and signed on the reverse – 27½ x 35½in.
(Sotheby's)   **$18,150**   **£12,100**

ANDREW SHEARBORN – Gathering Boughs – signed and dated 1869 – oil on canvas – 24 x 36in.
(Robert W. Skinner Inc.)   **$1,000**   **£666**

GEORGE SHEFFIELD – 'Winter, Church Lane, Wilmslow' – signed and dated – pastel and chalk drawing – 50 x 82cm.
(Reeds Rains)   **$585**   **£390**

GEORGE SHEFFIELD – 'A Country Walk' – signed and dated – watercolour – 15 x 23in.
(Reeds Rains)   **$495**   **£330**

GEORGE SHEPHERD – Carriage And Four On The Drive Of Battlesden Park, Bedfordshire – signed and dated 1825 – watercolour heightened with white – 10¾ x 16¾in.
(Sotheby's)   **$561**   **£374**

GEORGE SHEPHERD – The High Cross, Tottenham – signed and dated 1829 – pencil, pen and brown ink and watercolour – 3¼ x 2¼in.
(Christie's)   **$485**   **£324**

GEORGE SHEPHERD – View Of Chertsey, Surrey – signed and dated 1817 – 4¾ x 6in.
(Lawrence)   **$517**   **£352**

GEORGE SIDNEY SHEPHERD – St. Mary-Le-Strand – signed and dated 1836 – pencil and watercolour heightened with white – 17 x 22½in.
(Christie's)   **$9,396   £6,480**

GEORGE SIDNEY SHEPHERD – The Old George Tavern; and The Rose Inn, Farringdon St., Bloomfields Yard Opposite Stonecutter St. – both inscribed – watercolour – 6½ x 7½in.
(Christie's)   **$486   £324 Pair**

ALBERT SHERMAN – Still Life, Hydrangeas – signed – oil on canvas – 63 x 84cm.
*(Australian Art
   Auctions)*   **$550   £370**

DANIEL SHERRIN – Extensive River Landscape At Evening In Summer – signed – oil on canvas – 60 x 105cm.
*(Henry Spencer &
   Sons)*   **$1,200   £800**

DANIEL SHERRIN – 'A Woodland Clearing' – signed – oil – 19½ x 30in.
(Reeds Rains)   **$300   £200**

DANIEL SHERRIN – Near Cookham On The Thames – signed – on canvas – 23½ x 35½in.
(Sotheby's)   **$835   £572**

DANIEL SHERRIN – 'Upland River Scene' – signed – oil – 13 x 17in.
(Reeds Rains)   **$460   £320**

J. SHERRIN – Still Life With Bird's
Nest And Flowers – watercolour – 8 x
10in.
(Reeds Rains)   **$681**   **£470**

WALTER RICHARD SICKERT – L'Hotel
Royal, Dieppe – signed – oil on canvas –
19¾ x 24in.
(Christie's)   **$68,040** **£45,360**

WALTER RICHARD SICKERT –
Brighton Pierrots – signed and dated
1915 – oil on canvas – 25 x 30in.
(Christie's)   **$97,200** **£64,800**

HENRI LE SIDANER – La Sortie Du
Soir – signed – oil on panel – 8½ x
13¾in.
(Sotheby's)   **$6,600** **£4,400**

HENRI LE SIDANER – L'Entree Du
Village En Hiver – signed – 22¼ x 27½in.
(Sotheby's)   **$25,646** **£17,600**

BENJAMIN D. SIGMUND – Children
Outside A Cottage – signed – water-
colour – 13¾ x 9¾in.
(Sotheby's)   **$1,073** **£715**

BENJAMIN D. SIGMUND – A Street Scene In The Evening – signed – water-colour – 7 x 10½in.
(Sotheby's) **$280** **£187**

PAUL SIGNAC – Le Pont Des Arts – signed – watercolour and pencil on paper – 11 x 15½in.
(Christie's) **$14,191** **£9,720**

PAUL SIGNAC – Antibes-L'Eucalyptus – signed and dated 1910 – brush and indian ink and watercolour over pencil – 12½ x 17¼in.
(Sotheby's) **$29,700** **£19,800**

SIMKA SIMKHOVITCH – Island Beach – signed and dated 1934-35 – oil on canvas – 34 x 56½in.
(Christie's) **$7,150** **£4,765**

SIMKA SIMKHOVITCH – Ina – signed – oil on canvas – 50 x 29¼in.
(Christie's) **$4,180** **£2,785**

RICHARD SIMKIN – The Charge Of The Hussars – signed and dated '76 – watercolour with bodycolour – 13¾ x 21in.
(Sotheby's) **$627** **£418**

GUSTAVO SIMONI – The Halt Of The Caravan – signed and dated 1855 – 23 x 35in.
(Sotheby's) **$36,300** **£24,200**

MICHIEL SIMONS, Attributed to —
A Still Life Of Fruit On A Table Beside
A Window — inscribed — oil on canvas
— 24 x 33½in.
(Sotheby's) $8,833   £6,050

NIELS SIMONSEN — The Game Of Cards
— signed and dated 1838 — 18 x 23¾in.
(Sotheby's) $13,200   £8,800

WILLIAM SIMSON — A Camaldolese
Monk Showing The Relics In The Sacristy
Of A Roman Convent — signed and
dated 1838 — 51 x 41in.
*(Christie's &
    Edmiston's)* $1,040   £650

MAX SINCLAIR — Harbour Scene With
Shipping — signed — on canvas — 11½ x
19½in.
(Sotheby's) $742   £495

ELISABETTA SIRANI, Circle of — Saint
Catherine — 31½ x 25in.
(Sotheby's) $1,072   £715

MARIO SIRONI — Uomo Inginocchiato
E Il Papa — signed — gouache on paper
laid down on canvas — 17¼ x 13¾in.
(Christie's) $220   £151

MARIO SIRONI – Ritratto Urbano – indistinctly signed – pen and indian ink on paper – 5½ x 5¼in.
(Christie's) **$709** **£486**

ALFRED SISLEY – Les Oies – signed – pastel – 7½ x 9¾in.
(Sotheby's) **$28,875 £19,250**

ALFRED SISLEY – Saint-Mammes – signed and dated '85 – oil on canvas – 21¼ x 25½in.
(Christie's) **$194,400 £129,600**

M. NOEL SLANEY – The Red Hat – signed – watercolour over pencil – 17 x 12½in.
(Sotheby's) **$577** **£385**

C. H. SLATER – Bird's Nest – watercolour – 15 x 11in.
(Capes Dunn & Co.) **$188** **£130**

JOHN FALCONAR SLATER – The Mouth Of The Tyne, A View West From The Cliffs At Tynemouth Towards The Town Of North Shields – signed – 29½ x 49½in.
(Anderson & Garland) **$600** **£360**

STEPHEN SLAUGHTER, Attributed to
— A Gentleman Smoking His Pipe And
Taking Wine — oil on canvas — 31 x 52in.
(Sotheby's)   **$6,600   £4,400**

**JOHANNES CAROLUS BERNARDUS
SLUIJTERS** — A Portrait Of Martin
Kaufmann — signed and dated 1920 —
49½ x 37½in.
(Sotheby's)   **$1,650   £1,100**

EDWARD SLOCOMBE — Nude Seated
In A Cave — signed and dated 1908 —
watercolour — 20 x 13.5in.
(Lawrence)   **$726   £484**

WILLIAM SMALL — The Prince Of Wales
Out Driving A Sleigh On The Embankment — signed and dated 1881 — gouache
— 12½ x 20in.
(Sotheby's)   **$610   £418**

JOHN SMELLIE – The Harbour, Crail – signed, one inscribed on the reverse – 10 x 14in.
(Sotheby's) **$693** **£462 Pair**

LEON DE SMET – Autoportrait – signed, also signed with monogram and inscribed – pastel – 18¾ x 24in.
(Sotheby's) **$5,280** **£3,520**

JAMES SMETHAM – Friar Tuck – signed and dated 1858 – oil on board – 8 x 6in.
(Sotheby's) **$353** **£242**

FRANCISCUS SMIESENS – A Still Life With A Dead Hare – signed – 31¼ x 22¾in.
(Sotheby's) **$1,683** **£1,100**

JAMES DAVID SMILLIE – Etretat – signed and inscribed – oil on canvas – 10½ x 16½in.
(Robert W. Skinner Inc.) **$700** **£466**

ROBERT SMIRKE – The Rival Waiting Women (vide Tom Jones, vol. 1) – 72 x 54in.
(Sotheby's) **$2,692** **£1,870**

SMITH – Messrs. Beaufoy And Company's Vinegar And British Wine Manufactory; and Cuper's Gardens, Lambeth – signed, inscribed on reverse – pen and brown ink, and watercolour over pencil – 6¼ x 9¼in. and 5¼ x 7¾in.
(Sotheby's) **$1,567** **£1,045 Two**

CARLTON ALFRED SMITH — Sorry
For Herself — signed and dated 1901 —
oil on canvas laid on board — 10 x 8in.
(Sotheby's) $660   £462

CARLTON ALFRED SMITH — Taking
It Easy — signed and dated 1884 —
pencil and watercolour — 17¼ x 11¼in.
(Christie's) $626   £432

FRANCIS HOPKINSON SMITH — Street
Scene In Seville — signed and dated '82 —
watercolour, gouache and pencil on
paper on board — 14¼ x 24¾in.
(Christie's) $4,620   £3,080

CARLTON ALFRED SMITH — Fireside
Reflections — signed and dated 1906 —
pencil and watercolour — 20¼ x 13½in.
(Christie's) $3,565   £2,376

HENRY PEMBER SMITH — Cast On The
Shore — signed and dated 1883 — oil on
canvas — 18 x 28in.
(Robert W. Skinner
    Inc.) $1,500   £1,000

HENRY PEMBER SMITH – Home
Sweet Home – signed – oil on canvas
– 19½ x 27½in.
(Sotheby's) **$3,946** **£2,860**

JOHN BURRELL SMITH – A Northern
Waterfall – 31½ x 41½in.
(Christie's) **$4,183** **£2,808**

JAMES BURRELL SMITH – Landscape
With An Overshot Mill – signed and
dated 1877 – watercolour over traces
of pencil heightened with bodycolour
and gum arabic – 12½ x 19in.
(Sotheby's) **$528** **£352**

STEPHEN CATTERSON SMITH, JNR. –
A Promenade – signed and dated 1869 –
oil on panel – 16½ x 10¾in.
(Sotheby's) **$1,320** **£880**

JOHN BRANDON SMITH – Highland
Falls – signed and dated 1890 – 22 x
30in.
(Sotheby's) **$627** **£418**

WILLIAM COLLINGWOOD SMITH –
Rome, St. Peter's From The Vatican –
signed – pencil and watercolour heightened with white – 8½ x 13½in.
(Christie's) **$810** **£540**

WILLIAM COLLINGWOOD SMITH –
A Fisherman By A Mountain River –
signed – watercolour over pencil – 13¾
x 19½in.
(Sotheby's)   **$445   £297**

THOMAS SMYTHE – Horses Watering
In A Wooded Landscape – signed – 11½
x 17½in.
(Christie's)   **$1,931   £1,296**

EDWARD ROBERT SMYTHE, Circle of
– Stable Companions – 40 x 56in.
(Christie's)   **$3,862   £2,592**

THOMAS SMYTHE – Country Farmhouse With A Rustic By A Pond – signed
– oil on canvas – 11¼ x 17½in.
(Sotheby's)   **$2,569   £1,760**

THOMAS SMYTHE – Study Of A Cow
With Landscape Beyond – signed and
indistinctly dated – on canvas – 25 x
30in.
(Sotheby's)   **$462   £308**

THOMAS SMYTHE – The Day's Bag; and
The Plough Team – both signed – 14 x
17in.
(Sotheby's)   **$2,640   £1,760 Pair**

For the love of it.

SNAFFLES – 'For The Love Of It' –
signed – hand coloured print – 15 x
14½in. – together with a pen and ink
wash associated sketch.
*(Dreweatt Watson &
     Barton)*   **$646   £440**

PIETER SNAYERS – Spring – 32 x 47in.   *(Sotheby's)*   **$36,300**   **£24,200**

PIETER SNIJERS – A Cockerel Crowing
– signed – 43½ x 34in.
(Sotheby's)   **$13,200**   **£8,800**

GERARD SOEST – Portrait Of An
Officer, Possibly Sir Ralph Hare, 1st
Bt. Of Stow Bardolf, Norfolk –
inscribed and dated 1637 – oil on can-
vas – 56 x 44in.
(Sotheby's)   **$8,250**   **£5,500**

SIMEON SOLOMON – Sleep – signed with initials and dated 1886 – pencil and blue crayon – 10 x 8½in.
(Christie's)   **$7,047**   **£4,860**

PAUL VAN SOMER, Circle of – Portrait Of A Lady – oval – 20½ x 15¾in.
(Sotheby's)   **$1,430**   **£935**

SOLOMON JOSEPH SOLOMON – Portrait Of Violet, Lady Melchett With Her Two Daughters – 81 x 42in.
(Christie's)   **$11,188**   **£7,560**

THOMAS SOMERSCALES – In The Doldrums – signed and dated 1910 – oil on canvas – 23½ x 41½in.
(Sotheby's)   **$7,590**   **£5,060**

THOMAS SOMERSCALES – A Gaff-Rigged Ketch At Sea – signed – oil on panel – 10¼ x 15½in.
(Sotheby's)   **$2,580**   **£1,870**

OTTO SOMMERS – Deer By A Mountain
Stream – signed – oil on canvas – 27 x
39½in.
(Sotheby's)   **$1,445   £990**

JORIS VAN SON – A Still Life Of
Fruit And Oysters – on panel – 19¼ x
25¼in.
(Sotheby's)   **$11,550   £7,700**

HERMAN SONDERMANN – The Fair
Spinner – signed and dated 1865 – 25 x
28½in.
(Christie's)   **$15,390   £10,260**

JAN SONJE – Peasants Drinking By A
Roadside – signed – on panel – 12¼
x 10¾in.
(Sotheby's)   **$1,567   £1,045**

PIERRE SONNERAT – A Fish – signed
– brown ink and watercolour – 182 x
239mm.
(Sotheby's)   **$90   £60**

CARL FREDERIK SORENSEN – A
Ship In A Harbour – signed and dated
1848 – oil on board – 11¼ x 13¾in.
(Sotheby's)   **$1,116   £770**

SOTTOCORNOLA

GIOVANNI SOTTOCORNOLA – A
Shepherdess With Her Flock – signed
– oil on canvas – 15½ x 25¾in.
(Sotheby's) **$2,552 £1,760**

RAPHAEL SOYER – Pensive Model
– signed – oil on canvas – 25¾ x 20¼in.
(Christie's) **$5,500 £3,665**

RAPHAEL SOYER – Two Models Resting – signed and dated 1936 – oil on
canvas – 29¾ x 24¼in.
(Christie's) **$17,600 £12,222**

SPANISH Follower of Domenico Feti
– The Virgin Of The Seven Sorrows –
oil on canvas – 40 x 30½in.
(Sotheby's) **$1,284 £880**

THE SPANISH FORGER – A Courtly
Scene – on panel – 14½ x 9½in.
(Sotheby's) **$1,485 £990**

RUSKIN SPEAR – Seated Nude – signed
– 24 x 20in.
(Sotheby's)   **$1,815   £1,210**

CHARLES SPENCELAYH – 'Strangers'
– signed and dated 1899, and inscribed
on the reverse – 30 x 24¾in.
(Christie's)   **$3,540   £2,376**

CHARLES SPENCELAYH – Treasures – signed and dated 1945 – 16 x 20in.
(Sotheby's)   **$6,270   £4,180**

CHARLES SPENCELAYH – No Tick
– signed – 13 x 17in.
(Sotheby's) $7,755   £5,170

CHARLES SPENCELAYH – Darning A
Sock – signed – 30 x 20in.
(Sotheby's) $2,475   £1,650

CHARLES SPENCELAYH – The Clock-
maker – signed – 20 x 16in.
(Sotheby's) $3,300   £2,200

CHARLES SPENCELAYH – The Night-
light – signed and dated 1899 – 18 x
12in.
(Sotheby's) $3,630   £2,429

LILLY MARTIN SPENCER – The
Young Husband, First Marketing – signed and dated 1854 – oil on canvas –
29½ x 24¾in.
(Christie's) $99,000 £68,750

LILLY MARTIN SPENCER – Mother
And Child – signed and dated 1858 –
oil on board – 16 x 11¾in.
(Christie's) **$14,300 £9,930**

SIR STANLEY SPENCER – Portrait
Of Dorothy Hepworth – pencil – 14
x 10in.
(Sotheby's) **$707 £495**

BENJAMIN WALTER SPIERS – A
Studio Corner – signed with initials and
dated 1884 – watercolour heightened
with bodycolour – 16 x 26in.
(Sotheby's) **$5,940 £3,960**

RICHARD B. SPENCER, Attributed to –
The 'Wellington' Off Dover In Full Sail
– oil on canvas – 19¼ x 29¼in.
(Sotheby's) **$1,650 £1,100**

SIR STANLEY SPENCER – Nude
(Patricia Preece) – oil on canvas – 20 x
30in.
(Christie's) **$34,020 £22,680**

MARIA SPILSBURY, Circle of – Portrait
Of A Young Girl – oil on canvas – 30 x
24¾in.
(Sotheby's) **$907 £605**

JOHANNES FRANCISCUS SPOHLER –
A Dutch Street – signed – oil on panel
– 10 x 13¾in.
(Sotheby's)   **$5,263   £3,630**

CORNELIS SPRINGER – Street Scene In
Bolsward – signed and dated '71 – on
panel – 9¾ x 7¾in.
(Christie's)   **$11,340   £7,560**

CORNELIS SPRINGER – L'Hotel de Ville,
And Market Place, Halberstadt – signed
and dated '73 – on panel – 22¾ x 19in.
(Christie's)   **$19,440   £12,960**

MARTIN STAINFORTH – The Lion
Hunter – signed and dated '03 – on
board – 23 x 18in.
(Christie's)   **$1,539   £1,026**

CLARKSON STANFIELD – Tintagel
Castle, Coast Of Cornwall – signed and
dated 1866 – 33 x 51in.
(Sotheby's)   **$1,073   £715**

GEORGE CLARKSON STANFIELD –
On The Rhine – 20 x 30in.
(Sotheby's)   **$4,950   £3,300**

CHARLES JOSEPH STANILAND – The Lesson – signed and dated 1875 – watercolour over pencil heightened with bodycolour – 12½ x 17½in.
(Sotheby's) **$1,567** **£1,045**

ELOISE HARRIET STANNARD – A Still Life Study Of Poppies And A Jug On A Table – signed and dated 1890 – oil on canvas – 13½ x 16½in.
(Sotheby's) **$1,657** **£1,155**

ELOISE HARRIET STANNARD – A Still Life With Grapes, A Pineapple, A Melon, Figs And A Basket – signed and dated 1862 – 24½ x 29½in.
(Christie's) **$14,482** **£9,720**

EMILY STANNARD – A Jay And Other Dead Birds Hanging From A Nail In A Niche – on board – 12¼ x 9½in.
(Christie's) **$518** **£345**

ELOISE HARRIET STANNARD – Still Life Of A Basket Of Grapes With Pears, Apple And Butterfly On A Stone Ledge – signed and dated – oil on canvas – 18 x 21in.
(Morphets) **$5,100** **£3,400**

HENRY SYLVESTER STANNARD – 'Fishing' – signed – watercolour heightened with bodycolour and with scratching out – 15¾ x 27¾in.
(Sotheby's) **$2,367** **£1,650**

THERESA SYLVESTER STANNARD —
The Cottage Garden — signed — water-
colour — 13¾ x 9¾in.
(Sotheby's) **$957** **£638**

CLARK STANTON — Far Away
Thoughts — signed — oil on canvas —
30 x 20in.
(Sotheby's) **$748** **£506**

ARTHUR JAMES STARK, **Attributed
to** — A Girl Walking In A Cornfield — on
paper on canvas — 6½ x 9¼in.
(Christie's) **$730** **£486**

ARTHUR JAMES STARK — Cattle And
Milkmaid In An Extensive Landscape —
signed — on board — 11¾ x 18in.
(Sotheby's) **$803** **£550**

JAMES STARK — Horsemen On Mouse-
hold Heath, Norwich — indistinctly signed
— on panel — 8¾ x 6½in.
(Christie's) **$970** **£648**

DAVID GEORGE STEELL – The Dumfriesshire Otter Hounds Near Hoddon Castle With Mr Davidson The Huntsman – signed and dated 1909 – 62½ x 89in.
(Christie's)   **$14,482   £9,720**

JAN STEEN, After – The Doctor's Visit – on panel – 16¾ x 13in.
(Sotheby's)   **$4,125   £2,750**

JAN STEEN, After – A Kermesse – oil – 25 x 29½in.
(Lawrence)   **$1,023   £682**

JAN STEEN, Manner of – An Interior With A Peasant Family – oil on panel – 9 x 11¾in.
(Sotheby's)   **$2,248   £1,540**

PHILIP WILSON STEER – Girl In A Conservatory – oil on canvas – 18 x 14in.
(Christie's)   **$2,755   £1,836**

PHILIP WILSON STEER – Fisher-
children, Etaples – oil on canvas – 17¾
x 24in.
(Christie's) **$31,968 £21,600**

THEOPHILE-ALEXANDRE STEINLEN
– L'Hiver-Chat Sur Un Coussin – lithograph printed in colours – bearing pencil
signature – 19½ x 24¼in.
(Sotheby's) **$2,233 £1,540**

PHILIP WILSON STEER – Portrait Of
Miss Jennie Lee As 'Jo' – signed,
inscribed and dated 1887 – 36 x 28in.
(Sotheby's) **$19,800 £13,200**

THEOPHILE-ALEXANDRE STEINLEN
– Causserie – signed – charcoal and
coloured crayons – 18¼ x 24in.
(Sotheby's) **$9,075 £6,050**

**CARL CONSTANTIN HEINRICH
STEFFECK** – A Lady And An Officer,
Possibly The Crown Prince and Princess
Of Prussia – signed and dated 1861 – 39
x 48½in.
(Christie's) **$12,960 £8,640**

THEOPHILE-ALEXANDRE STEINLEN –
Deux Chats Endormis – signed – 21½ x
25½in.
(Sotheby's) **$26,499 £18,150**

JAMES STEPHANOFF – The Marriage
Of Othello And Desdemona – signed and
dated 1835 – watercolour over pencil –
20½ x 24½in.
(Sotheby's)   **$1,237   £825**

GEORGE STEVENS – A Game Larder
With Two Spaniels – 23¼ x 19¼in.
(Sotheby's)   **$792   £528**

WILLIAM LESTER STEVENS –
Winter Landscape – signed – oil on
board – 14 x 36in.
(Robert W. Skinner
Inc.)   **$900   £600**

ALBERT STERNER – Duncan Dancer
At Rest – signed and dated 1928 – pastel
on paper – 17¼ x 14¼in.
(Christie's)   **$880   £637**

GEORGE STEVENS – Game Larder
Still Lives – 7½ x 9½in.
(Sotheby's)   **$990   £660 Pair**

JOSEPH STIELER – A Portrait Of
Katharina Bozzario – oil on canvas – 28
x 22½in.
(Sotheby's)   **$82,500 £55,000**

MARIE SPARTALI STILLMAN –
A May Feast At The House Of Folco
Portinari – signed with monogram and
dated 1887 – watercolour heightened
with bodycolour – 15 x 20in.
(Sotheby's) **$10,725 £7,150**

MARCUS STONE – A Passing Cloud –
signed and dated 1882 – 20 x 27½in.
(Sotheby's) **$3,533 £2,420**

JACOBUS VAN DER STOK – Skaters
On A Frozen Waterway By A Tower –
signed – 14½ x 19½in.
(Christie's) **$9,590 £6,480**

W. R. STONE – Children Outside A
Cottage – signed – on canvas – 29½
x 49¾in.
(Sotheby's) **$1,606 £1,100**

JAMES STOKELD – Fatherly Advice
– signed – oil on canvas – 24 x 19in.
(Sotheby's) **$1,887 £1,320**

ABRAHAM STORCK – A Southern
Port Scene With Numerous Figures On
A Quayside – signed – oil on canvas –
31½ x 25in.
(Sotheby's) **$77,088 £52,800**

ABRAHAM STORCK – A Harbour
Scene – signed – oil on canvas – 24
x 29½in.
(Sotheby's)   **$13,651   £9,350**

JACOBUS STORCK – A River Landscape
With A States Yacht And Other Shipping,
A Walled Town Beyond – signed with
initials – 26 x 36in.
(Christie's)   **$7,290   £4,860**

**ABRAHAM STORCK, 18th century
Follower of** – A View Of Amsterdam
And The River Amstel – oil on canvas
– 51 x 52½in.
(Sotheby's)   **$5,139   £3,520**

**ROBERT THOMAS STOTHARD, Attri-
buted to** – The Departure – oil on panel
– 9½ x 11¾in.
(Sotheby's)   **$642   £440**

ABRAHAM STORCK, Manner of – A
Southern Harbour Scene – inscribed –
oil on canvas – 24¾ x 30in.
(Sotheby's)   **$4,232   £2,860**

EDWARD STOTT – The Team – signed
– oil on canvas – 16¼ x 24in.; together
with three letters relating to the picture.
(Sotheby's)   **$13,890   £9,680**

ARTHUR CLAUDE STRACHAN –
An Old Gateway At Evesham – signed –
watercolour heightened with white –
13¼ x 9in.
(Sotheby's)   **$2,475   £1,650**

FRANK STRATFORD – Gun Dogs –
signed – oil on canvas – 35 x 27in.
(Sotheby's)   **$1,036   £715**

CLAUDE STRACHAN – A Mill – watercolour.
(Andrew Grant)   **$2,250   £1,500**

CLAUDE STRACHAN – At Dunster,
Feeding Doves In A Cottage Garden –
signed – watercolour and bodycolour
– 13½ x 19½in.
(Christie's)   **$2,754   £1,836**

JOHN STREVENS – A Petite Modiste –
signed, also signed and inscribed on the
reverse – 19½ x 15¾in.
(Sotheby's)   **$825   £550**

JOHN STREVENS – Beaux Amis –
signed, also signed and inscribed on the
reverse – 19½ x 29½in.
(Sotheby's)   **$1,155**   **£770**

**FRANCES STRICKLAND, Attributed
to** – Winter Hunt – oil on board –
oval 12½ x 16½in.
(Butterfield's)   **$600**   **£355**

C. F. GORDON STUART – There's A
Stone In My Shoe – signed and dated
1888, inscribed on the stretcher – 24 x
18in.
(Sotheby's)   **$907**   **£605**

G. MURRIE STUART – Spring In The
Weald Of Surrey – 19 x 29in.
*(Sotheby Beresford
     Adams)*   **$170**   **£99**

JOHN MELHUISH STRUDWICK –
When Sorrow Comes In Summer Days
– signed, inscribed on the reverse – 35
x 21½in.
(Sotheby's)   **$25,575 £17,050**

GEORGE STUBBS – Mr. Ogilvy's
Trentham At Newmarket With Jockey Up
– signed and dated 1771 – 40 x 52in.
(Sotheby's)   **$189,750 £126,500**

GEORGE STUBBS – Lion And Lioness
– signed and dated 1770 – enamel on
copper – 9½ x 11in.
(Sotheby's)   **$74,250   £49,500**

JINDRICH STYRSKY – Composition
– inscribed – collage – 12½ x 9¼in.
(Sotheby's)   **$2,310   £1,540**

PIERRE SUBLEYRAS, Circle of –
Saint Luke – 37 x 61in.
(Sotheby's)   **$742   £495**

LEOPOLD SURVAGE – La Porteuse
D'Eau – signed and dated '34 – oil on
canvas – 15¾ x 12½in.
(Sotheby's)   **$1,754   £1,210**

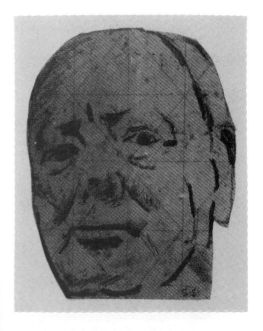

GRAHAM SUTHERLAND – Portrait
Study Of Sir Winston Churchill –
signed – black and grey wash, black chalk
and pencil on brown paper, squared – 9¼
x 7¼in.
(Christie's)   **$1,944   £1,296**

FRANCIS SWAINE – Shipping In A Light Breeze; and Frigates In A Heavy Sea – on panel – 4¼ x 5¾in.
(Christie's)   **$1,134**   **£756 Pair**

ROBERT SUTZ – Lady In Red Viewing A Painting – signed – oil on canvas – 40¼ x 29¼in.
(Christie's)   **$8,800**   **£6,376**

R. SWAINSON – The Model Boat – signed and dated 1867 – oil on canvas – 15¼ x 11¼in.
(Sotheby's)   **$1,973**   **£1,375**

FRANCIS SWAINE – British Men Of War And Other Vessels Off Gibraltar – signed – oil on canvas – 13½ x 17in.
(Sotheby's)   **$7,425**   **£4,950**

CUTHBERT EDWARD SWAN – Lion And Cub – signed and dated 1900 – oil on canvas – 15½ x 19in.
(W. H. Lane & Son)   **$277**   **£190**

FRANCIS SWAINE – Sailing Vessels At Anchor In A Bay; and An English Man O' War Off The Dutch Coast – signed or inscribed, one dated 1781 – gouache – 7¼ x 9in.
(Sotheby's)   **$2,145**   **£1,430 Pair**

JOSEPH HAROLD SWANWICK – A Street In Tunis – signed with initials – pencil and watercolour – 6½ x 9¼in.
(Christie's)   **$339**   **£216**

GEORGE HILLYARD SWINSTEAD – Rats, Toby! – signed – 42 x 15in.
(Sotheby's) $6,930 £4,620

SWISS SCHOOL, 17th century – Portrait Of Ulrich Zwingli – inscribed – 9½ x 7½in.
(Sotheby's) $1,683 £1,100

JAMES BRADE SWORD – My Guardian – signed – oil on canvas – 18 x 14in.
(Christie's) $1,210 £805

JOHN SYER, JNR. – Castle Above A River At Sunset – signed and dated 1880 – oil on canvas – 30 x 50in.
(Sotheby's) **$1,237** **£825**

HENRY SYKES – Heavy Horses – signed – watercolour heightened with bodycolour – 18½ x 9in.
(Sotheby's) **$990** **£660**

JOHN GUTTRIDGE SYKES – 'Seascape In Grey' – watercolour – 5 x 7in.
(W. H. Lane & Son) **$69** **£40**

WILLIAM ROBERT SYMONDS – 'Heather', Portrait Of A Girl Wearing A White Dress With A Blue Sash, With Her Terrier, In A Landscape – signed and dated 1904 – 43¾ x 36¾in.
(Christie's) **$11,340** **£7,560**

GEORGE GARDNER SYMONS – Early Spring Landscape – oil on canvas – 50 x 60¼in.
(Christie's) **$12,100** **£8,066**

AGNES AUGUSTA TALBOYS – The New
Arrival – signed, inscribed on the reverse
– 20 x 30in.
(Sotheby's)   **$1,452   £968**

LADY LAURA ALMA TADEMA – Still
Life With Lilies and Mimosa – signed
and inscribed –.25 x 19in.
(Sotheby's)   **$3,135   £2,090**

FRANZ WERNER VON TAMM, Circle of
– Still Life Of Fruit And Flowers – 29 x
24in.
(Sotheby's)   **$2,475   £1,650**

FRANCIS TAILLEUX – Dieppe,
L'Arrivee De Paquebots – signed –
21¼ x 25¾in.
(Sotheby's)   **$877   £605**

ARTHUR FITZWILLIAM TAIT –
Solitude – signed and dated '85, also
signed, dated and inscribed on the
reverse – oil on canvas – 20½ x 30¼in.
(Christie's)   **$16,500   £11,458**

YVES TANGUY – Genèse – signed and
dated '26 – oil on canvas – 39¼ x 31¾in.
(Sotheby's)   **$222,750 £148,500**

DOROTHEA TANNING – Moi Et
Katchina – signed and dated '55 – oil
on canvas – 14 x 9½in.
(Sotheby's)   **$5,775   £3,850**

NICOLAS TARKHOFF – Maternite –
signed – oil on canvas – 85.5 x 110.5cm.
*(Germann
    Auktionshaus)* **$23,616   £16,176**

PERCY TARRANT – Painting A Train
– signed – on board – 6 x 8in.
(Sotheby's)   **$1,043   £715**

PERCY TARRANT – An Upland Song
– signed and dated 1916 – 22 x 29in.
(Sotheby's)   **$17,666   £12,100**

PERCY TARRANT – Wet Weather –
signed with initials – oil on board – 7½
x 5in.
(Sotheby's)   **$3,630   £2,420**

ALBERT CHEVALLIER TAYLER –
Dinners And Diners – signed and dated
1902 – 40 x 50in.
(Sotheby's)   **$29,700   £19,800**

JOHN FREDERICK TAYLER – The
Hunting Party – pencil and watercolour
heightened with white – 14 x 19in.
(Christie's) $890   £594

LEONARD CAMPBELL TAYLOR –
A Game Of Chess – signed – on canvas
– 36¼ x 28in.
(Sotheby's) $6,930   £4,620

STEPHEN TAYLOR – A Brace Of
Mallard And A Rabbit On A Ledge, In An
Interior – signed and dated 1818 – 31 x
25¾in.
(Christie's) $2,268   £1,512

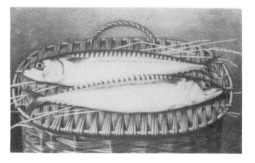

WILLIAM TAYLOR – A Still Life Of
Mackerel On A Basket – signed and
dated 1832 – canvas on board – 11¼ x
16½in.
(Sotheby's) $990   £660

HENRI TEBBIT – 'Landscape With
Stream' – signed – watercolour – 20
x 30cm.
(Geoff K. Gray) $180   £107

ABRAHAM TENIERS – Monkeys At An
Inn – dated 1662 – on panel – 9 x 13¼in.
(Sotheby's) $14,850   £9,900

DAVID TENIERS, The Younger – A Man
And A Peasant Woman Seated Near A
Building – signed – on panel – 7 x 9in.
(Sotheby's) $21,450   £14,300

DAVID TENIERS, The Younger – A
Singerie: Cats In A Monkey Barber Shop
– signed or inscribed – 11¾ x 16¼in.
(Sotheby's)   **$15,675 £10,450**

HENRY JONES THADDEUS – A
Bearded Man – signed and dated 1898 –
40 x 30¾in.
(Sotheby's)   **$462   £308**

DAVID TENIERS, The Elder – The
Judgement Of Paris – inscribed – oil
on panel – 16 x 22in.
(Sotheby's)   **$21,164 £14,300**

HENRY HERBERT LA THANGUE –
Sussex Hayricks – signed – oil on canvas
– 20½ x 28½in.
(Sotheby's)   **$8,208   £5,720**

ALFRED J. TERNOUTH – Views In
Cairo – signed – watercolour – 28 x
18in.
(Sotheby's)   **$2,884   £2,090 Pair**

FRITZ THAULOW – Cottages By A
River In Summer – signed – 17¼ x 21in.
(Sotheby's)   **$37,950 £25,300**

FRITZ THAULOW – The Accademia Steps, Venice – signed – 21 x 25in.
(Christie's)   **$21,060 £14,040**

FRITZ THAULOW – Slottet – signed and dated '80 – on panel – 25 x 31in.
(Christie's)   **$67,132 £45,360**

BERT THOMAS – George Bernard Shaw – signed – brush and black ink and water-colour – on thin card – 11¼ x 8¼in.
(Christie's)   **$567   £378**

CEPHAS GIOVANNI THOMPSON – Country Boy – oil on canvas – 26¾ x 22¼in.
(Christie's)   **$2,860   £1,905**

E. D. H. THOMPSON – Clearing After Rain, The River Derwent In Borrowdale At Grainger With The Gate Crag – signed – 10 x 14in.
(Reeds Rains)   **$435 £290**

ARCHIBALD THORBURN — A Common
Tern — signed — watercolour heightened
with bodycolour — 3½ x 5in.
(Sotheby's) **$749** **£528**

ARCHIBALD THORBURN — Tree
Sparrow And Bullfinches On A Bough
Of Blossom — signed and dated 1924 —
watercolour and bodycolour — 7½ x
11in.
(Christie's) **$7,830** **£5,400**

HENRY RAYMOND THOMPSON — 'O
holy Night! from thee I learn to bear
What man has borne before! etc. —
signed and dated 1897-98 — watercolour
— 50 x 20in.
(Christie's) **$8,613** **£5,940**

ED. H. THOMSON — Lake Scenes —
signed — watercolour — 10 x 14in.
(Warren &
Wignall) **$555** **£370**

ARCHIBALD THORBURN — The
Morning Call — signed and dated 1911 —
watercolour with touches of white heightening — 22¼ x 30in.
(Christie's) **$12,150** **£8,100**

ARCHIBALD THORBURN – A
Grouse In Flight – signed – watercolour
heightened with white on buff paper –
16¾ x 24in.
(Christie's) **$2,192 £1,512**

WILLIAM THORNBERY – Seascapes
With Vessels – signed – 7½ x 15½in.
(Edgar Horn) **$765 £510 Pair**

ARCHIBALD THORBURN – A Cock
Pheasant – signed – watercolour
heightened with bodycolour -- 18½ x
14½in.
(Sotheby's) **$2,279 £1,540**

HUBERT THORNLEY – Estuary Scene
With A Hay Barge – signed – on panel –
10 x 7¾in.
(Sotheby's) **$726 £484**

ARCHIBALD THORBURN – Oyster
Catchers On The Foreshore – signed with
initials – watercolour, heightened with
bodycolour and scratching out – 7 x
11¼in.
(Sotheby's) **$3,256 £2,200**

HUBERT THORNLEY – An Estuary
Scene With Shipping At Sunset; and An
Estuary Scene By Moonlight – one
signed – oil on panel – 6¾ x 9¾in.
(Sotheby's) **$2,489 £1,705 Pair**

HUBERT THORNLEY – Towing Out Of Dover – signed – oil on canvas – 13½ x 11½in.
(Sotheby's)   **$1,499   £1,045**

WILLIAM THORNLEY – A Beached Fishing Vessel On The Coast At Evening With A Distant View Of A Castle Beyond – signed – oil – 15 x 23½in.
(Anderson & Garland)   **$1,500   £1,000**

WILLIAM THORNLEY – Hay Barges And Other Shipping In The Thames Estuary – signed – 16 x 23¼in.
(Christie's)   **$1,295   £864**

JOSEPH THORS – Country Paths By Cottages – signed – oil on canvas – 8 x 12in.
(Sotheby's)   **$1,196   £825 Pair**

JOSEPH THORS – Rural Scene With Horse And Cart – signed – on canvas – 9 x 12in.
(Sotheby's)   **$562   £385**

GILLIS VAN TILBORCH – Elegant Company In An Interior – indistinctly signed and dated – 21½ x 27in.
(Sotheby's)   **$9,570   £6,380**

JOHAN TILL – A Young Flower Girl With Turkeys And Ducks In An Open Landscape – signed – oil on canvas – 30 x 45in.
(Morphets)   **$16,200 £10,800**

BENVENUTO TISI, Called Il Garofalo –
Self Portrait As A Musician – inscribed
– oil on canvas – 35½ x 31½in.
(Sotheby's)   **$13,024   £8,800**

VIKTOR TISCHLER – Girl With A Cat
– signed – pencil drawing – 16¾ x
12¾in.
(Lawrence)   **$226   £154**

JAMES JOSEPH TISSOT – Portrait Of
Algernon Moses Marsden In His Study –
signed and dated 1877 – 19½ x 29in.
(Christie's)   **$71,928 £48,600**

JAMES JOSEPH TISSOT – Le Banc de Jardin, or The Garden Bench – signed –
39 x 56in.
(Christie's)   **$842,400 £561,600**

HENRY GEORGE TODD – A Bird's Nest, With Grapes, A Pear And Other Fruit On A Mossy Bank – signed and dated 1878 – 10 x 12in.
(Christie's)   **$730**   **£486**

JAMES JOSEPH TISSOT – Reading A Book – signed – on panel – 16½ x 11½in.
(Christie's)   **$19,440 £12,960**

MARK TOBEY – Untitled – signed and dated '66 – watercolour on paper – 13¼ x 15¼in.
(Christie's)   **$2,021**   **£1,296**

HENRY GEORGE TODD – A Still Life Study Of Fruit, A Goblet And A Vase On A Table – signed and dated 1879 – on canvas – 17½ x 14½in.
(Sotheby's)   **$1,204**   **£825**

TITIAN, Follower of – Danae – oil on canvas – 16½ x 27½in.
(Sotheby's)   **$3,256 £2,200**

HON. DUFF TOLLEMACHE –
Schooners In Choppy Seas – signed
and dated 1919 – oil on canvas on board
– 20 x 30in.
(Sotheby's)   **$693**   **£462**

EDOUARD TOFANO – Girl In Blue –
signed – 10½ x 8½in.
(Lawrence)   **$582**   **£396**

FRANK HECTOR TOMPKINS – In
Contemplation – signed – oil on canvas
– 26 x 32in.
*(Robert W. Skinner
Inc.)*   **$1,200**   **£1,133**

VIRGILIO TOJETTI – 'Judith' –
signed and dated '85 – oil on canvas –
17½ x 10½in.
*(Robert W. Skinner
Inc.)*   **$1,200**   **£800**

JACOB TOORENVLIET – The Mocking
Of Christ – signed with initials – on
panel – 14½ x 12½in.
(Sotheby's)   **$1,514**   **£990**

JACOB TOORENVLIET – A Grimacing
Man – oil on panel – 9½ x 6½in.
(Sotheby's)   **$1,927**   **£1,320**

TOMAS MORAGAS Y TORRAS –
Strassenansicht – signed and dated 1878
– oil on canvas – 69 x 52cm.
*(Germann
    Auktionshaus)* **$2,146**   **£1,470**

TOPOR – Senza Titolo, 1967 – charcoal on paper – 26.5 x 21cm.
(Christie's)   **$149**   **£102**

**MICHELE TOSINI, Known As Michele
Di Ridolfo** – The Madonna And Child
With Saint John – oil on panel – 37¾
x 28½in.
(Sotheby's)   **$12,698**   **£8,580**

CHARLES TOWNE, Attributed to —
Two Shorthorn Bulls In A Hilly Land-
scape — 28 x 41½in.
(Sotheby's)   **$3,135**   **£2,090**

CHARLES TOWNE, Circle of — A
Retriever About To Set Up A Pheasant
— on panel — 8¼ x 10¼in.
(Sotheby's)   **$1,485**   **£880**

HENRY SPERNON TOZER — The
Evening Meal — signed and dated 1925
— watercolour — 9 x 13in.
(Sotheby's)   **$742**   **£495**

FRANCIS D. TRAIES — Home From
Harvesting — signed and dated 1853 —
22½ x 32in.
(Lawrence)   **$1,732**   **£1,155**

G. TRAVERSI — Portrait Of The Abbate
Adriano Marco Vicentini, In Black Costume, Holding A Letter — inscribed —
38 x 28¼in.
(Christie's)   **$1,944**   **£1,296**

**ANTONIO TRAVI, Called Il Sestri,
Circle of** — The Head Of An Old Man —
23¼ x 18in.
(Sotheby's)   **$1,650**   **£1,100**

JULES TRAYER – Mother And Child
– signed – oil on thin panel – 16¼ x
12¼in.
(Robert W. Skinner
Inc.) **$3,900 £2,600**

FRANCESCO TREVISANI – The
Penitent Magdalen – 52 x 37½in.
(Sotheby's) **$7,920 £5,280**

CLOVIS TROUILLE – L'Heure Senti-
mentale – signed, and signed and inscribed
on the reverse – oil on canvas – 15 x 24in.
(Christie's) **$3,240 £2,160**

CLOVIS TROUILLE – La Voyeuse –
signed, and signed and inscribed on the
reverse – oil on canvas – 18 x 15in.
(Christie's) **$8,100 £5,400**

PAUL TROUILLEBERT – Moulin A
Vent Au Bord D'Une Riviere – signed –
oil on canvas – 37 x 53.5cm.
(Germann
Auktionshaus) **$5,838 £3,892**

HENRY SCOTT TUKE – Reading –
signed and dated 1920, also inscribed
– watercolour – 9½ x 6½in.
(Sotheby's) **$610** **£418**

PAUL DESIRE TROUILLEBERT –A
Seated Arab Girl Holding A Sword, With A
Shield Behind Her – signed – 66 x 41¾in.
(Christie's) **$7,290** **£4,860**

ALBERT TUCKER – 'Rosella In A Rain-
forest' – signed – oil on board – 51 x
64cm.
*(Australian Art
Auctions)* **$3,700** **£2,470**

JAMES TUCKER – Rest After Toil –
signed, inscribed on the backboard –
tempera – 15 x 19½in.
(Sotheby's) **$990** **£660**

HENRY SCOTT TUKE – Boy In A Rowing Boat – signed and dated 1909 –
watercolour – 8¼ x 5¼in.
(Sotheby's) **$330** **£220**

HENRY SCOTT TUKE – Falmouth –
signed and dated 1925, and inscribed on
the reverse – watercolour – 9¾ x 13¾in.
(Sotheby's) **$1,353** **£902**

CHARLES TUNNICLIFFE – Twenty-
Two Illustrations for 'Both Sides of the
Road' – inscribed – watercolour and
gouache – 13 x 9¼in.
(Christie's) **$9,720** **£6,480**

CHARLES FREDERICK TUNNICLIFFE
– A Tawny Owl – signed – on board –
26 x 14½in.
(Sotheby's) **$742** **£495**

ALESSANDRO TURCHI, Circle of –
The Virgin And Child With Saint
Catherine – on panel – 35¾ x 29¾in.
(Sotheby's) **$1,815** **£1,210**

ELIZA TURCK – The Doll's Tea Party – signed – oil on canvas – 17 x 30in.
(Sotheby's)   **$6,380 £4,400**

DANIEL TURNER – A View Of London Bridge – signed – on panel – 5¼ x 8in.
(Sotheby's)   **$610**   **£418**

GEORGE TURNER – Callon Trough, Derbyshire; and Derbyshire Lane – signed, signed and inscribed and dated 1898 on the reverse – oil on canvas – 20 x 16in.
(Sotheby's)   **$797**   **£550 Pair**

GEORGE TURNER – 'A Lane Near Dovedale' – signed and inscribed on reverse, dated 1904 – oil on canvas – 24 x 36in.
(Sotheby, King & Chasemore)   **$1,386**   **£792**

FRANCIS CALCRAFT TURNER – The Fox – signed and dated 1837 – 16¾ x 20½in.
(Sotheby's)   **$6,270**   **£4,180**

GEORGE TURNER – The Trent Near Anchor Church – signed – oil on canvas – 12 x 20in.
(Sotheby's)   **$2,711**   **£1,870**

JOSEPH MALLORD WILLIAM TURNER – 'Harlech Castle' – watercolour – 7 x 10½in.
(Reeds Rains)   **$1,160**   **£800**

JAMES A. TURNER – The Kangaroo Hunt – signed and dated 1873 – oil on canvas – 19½ x 23½in.
(Sotheby's)   **$7,590**   **£5,500**

JOSEPH MALLORD WILLIAM TURNER, After – Martello Towers Near Bexhill – 23½ x 32in.
(Sotheby's)   **$554**   **£385**

JOSEPH MALLORD WILLIAM TURNER – View Of Cottages By A River, Fishermen And A Dog By The Water – inscribed – watercolour over pencil – 7¼ x 10in.
(Sotheby's)   **$15,675   £10,450**

JOSEPH MALLORD WILLIAM TURNER – Gibside, County Durham, The Seat Of The Earl Of Strathmore – watercolour and gum arabic – 10¾ x 17¾in.
(Sotheby's)   **$66,000   £44,000**

JOSEPH MALLORD WILLIAM TURNER – Neapolitan Fisher-Girls Surprised Bathing By Moonlight – on panel – 25 x 31in.
(Sotheby's)   **$313,500 £209,000**

JOSEPH MALLORD WILLIAM TURNER
– Tamworth Castle, Warwickshire –
watercolour – 11½ x 17½in.
(Christie's)   **$113,400 £75,600**

MARTIN L. TURNER – Still Life Of
Fruit – signed and dated 1886 – 15½ x
19in.
(Sotheby's)   **$330   £220**

ROSS STERLING TURNER – The
White House – signed – watercolour –
25 x 38in.
(Robert W. Skinner
Inc.)   **$800   £533**

W. EDDOWES TURNER – A Mare And
Foal In A Paddock – signed and dated
1889 – 24 x 29in.
(Christie's)   **$1,620   £1,080**

WILLIAM TURNER OF OXFORD – In
Dorchester Field, Oxfordshire – signed
and inscribed on the verso – watercolour over pencil heightened with bodycolour – 6¾ x 11in.
(Sotheby's)   **$7,920   £5,280**

JAMES GALE TYLER – Yachting –
signed – oil on canvas – 36 x 53¾in.
(Christie's)   **$15,400   £10,265**

THOMAS NICHOLSON TYNDALE –
North Mundham, Sussex – signed – 7 x
10in.
(Sotheby's)   **£440   £286**

W. E. TURNER – A Favourite Chestnut
Hunter – indistinctly signed – 20 x 25in.
(Sotheby's)   **$931   £638**

WALTER FREDERICK ROOFE TYNDALE – A Spanish Fruit Stall – signed – watercolour – 10 x 14in.
(Sotheby's) **$1,525 £1,045**

WALTER FREDERICK ROOFE TYNDALE – A Fruit Stall In The Salizzada, S. Polo – signed – watercolour – 10 x 14in.
(Sotheby's) **$2,328 £1,595**

WALTER FREDERICK ROOFE TYNDALE – The Sok El Kebir, Jerusalem – signed, inscribed on the reverse – watercolour over traces of pencil heightened with bodycolour – 13¾ x 9¾in.
(Sotheby's) **$9,411 £6,820**

WALTER FREDERICK ROOFE TYNDALE – An Eastern Street Scene – signed – watercolour – 14¾ x 7in.
(Sotheby's) **$2,888 £1,925**

RAOUL UBAC – Soleil Et Pierre –
signed and dated – oil, tempera and
gouache on card – 9½ x 11¾in.
(Christie's) **$630** **£432**

FRANZ RICHARD UNTERBERGER –
Amalfi, Street Scene – signed – oil –
33 x 28in.
(Woolley &
Wallis) **$7,250** **£5,000**

FRANZ RICHARD UNTERBERGER –
A Lake Scene – signed – 7¾ x 14in.
(Christie's) **$1,255** **£810**

JOHN WILLIAM UPHAM – Cerne
Abbey – signed and dated 1802, and
inscribed on reverse – watercolour –
12½ x 15in.
(Lawrence) **$1,389** **£945**

LESSER URY – Sonntagmorgen im
Tiergarten, Berlin – signed – pastel on
paper – 19¾ x 13¼in.
(Christie's) **$22,042** **£14,040**

ADRIAEN VAN UTRECHT, Follower
of – A Still Life With Fruit, Fish And
A Cat – oil on canvas – 42 x 57in.
(Sotheby's) **$4,336** **£2,970**

MAURICE UTRILLO – Le Jardin Public
– signed and dated 1922 – watercolour
and gouache – 6¼ x 9½in.
(Sotheby's) **$8,745** **£5,830**

MAURICE UTRILLO – Le Lapin Agile
Sous La Neige – signed – 13¼ x 16¼in.
(Sotheby's)   **$4,950   £3,300**

MAURICE UTRILLO – Rue Saint-
Rustique – signed and inscribed –
gouache – 26 x 20¼in.
(Sotheby's)   **$35,887   £24,750**

MAURICE UTRILLO – Rue A Asnieres
– signed – oil on canvas – 23½ x 28¾in.
(Christie's)   **$63,504   £43,200**

MAURICE UTRILLO – Eglise De La
Ferte-Milon (Aisne) – signed – 25¼ x
21½in.
(Sotheby's)   **$64,350   £42,900**

MAURICE UTRILLO – La Chaumiere
De Henri IV, Rue Saint-Vincent –
signed – oil on canvas – 12 x 21¼in.
(Sotheby's)   **$54,450   £36,300**

ANDREA VACCARO, Circle of – A Shepherd By A Well – 58 x 77in.
(Sotheby's)   **$2,640**   **£1,760**

WALLERANT VAILLANT – Portrait Of A Young Man In A Brown Cape – on panel – 13½ x 10¾in.
(Sotheby's)   **$3,630**   **£2,420**

SUZANNE VALADON – Femme Se Peignant – signed and dated 1920 – charcoal and coloured crayons on cardboard – 21½ x 16in.
(Sotheby's)   **$4,950**   **£3,300**

SUZANNE VALADON – Bouquet De Fleurs Dans Un Vase Empire – signed and dated 1920 – 28¾ x 21¼in.
(Sotheby's)   **$15,257**   **£10,450**

FELIX VALLOTTON – Femmes Jouant Dans Un Paysage – signed and dated '05 – oil on canvas – 19¼ x 25½in.
(Christie's)   **$12,960**   **£8,640**

FELIX VALLOTTON – Liseuse Au Collier Jaune – signed and dated – oil on canvas – 25½ x 31¾in.
(Christie's) **$18,921 £12,960**

LOUIS VALTAT – Les Baigneuses – signed – 51½ x 63½in.
(Sotheby's) **$28,050 £18,700**

FLORENCE E. VALTER – Springtime – signed – watercolour – 14 x 20¾in.
(Sotheby, King & Chasemore) **$500 £295**

FREDERICK E. VALTER – Unwelcome Intruders – signed and dated 1888 – oil on canvas – 19 x 30in.
(Sotheby's) **$925 £638**

JOHN VANDERBANK – Portrait Of Mary Somerset – signed and dated 1722 – 29¼ x 24¼in.
(Sotheby's) **$1,155 £770**

JOHN VANDERBANK, Attributed to – Hudibras In Tribulation – inscribed on the reverse – on panel – 20¼ x 26½in.
(Sotheby's) **$627 £418**

JOHN VARLEY – Cashel Of The Kings, County Tipperary – signed and dated 1834 – watercolour over pencil – 6 x 9¼in.
(Sotheby's) **$990 £660**

JOHN VARLEY – Old Houses In
Coventry – signed, indistinctly dated
1808(?) and inscribed – watercolour over
pencil – 13½ x 10½in.
(Sotheby's) **$1,122** **£748**

VICTOR VASARELY – Mimas – signed,
inscribed and dated 1958 on the reverse –
oil on canvas – 76¾ x 45in.
(Christie's) **$8,100** **£5,400**

MARIE VASSILIEF – Les Artistes
De Cirque – signed – 28 x 35½in.
(Sotheby's) **$6,380** **£4,400**

LEWIS VASLET – The Brydges Children – signed with monogram and dated
1796, indistinctly inscribed on the reverse – 35½ x 40in.
(Sotheby's) **$3,960** **£2,640**

KEITH VAUGHAN – Miners – signed and dated /52 – indian ink and gouache – 14¾ x 11in.
(Sotheby's) **$2,145 £1,430**

ELIHU VEDDER – 'Dawn On The Arno' – signed with monogram and dated '69 – oil on canvas – 7½ x 10½in.
(Robert W. Skinner Inc.) **$850 £566**

AUGUSTE-LOUIS VEILLON – Agyptische Abendlandschaft Am Schubratkanal – signed – oil on canvas – 81 x 140cm.
(Germann Auktionshaus) **$5,366 £3,676**

NICOLAES VAN VEERENDAEL – Poppies, Tulips, Roses And Marigolds In A Vase – signed – 30 x 23½in.
(Sotheby's) **$105,600 £70,400**

DIEGO VELASQUEZ, Follower of – Portrait Of The Infante Don Carlos – 47 x 35in.
(Sotheby's) **$1,211 £792**

VELASQUEZ

DIEGO VELASQUEZ, After – A
Bacchanalian Scene – oil on canvas –
35¾ x 48¾in.
(Sotheby's)   **$3,212**   **£2,200**

ADRIAEN VAN DE VELDE – Cattle,
Sheep And A Horse With A Herdsman In
A Wooded Landscape – oil on canvas –
18¾ x 22½in.
(Sotheby's)   **$16,280**   **£11,000**

CAMILLE VENNEMAN – A Family
At A Cottage Door – signed and
dated 1867 – oil on panel – 13 x
10½in.
(Sotheby's)   **$4,466**   **£3,080**

**SCHOOL OF THE VENETO, 17th
century** – The Rape Of Europa – 71 x
81in.
(Sotheby's)   **$2,640**   **£1,760**

SPIRIDON VENTURAS – Portrait Of A
Phanariot Greek Administrator – signed
– oil on canvas – 27½ x 22½in.
(Sotheby's)   **$2,007**   **£1,375**

EUGENE JOSEPH VERBOECKHOVEN –
Sheep And Poultry In A Barn – signed and
dated 1867 – 29 x 40in.
(Christie's) **$12,150** **£8,100**

EUGENE JOSEPH VERBOECKHOVEN –
An Extensive Winter Landscape With
Figures By A Windmill – signed and dated
1865 – on panel – 8 x 12¼in.
(Christie's) **$8,910** **£5,940**

JOHN VERELST – Portrait Of A Gentleman In A Landscape – 49¾ x 40in.
(Christie's) **$1,458** **£972**

NICHOLAS VERKOLJE – The Death
Of Lucretia – 33¾ x 29¾in.
(Christie's) **$1,853** **£1,296**

ANDRIES VERMEULEN – Winterfreu-
den Auf Dem Eis – signed – oil on wood
– 53.5 x 69.5cm.
*(Germann
Auktionshaus)* **$6,869** **£4,705**

FREDERICK ARTHUR VERNER –
Bison At Dawn – signed and dated
1912 – watercolour – 14 x 21in.
(Sotheby's) **$1,821** **£1,320**

VERNON

PROF. EMILE VERNON – 'Marguerite'
– signed, dated 1916 and inscribed –
25 x 21in.
(Sotheby's)   **$7,387**   **£5,060**

BONIFAZIO VERONESE, Follower of –
The Madonna And Child – on panel –
10 x 8¼in.
(Sotheby's)   **$1,851**   **£1,210**

EMILE VERNON – A Sea Nymph –
signed – 24 x 18in.
(Christie's)   **$4,860**   **£3,240**

UMBERTO VERUDA – Portrait Of
Giacomo Puccini, Seated Three-Quarter
Length – signed and dated '90 – 53½ x
38½in.
(Christie's)   **$7,290**   **£4,860**

ALFRED H. VICKERS – A River Scene
With A Castle Keep – signed – oil on
canvas – 12¼ x 24in. and another.
(Sotheby's) **$1,525 £1,045**

ALFRED H. VICKERS – Lake Scene
With Cottage And Figures In The Foreground – signed and dated 1880 – oil
on canvas – 12 x 23in.
(Sotheby's) **$963 £660**

ALFRED H. VICKERS – Limerick –
signed, inscribed on the stretcher – 16
x 24in.
(Sotheby's) **$1,485 £990**

ALFRED VICKERS, SNR. – Reigate,
Surrey – signed and inscribed on the
reverse – on canvas – 7¾ x 9½in.
(Sotheby's) **$1,072 £715**

ROBERT VICKREY – Two Yo-Yo's –
signed, also inscribed – oil on masonite
– 24¾ x 19¾in.
(Christie's) **$2,860 £1,986**

JAN VAN DER VINNE – A Roman
Emperor, Head And Shoulders – on
panel – 20 x 16¼in.
(Christie's) **$772 £540**

FILIPPO VITTARI – A View Of Messina
– inscribed and dated 1732 – 31½ x
62½in.
(Sotheby's) **$3,300 £2,200**

VIVIAN

J. VIVIAN – The Mouth Of The Grand Canal, Venice, With Santa Maria Della Salute – signed – 18 x 32in.
(Christie's)   **$1,206   £810**

MAURICE DE VLAMINCK – Scene de Village – signed – watercolour, brush and indian ink on paper – 14¾ x 18¼in.
(Christie's)   **$7,776   £5,184**

MAURICE DE VLAMINCK – Poupee Et Vase – signed – oil on canvas – 21½ x 18in.
(Sotheby's)   **$103,950   £69,300**

MAURICE DE VLAMINCK – Le Remorqueur, Rouen – signed – oil on canvas – 21½ x 25¾in.
(Sotheby's)   **$70,950   £47,300**

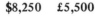

MAURICE DE VLAMINCK – Nature Morte Aux Fruits, A La Bouteille Et Au Verre – watercolour over pen and indian ink – 15 x 20½in.
(Sotheby's)   **$8,250   £5,500**

MAURICE DE VLAMINCK – La Maison Sur La Riviere – signed – brush and ink and watercolour heightened with gouache – 17¾ x 21¼in.
(Sotheby's)   **$16,500   £11,000**

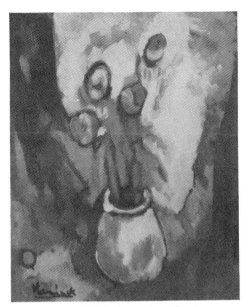

MAURICE DE VLAMINCK – Quatre
Tulipes Dans Un Vase – signed – oil
on canvas – 21½ x 17¼in.
(Sotheby's)   **$41,250 £27,500**

FERDINAND VOET – Portrait Of
Maria Mancini – oil on canvas – 23 x
28¼in.
(Sotheby's)   **$2,930   £1,980**

SIMON DE VOS – The Martyrdom Of A Male Saint – signed – oil on copper –
27 x 34in. *(Sotheby's)*   **$4,496 £770**

SYDNEY CARNOW VOSPER – A Dutch
Loom – signed and dated 1902 – water-
colour – 8¼ x 7¼in.
(Christie's)   **$783   £540**

HANS VREDEMAN DE VRIES – The
Interior Of A Gothic Cathedral With Figures
– indistinctly signed and dated – on panel
– 24½ x 37½in.
(Sotheby's)   **$2,845   £1,650**

ROELOF VAN VRIES – A View Of
The Outskirts Of A Village – signed –
oil on canvas – 12½ x 10½in.
(Sotheby's)   **$3,051   £2,090**

EDOUARD VUILLARD – Portrait De
Madame Leopold Marchand – signed –
pastel on grey paper – 9 x 9in.
(Christie's)   **$4,380   £2,808**

ROELOF VAN VRIES – A Country
Church With Travellers In The Foreground
– signed – oil on panel – 12½ x 11in.
(Sotheby's)   **$3,212   £2,200**

EDOUARD VUILLARD – Fidette
Laroche Au Restaurant – signed – pastel
on buff paper – 9 x 12in.
(Christie's)   **$53,460   £35,640**

THOMAS WADSWORTH — Two Children With Their Horse — signed — oil on canvas — 24 x 19½in.
(Sotheby's) **$2,805** **£1,870**

LOUIS WAIN — Lady Dainty — signed and inscribed — pen and ink and grey washes, heightened with white — 17 x 12in.
(Sotheby's) **$503** **£352**

LOUIS WAIN — In The Hielans — signed — watercolour and gouache — 15 x 10½in.
(Sotheby's) **$707** **£495**

LOUIS WAIN — To My Dearest Heart — signed — red crayon — 15¾ x 12½in.
(Christie's) **$891** **£594**

LOUIS WAIN – The New Arrivals –
signed – watercolour heightened with
white – 9½ x 13in.
(Sotheby's)   **$1,650   £1,100**

LOUIS WAIN – Cat In A Garden –
signed – gouache – 12 x 13in.
(Sotheby's)   **$865   £605**

LOUIS WAIN – A Bouquet – signed –
watercolour heightened with bodycolour
– 7 x 9in.
(Sotheby's)   **$550   £385**

EDWARD WILKINS WAITE – Punting
On A River – signed – oil on canvas –
16 x 24in.
(Sotheby's)   **$4,466   £3,080**

ROBERT THORNE WAITE – A Harvesting Scene – signed – watercolour
– 13¾ x 20½in.
(Sotheby's)   **$1,686   £1,155**

ROBERT THORNE WAITE – The
Harvester's Picnic – signed and dated
1860 – pencil and watercolour
heightened with white – 12½ x 16¾in.
(Christie's)   **$2,494   £1,620**

ERNEST WALBOURN – Moonlit Coastal
Scene With Church And Cottages Nestled
In The Hillside – signed – on canvas –
14 x 18in.
(Morphets)   **$540   £360**

ERNEST WALBOURN – Outside A
Cottage – signed – 20 x 30in.
(Sotheby's)   **$2,730   £1,870**

THOMAS WALCH – Frauen An Spinn-
radern – signed – oil – 49 x 69cm.
(Germann
Auktionshaus) **$1,822 £1,215**

FERDINAND GEORG WALDMULLER
– Am Palmsonntag – on panel – 21½ x
26¾in.
(Sotheby's)   **$46,200 £30,800**

ANTONIE WALDORP – Abendstimmung
Am Hafen – signed with monogram – oil
on canvas – 48 x 60cm.
(Germann
Auktionshaus) **$6,010 £4,117**

CLAUDE WALKER – The Factory,
Near Brook Green, Hammersmith –
signed and dated 1911 – watercolour
over pencil heightened with bodycolour
– 25 x 21in.
(Sotheby's)   **$3,460 £2,420**

DAME ETHEL WALKER – Flower
Piece – oil on canvas – 33 x 25¼in.
(Christie's)   **$841 £561**

DAME ETHEL WALKER – Mandolin
Player – signed – 26 x 22in.
(Sotheby's)   **$495 £330**

DAME ETHEL WALKER – Music Of The Vales – inscribed on the reverse – oil on canvas – 36 x 56in.
(Sotheby's) $786   £550

JAMES ALEXANDER WALKER – The Brave Trumpeter – signed – 46 x 35in.
(Sotheby's) $4,200   £2,860

ROBERT WALKER – Portrait Of General John Lambert And Oliver Cromwell – 54½ x 64½in.
(Sotheby's) $19,800   £13,200

ROBERT WALKER – Portrait Of Oliver Cromwell – 49 x 39½in.
(Sotheby's) $6,270   £4,180

ABRAHAM WALKOWITZ – Flapper; and Woman With Brown Hat – one signed and dated 1927, the other signed and dated 1912 – one pastel on paper, the water-colour, pencil and pen and black ink on paper – one 12½ x 9½in., the other 6 x 4¾in.
(Christie's) $825   £550 **Two**

ROBERT CRAIG WALLACE – The Front At Largs – signed – watercolour – 17 x 27in.
(Sotheby's)   **$693**   **£462**

ROBERT CRAIG WALLACE – Bathers – signed, inscribed and dated 1934 on the reverse – watercolour – 14 x 18in.
(Sotheby's)   **$276**   **£187**

ROBERT CRAIG WALLACE – Sea Anglers, Off Barmore, Loch Fyne – signed, inscribed on the reverse – water-colour – 20 x 30in.
(Sotheby's)   **$293**   **£198**

ALFRED WALLIS – A Steamer – signed – on board – 7 x 12½in.
(Sotheby's)   **$1,415**   **£990**

THOMAS WALMSLEY – An Old Stone Bridge – gouache – 13¼ x 19in.
(Sotheby's)   **$280**   **£198**

JAN WALRAVEN – The Broken Pitcher – signed – on canvas – 27 x 22in.
(Sotheby's)   **$1,525**   **£1,045**

JOSEPH WALTER – Three West Indiamen In The Bristol Channel – signed – 16 x 22in.
(Sotheby's)   **$5,940**   **£3,960**

GEORGE STANFIELD WALTERS — A
Dutch Estuary Scene — signed, dated
1886 and inscribed — watercolour — 13½
x 19¾in.
(Sotheby's)   **$660**   **£440**

SAMUEL WALTERS — Sailing Vessels At
Sea Off Anglesey — signed and dated
1834 — 27¼ x 43in.
(Sotheby's)   **$14,850**   **£9,900**

GEORGE STANFIELD WALTERS —
Hay Barges On The Medway — signed
and dated 1877 — oil on canvas — 24 x
42in.
(Sotheby's)   **$4,290**   **£2,860**

GEORGE STANFIELD WALTERS —
Fishing Boats At Sea — signed — on
panel — 7½ x 11¾in.
(Sotheby's)   **$1,124**   **£770**

EDWARD ARTHUR WALTON — Herd
Boy — signed and dated '86 — water-
colour — 22 x 23½in.
(Sotheby's)   **$25,234**   **£17,050**

GEORGE STANFIELD WALTERS —
A Harbour Scene — signed — on panel
— 7½ x 11¾in.
(Sotheby's)   **$2,007**   **£1,375**

FRANK WALTON — Ben Eay, Kinlochewe,
Ross-shire — signed and dated 1904 —
watercolour — 16 x 22½in.
(Dreweatt Watson &
     Barton)   **$441**   **£300**

FRANK WALTON – Sheepdipping In A River – signed and dated '65, and indistinctly inscribed on reverse – watercolour heightened with bodycolour – 8 x 16½in.
(Sotheby's) $505 £352

ARY VAN WANUM – A Dutch States Yacht And Other Vessels In A Breeze – signed – 23¾ x 39½in.
(Sotheby's) $2,970 £1,980

JAMES WARD – Still Life With Axe, Bill-Hook And Two Dogs – signed with monogram and dated 1827 – on panel – 9 x 12in.
(Sotheby's) $1,237 £825

JAMES WARD – Landscape With Cattle And A Haywagon Passing A House – signed with monogram – oil on canvas – 12½ x 17in.
(Sotheby's) $825 £550

JAMES WARD – Christmas Carols – inscribed and dated '90 – 25½ x 34in.
(Sotheby's) $9,900 £6,600

JOHN WARD of Hull – A Keel In The Humber – signed – on panel – 5½ x 7¾in.
(Christie's) $4,860 £3,240

JOHN WARD of Hull – A Riverside Capriccio With A Dutch Galliot And Two Sailors In The Foreground – 9 x 7in.
(Sotheby's) $1,661 £1,100

MARTIN THEODORE WARD – Puppies At Play – signed and dated 1820 – 24½ x 29½in.
(Sotheby's) $6,270 £4,180

VERNON WARD – Winter Circle –
signed – oil on canvas – 19½ x 19¾in.
(Sotheby's) **$2,248 £1,540**

ARTHUR WARDLE – At The Rabbit
Warren: Two Children Ferreting –
signed – watercolour – 19 x 24¼in.
(Christie's) **$1,050 £626**

ARTHUR WARDLE – Terriers After
A Rabbit – signed – oil on canvas –
18 x 14in.
(Sotheby's) **$1,966 £1,375**

ANDY WARHOL – Portrait Of Joseph
Beuys – signed on the reverse – silkscreen
and acrylic on canvas – executed in 1980
– 40 x 40in.
(Christie's) **$6,480 £4,320**

ANDY WARHOL – Marilyn – each
print signed on the reverse – silkscreen
on thick paper – 36 x 36in.
(Christie's) **$21,286 £14,580 Ten**

ANDY WARHOL – Jackie – signed and
dated '64, also signed and dated on the
reverse – silk screen – 20 x 16in.
(Sotheby's) **$5,263 £3,630**

R. E. WARMINGTON – Rydal Lake –
watercolour – 13 x 26in.
(Edgar Horne) **$234 £155**

EDMUND GEORGE WARREN – The Vale Of Chudleigh, Devon – signed and dated 1891 – oil on canvas – 30 x 48in.
(Sotheby's)   **$6,930   £4,620**

MARCUS WATERMAN – The Old Orchard – signed – oil on canvas – 25 x 30in.
(Robert W. Skinner Inc.)   **$750   £500**

GEORGE ROBERT WATERHOUSE – A Cavia – inscribed – watercolour over pencil – 7¾ x 13¼in.
(Sotheby's)   **$4,857   £3,520**

GEORGE SPENCER WATSON – Prometheus Consoled By The Spirits Of The Earth – signed and dated 1900 – oil on canvas – 57 x 82in.
(Sotheby's)   **$9,240   £6,160**

MARCUS WATERMAN – Banana Seller – signed – oil on canvas – 18 x 14in.
(Robert W. Skinner Inc.)   **$2,500   £1,666**

JOHN DAWSON WATSON – Little Miss Orange – signed with monogram and dated 1857 – watercolour – 10 x 7in.
(Christie's)   **$6,264   £4,320**

ROBERT WATSON – Sheep On The Cliffs – signed and dated 1915 – oil on canvas – 20 x 30in.
(Sotheby's)   **$895   £605**

ROBERT WATSON – Sheep In A Highland Landscape – signed and dated 1904 – 24 x 36¼in.
(Christie's)   **$1,770   £1,188**

ROBERT WATSON – Highland Rovers – signed and dated 1894 – 47 x 39in.
(Sotheby's)   **$1,980   £1,320**

FREDERICK WATERS WATTS – A Lane Beside A River – 19½ x 29½in.
(Sotheby's)   **$7,590   £5,060**

FREDERICK WATERS WATTS – A View Of Strand On The Green, Kew – 12 x 17¾in.
(Christie's) **$4,860 £3,240**

FREDERICK WATERS WATTS – A View On The Isle Of Wight Between Ventnor And Niton – signed, and signed and inscribed on an old label on the reverse – 17¼ x 32¼in.
(Christie's) **$5,184 £3,456**

FREDERICK WATERS WATTS – The Lock Gate – oil on canvas – 27 x 43in.
(Sotheby's) **$7,590 £5,060**

FREDERICK WATERS WATTS – 'The Watermill' – inscribed on an old label on the reverse – 13½ x 22¼in.
(Christie's) **$5,184 £3,456**

FREDERICK WATERS WATTS – A River Landscape With Figures On A Jetty By A Village – 20½ x 29½in.
(Christie's) **$5,670 £3,780**

FREDERICK WATERS WATTS – A Lock On The River Waveney, Near Shipmeadow Suffolk – 36 x 48¼in.
(Sotheby's)   **$26,400   £17,600**

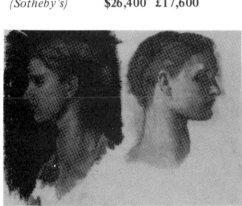

GEORGE FREDERICK WATTS – Portrait Of Alexander Constantine Ionides – oil on canvas – 30 x 25in.
(Sotheby's)   **$907   £605**

GEORGE FREDERICK WATTS – Study Of Two Female Heads – oil on canvas – 21 x 26in.
(Sotheby's)   **$478   £330**

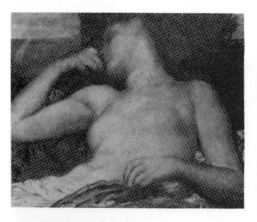

GEORGE FREDERICK WATTS – Study Of A Reclining Nude – oil on canvas – 25 x 30in.
(Sotheby's)   **$957   £660**

GEORGE FREDERICK WATTS – A Study For The Judgement Of Paris – oil on canvas – circa 1870 – 30 x 26in.
(Sotheby's)   **$1,515   £1,045**

GEORGE FREDERICK WATTS –
Portrait Of A Girl Holding A Violin
– signed with initials and dated 1875 –
25½ x 20½in.
(Christie's)   **$8,046   £5,400**

JAMES THOMAS WATTS – Woodland
Scene With A Stream – signed – water-
colour – 12¾ x 10¼in.
(Dreweatt Watson &
Barton)   **$529   £360**

JAMES THOMAS WATTS – The Pet
Bunny – signed – watercolour height-
ened with white – 14 x 10in.
(Sotheby's)   **$825   £550**

WILLIAM HARRIS WEATHERHEAD –
The Puritan Girl – signed with monogram
and dated 1872 – on canvas – 23½ x
17½in.
(Sotheby's)   **$363   £242**

WILLIAM HARRIS WEATHERHEAD –
Fishergirls By A Window – signed –
watercolour heightened with white – 19½
x 28in.
(Sotheby's)   **$1,320   £880**

WILLIAM HARRIS WEATHERHEAD –
As Busy As A Bee – signed and dated
1884, also inscribed – on board – 15 x
11in.
(Sotheby's)   **$1,567   £1,045**

GEORGE WEATHERILL – Whitby Harbour – watercolour – 13¼ x 20¾in.
(Sotheby's)   **$4,455   £2,970**

JAMES WEBB – Pulborough, Sussex –
signed and inscribed on the reverse – oil
on canvas – 5½ x 6¼in.
(Sotheby's)   **$662   £462**

JAMES WEBB – Evening Off Dordrecht,
Holland – signed, inscribed and dated
1874-75, inscribed on the reverse – oil
on canvas – 14 x 24in.
(Sotheby's)   **$3,828   £2,640**

JAMES WEBB – Holland – signed and
dated '83 and inscribed on label on the
reverse – oil on panel – 13¾ x 24in.
(Sotheby's)   **$5,682   £3,960**

JAMES WEBB – A Coastal Landscape
With Beached Fishing Vessels – signed –
on panel – 6½ x 9½in.
(Christie's)   **$3,565   £2,376**

JAMES WEBB – Evening – signed and
dated '75, also inscribed – 14 x 24in.
(Sotheby's) **$2,805 £1,870**

JAMES WEBB – At Rennes – signed,
inscribed and dated 1883 on the reverse –
on board – 8 x 5½in.
(Sotheby's) **$1,072 £715**

JAMES WEBB – A Mediterranean
Port – signed and indistinctly dated
– 32 x 45in.
(Sotheby's) **$6,380 £4,400**

JAMES WEBB – Paris, Pont Neuf, Looking Towards The Quai Des Orfevres –
signed and inscribed – 24 x 36in. *(Sotheby's)* **$12,375 £8,250**

WEBB

JAMES WEBB – 'A Bit In Holland' –
signed and dated 65? – 7½ x 13½in.
(Christie's) **$1,206** **£810**

JAMES WEBB – 'Wye Valley' – signed
and dated '78, and signed and inscribed on
the reverse – on panel – 14½ x 20½in.
(Christie's) **$729** **£486**

JAMES WEBB – On The Rhine –
signed and dated '81 – on panel – 13 x
18in.
(Sotheby's) **$2,970** **£1,980**

W. WEBB – The 'Pekina' Off The Coast
– signed and inscribed – 20 x 30in.
(Sotheby's) **$1,766** **£1,210**

WILLIAM EDWARD WEBB – Working
With The Tide Out – signed – oil on
canvas – 22 x 38in.
(Sotheby's) **$2,062** **£1,375**

CARL WEBER – Stream In The Woods
– signed – oil on canvas – 15 x 26in.
*(Robert W. Skinner
Inc.)* **$550** **£366**

WERNER WEBER – Apfel Und Bananen
– signed and dated '29 – oil on plywood
– 37 x 52cm.
*(Germann
Auktionshaus)* **$3,004** **£2,058**

THOMAS WEBSTER – Going To School – signed and dated 1842 – on panel – 27¼ x 41¼in. *(Christie's)*   **$10,389 £7,020**

THOMAS WEBSTER – The Pedlar – signed and indistinctly dated – on panel – 28 x 36in. *(Sotheby's)*   **$6,600 £4,400**

HENRY WEEKES – Duck Shooting – signed – 20 x 30in. *(Sotheby's)*   **$6,102 £4,180**

HENRY WEEKES – Waiting For Hire, Hampstead Heath – signed and dated 1874 – 30 x 50in. *(Sotheby's)*   **$4,950 £3,300**

WILLIAM WEEKES – A Gaggle Of Geese – oil on canvas – 24 x 36in. *(Sotheby's)*   **$925 £638**

WEEKES

WILLIAM WEEKES – The Interloper –
signed – oil on board – 10 x 8in.
(Sotheby's)   **$1,485**   **£990**

CAREL WEIGHT – The Amazing Aero-
naut or Sun, Steam and Speed – oil on
panel – 19 x 16in.
(Christie's)   **$2,592**   **£1,728**

WILLIAM WEEKES – A New Friend –
signed – on panel – 12 x 8in.
(Sotheby's)   **$1,567**   **£1,045**

LUCY ELISABETH KEMP WELCH –
Portrait Of A Woman, recto; Portrait
Of A Man Wearing A Hooded Cape,
verso – signed – pencil on wove paper
– 9¾ x 6¾in.
*(Robert W. Skinner
Inc.)*   **$100**   **£66**

LUCY KEMP WELCH – The Finish –
signed – pastel – 17¼ x 25½in.
(Sotheby's)   **$7,387   £5,060**

WILLIAM PAGE ATKINSON WELLS –
The Marsh, Topsham, South Devon –
signed – oil on canvas – 24 x 30in.
(Sotheby's)   **$9,116   £6,160**

JOHN E. SANDERSON WELLS – The
End Of A Day's Sport – signed – black
chalk and watercolour heightened with
white – 18¼ x 27½in.
(Christie's)   **$751   £518**

JOSEPH WENGLEIN – On The Banks Of
The Isar Near Munich – signed and dated
1876 – 24½ x 37in.
(Sotheby's)   **$33,000   £22,000**

WILLIAM FREDERICK WELLS –
Malvern – pencil and watercolour – 12¾
x 16¼in.
(Christie's)   **$775   £518**

WILLIAM FREDERICK WELLS – View
Of York – signed – watercolour – 10¾
x 16¾in.
(Sotheby's)   **$1,027   £704**

**ADRIAEN VAN DER WERFF, Attri-
buted to** – A Bacchanal – oil on
canvas – 19½ x 16¼in.
(Sotheby's)   **$1,927   £1,320**

TOM WESSELMANN – Embossed
Nude, No. 3 – signed and dated 1968
– pencil outline and thinned liquitex
on embossed paper – 15 x 18in.
(Christie's) **$1,734** **£1,188**

EDGAR E. WEST – Looking Across The
Severn Valley – signed – watercolour
heightened with bodycolour – 28 x 48in.
(Sotheby's) **$3,960** **£2,640**

JOSEPH WALTER WEST – 'A Bit
Of Blue' – signed with monogram and
dated 1901 – watercolour with gum
arabic and heightened with bodycolour
– 15½ x 11¼in.
(Sotheby's) **$1,284** **£880**

WILLIAM WEST – A Norwegian Waterfall – signed, indistinctly inscribed on
a label on the stretcher – 28 x 36in.
(Sotheby's) **$3,300** **£2,200**

WESTPHALIAN SCHOOL, circa 1500 –
The Flagellation – oil on panel – 43 x
29½in.
(Sotheby's) **$16,280** **£11,000**

JACOB DE WET – Christ Preaching From
Lake Galilee – signed – oil on panel –
24 x 33½in.
(Sotheby's) **$3,212** **£2,200**

ROGIER VAN DER WEYDEN, After – The Descent From The Cross – oil on panel – 42 x 56¾in. *(Sotheby's)* **$1,686 £1,155**

WHEATLEY – Portrait Of An Artist, Sketching In A Landscape – 22¼ x 17¼in. *(Christie's)* **$1,377 £918**

EDITH GRACE WHEATLEY – The Turning Mill – signed – 49½ x 39½in. *(Sotheby's)* **$1,980 £1,320**

FRANCIS WHEATLEY – Antipholis Of
Ephesus, Dromio And A Courtesan
(Comedy of Errors, Act IV, Scene 4) –
·30½ x 21¼in.
(Sotheby's)   **$1,204   £825**

FRANCIS WHEATLEY, After – Interior
Scene – oil.
(Andrew Grant)   **$750   £500**

ALFRED WHEELER – Hounds; and
Terriers – signed, also one with initials
and dated '89 – oil on board – 10½ x
18in.
(Sotheby's)   **$1,036   £715**

JOHN ALFRED WHEELER – A Bay
Horse In A Stable – signed and dated
·1874 – 28 x 36in.
(Lawrence)   **$1,455   £990**

JOHN ARNOLD WHEELER – Forrester Britten On Horseback – signed and
dated 1881 – oil on canvas – 24 x
18¼in.
(Sotheby's)   **$1,204   £825**

JOHN ARNOLD WHEELER — Forrester Britten On A Grey Hunter At Shermanbury Grange, Henfield, Sussex — signed and dated 1881 — 24½ x 18½in.
(Christie's) **$890** **£594**

JOHN ARNOLD WHEELER — Minoru, A Dark Bay Racehorse With Jockey Up On A Racecourse — signed and inscribed — 19¾ x 23½in.
(Sotheby's) **$1,155** **£770**

ROWLAND WHEELWRIGHT — Light Literature — signed, inscribed on the reverse — oil on canvas — 25 x 30in.
(Sotheby's) **$742** **£495**

ROLAND WHEELWRIGHT — New Friends, A Young Girl And Donkey In Springtime Landscape, Village Beyond — signed — oil — 20 x 30in.
(Neales) **$2,250** **£1,500**

GEORGE WHITAKER — A Squall Off The Pier — signed and dated 1871 — watercolour over pencil, heightened with scratching out — 24 x 37in.
(Sotheby's) **$1,204** **£825**

THOMAS WHITCOMBE — A Frigate And Two Luggers Off The Coast — 17 x 23¼in.
(Sotheby's) **$3,630** **£2,420**

THOMAS WHITCOMBE — Shipping Making For Port, Stormy Day — signed with initials and dated 1819? — oil on panel — 7¾ x 11½in.
(W. H. Lane & Son) **$1,606** **£1,100**

JOHN WHITE — Donkeys — signed and dated 1912 — oil on canvas — 20 x 30in.
(Sotheby's) **$915** **£638**

ROBERT WHITFORD, Style of — A
Prize White Shorthorn Bull — oil on
canvas — 20 x 24in.
(Sotheby's)   **$1,320   £880**

JOHN WHORF — Bather (Twilight) —
signed, inscribed on the reverse — watercolour on paper — 21 x 14½in.
(Christie's)   **$1,100   £730**

JOHN WHORF — 'Fishing' — signed —
watercolour — 15 x 22in.
*(Robert W. Skinner
    Inc.)*   **$2,200   £1,375**

C. H. WHITTENBURY — An English
Traveller With A Native Soldier Riding A
Camel — signed — 13¾ x 16¾in.
(Sotheby's)   **$11,550   £7,700**

JOSIAH WOOD WHYMPER — Landscape
With River, Ruins And Seated Figures —
dated 1851 — 20 x 29in.
*(Dacre, Son &
    Hartley)*   **$600   £400**

JOHN WHORF — A Discussion — signed
— watercolour on cream paper — 14½
x 22in.
*(Robert W. Skinner
    Inc.)*   **$2,500   £1,666**

GUY CARLTON WIGGINS — Cafe In
Snow — signed — oil on canvas — 16 x
20in.
(Christie's)   **$3,850   £2,566**

GUY CARLTON WIGGINS – Farm In Winter, Kent, Connecticut – signed, also signed and inscribed on the reverse – oil on canvas – 20 x 24in.
(Christie's) **$2,970** **£1,980**

GUY CARLTON WIGGINS – Blizzard On Wall Street – signed, also signed and inscribed on the reverse – oil on canvas – 24 x 20in.
(Christie's) **$9,350** **£6,235**

SIR DAVID WILKIE, After – The Tavern – bears a signature – oil on canvas – 37 x 50in.
(Sotheby's) **$2,279** **£1,540**

N. WILKINSON – A River Scene With Anglers – watercolour – 9 x 14in.
(G. H. Bayley & Sons) **$484** **£280**

MAURICE C. WILKS – A Breezy Day, Cushenden, Co. Antrim – signed, inscribed on the reverse – oil on canvas – 14½ x 18½in.
(Sotheby's) **$495** **£330**

MAURICE CANNING WILKS – Galway Cottages – signed and inscribed on reverse – on canvas – 13½ x 17¾in.
(Sotheby's) **$481** **£330**

ADAM WILLAERTS – A Dutch Whaling Fleet Off A Rocky Coast – signed – 37¾ x 52¼in.
(Christie's) **$2,916** **£1,944**

ADAM WILLAERTS – Pioneers On A
Rocky Shore With Shipping Offshore –
signed and dated 1624 – 38¾ x 63in.
(Christie's)   **$1,944**   **£1,296**

FLORENT WILLEMS – Watering The
Geraniums – signed – oil on panel –
15 x 12in.
(Sotheby's)   **$1,156**   **£792**

B. WILLEMONT – A Youth With A
Bottle; and A Girl With A Cooking Pot
And A Cabbage – signed and dated
1813, also inscribed – pastel – 19 x 12in.
(Dreweatt Watson &
* Barton)*   **$558**   **£380 Pair**

ALFRED WALTER WILLIAMS – The Toll House, Woodhatch, Reigate – signed with monogram and dated 1881 – oil on canvas – 7¾ x 11¾in.
(Sotheby's)   **$789**   **£550**

TERRICK JOHN WILLIAMS – The Piazzetta, Twilight – signed and inscribed on the reverse – oil on canvas – 23½ x 35½in.
(Sotheby's)   **$1,578**   **£1,100**

EDWARD CHARLES WILLIAMS – Returning From Market – on panel – 18 x 20in.
(Sotheby's)   **$825**   **£550**

TERRICK WILLIAMS – Lagoons, Venice – signed and inscribed – pastel – 9 x 11.2in.
(Woolley & Wallis)   **$601**   **£360**

W. WILLIAMS – Portraits Of A Lady And Gentleman Of The Crowther Family Of Heaton Norris, With Their Young Daughter – 35 x 27in.
(Christie's)   **$2,754**   **£1,836**

TERRICK WILLIAMS – Sailing Boats – signed – 12 x 18in.
(Sotheby's)   **$907**   **£605**

WALTER WILLIAMS – Sunset On The Lakes – signed and dated 1881 – 24 x 36in.
(Christie's)   **$885**   **£594**

WALTER WILLIAMS – In The Highlands – signed – oil on canvas – 14 x 18in.
(Sotheby's)   **$495**   **£330**

HENRY BRITTAN WILLIS – Sunset – signed, dated 1857 and inscribed on the reverse – watercolour – 10½ x 15½in.
(Sotheby's)   **$546**   **£374**

JOHN WILLIS – A Family Meal In An Interior – signed and dated 1836 – on panel – 8 x 10in.
(Christie's)   **$810**   **£540**

WALTER WILLIAMS – Views Near Gomshall, Surrey – both signed, one inscribed on the stretcher – 24 x 36in.
(Sotheby's)   **$8,250**   **£5,500 Pair**

HENRY BRITTAN WILLIS – River Landscape With Cattle Watering – signed – oil on canvas – 17¾ x 26¾in.
(Sotheby's)   **$1,231**   **£858**

CHARLES EDWARD WILSON – Feeding The Ducks – signed – watercolour – 15 x 10in.
(Sotheby's)   **$4,175**   **£2,860**

JOHN H. WILSON, Attributed to – A Harbour Scene At Low Tide – indistinctly signed – on canvas – 18 x 24in.
(Sotheby's)   **$792**   **£528**

JOHN J. WILSON – Shipping Off The Coast – signed and dated 1877 – on canvas – 11½ x 19½in.
(Sotheby's)   **$1,733**   **£1,155**

JOHN JAMES WILSON – A Wooded Landscape With A Peasant By A Cottage – indistinctly signed – 11½ x 19½in.
(Christie's)   **$648**   **£432**

JOHN JAMES WILSON – A Farmyard – signed with initials and dated '39, also signed and dated on the reverse – oil on board – 8 x 11in.
(Sotheby's)   **$1,036**   **£715**

JOHN JAMES WILSON – Lighting The Beacon – signed – oil on canvas – 12½ x 30½in.
(Sotheby's)   **$883**   **£605**

JOHN 'JOCK' WILSON, Attributed to – Edge Of The Wood With Gypsy Camp And Tower – bears signature – on panel – 7 x 9in.
(Sotheby's)   **$462**   **£308**

OSCAR WILSON – A Belgian Flower Market – signed and dated 1892 – linen on original panel – 8 x 11in.
(Sotheby's)   **$3,460**   **£2,420**

RICHARD WILSON, After – Evening, Peasants Dancing Above A River Estuary – on panel – 22 x 29in.
(Sotheby's)   **$760**   **£528**

THOMAS FREEBAIRN WILSON – 'The Jup', Gandy And St. John – A Prize Sheep, And A Prize Shorthorn Bull And Cow In A Landscape – inscribed on the reverse – 31½ x 47¼in.
(Sotheby's) **$14,850 £9,900**

THOMAS WALTER WILSON – Home Again – signed and dated 1877 – watercolour heightened with white – 24 x 33in.
(Christie's) **$890 £594**

CHARLES WIMAR – Reconnoitering – signed – oil on canvas – 10 x 14in.
(Christie's) **$18,700 £12,986**

CALEB WING – Elegant Couples In A Garden; and A Boar Hunt – gouache on vellum – 146 x 100mm.
(Sotheby's) **$307 £209 Two**

SIR JAMES LAWTON WINGATE – Sheep Shearing – signed – oil on canvas – 18½ x 30in.
(Sotheby's) **$2,116 £1,430**

FREDERICK A. WINKFIELD – The River Weir, Sunderland – signed and inscribed – on board – 7½ x 11½in.
(Sotheby's) **$963 £660**

HAMLET WINSTANLEY, Attributed to – Portrait Of Mrs Peter How With Her Children, Peter And Christian – oil on canvas – 59¼ x 89in. *(Sotheby's)*
$8,250 £5,500

PETER DE WINT – Two Farmworkers With Their Horses On A Track Near Watford – signed, inscribed on reverse – watercolour over pencil – 17¼ x 23¼in. *(Sotheby's)* **$3,630 £2,420**

W. TATTON WINTER – 'The Shadowed Heath' – watercolour – 29 x 17in. *(Riddetts)* **$345 £230**

WINTERHALTER – Portrait Of Louis Philippe of France – 24 x 20in. *(Taylors)* **$135 £90**

WILLIAM FREDERICK WITHERINGTON,
After Constable – The Young Waltonians
– signed – on board – 14½ x 18¾in.
(Christie's)   **$965**   **£648**

EDWARD WOLFE – Still Life Of
Flowers And Book – on board – 20½ x
15in.
(Sotheby's)   **$907**   **£605**

MRS. AUGUSTA INNES WITHERS – A
Parrot Taking Fruit – signed – watercolour heightened with gum arabic –
22¾ x 17¾in.
(Sotheby's)   **$990**   **£660**

MARTHA WITTWER-GELPKE – Der
Geiger (Mann Der Kunstlerin) – oil
on board – 49.5 x 72cm.
(Germann
Auktionshaus) **$1,795** **£1,197**

FRANZ XAVIER WOLFE – The Pipe
Smoker – signed – on panel – 7 x
5¼in.
(Sotheby's)   **$770**   **£528**

GEORGE WOLFE – Clovelly – signed
– 13¾ x 20¾in.
(Lawrence) **$1,617 £1,100**

GEORGE WOLFE – Fishing Boats, St
Michael's, Mount Bay – signed – 13¼
x 19½in.
(Lawrence) **$679 £462**

CHRISTOPHER WOOD – Flowers In A
Pot – signed and dated '26 – oil on
canvas – 24 x 18in.
(Christie's) **$1,295 £864**

WILLIAM CLARKE WONTNER – Portrait Of A Lady In Arab Dress – signed
and dated 1922 – oil on canvas – 62 x
52cm.
*(Henry Spencer &
Sons)* **$5,840 £4,000**

JOHN WOOD – Psyche Wafted By
Zephyr To The Valley Of Pleasure –
signed, dated 1844 and inscribed on the
reverse – on panel – 21½ x 16½in.
(Sotheby's) **$495 £330**

WOOD

JOHN WOOD – The Smuggler Surprised – signed – on board – 18¾ x 13¾in.
(Sotheby's) **$363** **£242**

THOMAS WATERMAN WOOD – Who's There? – signed and dated 1856 – oil on canvas – 24¼ x 18½in.
(Christie's) **$22,000** **£15,277**

LAWSON WOOD – 'Golf!' – signed and dated 1922 – watercolour – 19½ x 17¼in.
(Sotheby's) **$1,122** **£748**

LEWIS JOHN WOOD – Rue Du Bac, Rouen – inscribed.
(Sotheby's) **$411** **£286**

DAVID WOODLOCK – Outside The Cottage – signed – watercolour heightened with bodycolour – 14 x 10in.
(Sotheby's) **$2,970** **£1,980**

HENRY CHARLES WOOLLETT – Outside The Tavern – signed – 20 x 36in.
(Sotheby's)   **$2,007   £1,375**

MABEL M. WOODWARD – Picking
Dandelions – signed and dated 1919
– oil on canvas – 22 x 16in.
(Robert W. Skinner
Inc.)   **$16,500   £11,000**

HENRY CHARLES WOOLLETT –
Timber Haulers – signed and dated
1867 – 30 x 25in.
(Sotheby's)   **$1,043   £715**

THOMAS WOODWARD, Circle of – Two
Squirrels With A Bullfinch – 16 x 13in.
(Sotheby's)   **$825   £550**

ALFRED JOSEPH WOOLMER –
Mother And Child – signed and dated
1863 – oil on canvas – 24 x 19in.
(Sotheby's)   **$1,196   £825**

CHARLES NICHOLLS WOOLNOTH – Boats On A Lake – signed – watercolour – 12½ x 18½in. *(Sotheby's)*   **$330 £220**

GEORGE R. WOOLWAY – Portrait Of Walter Travis – signed and inscribed on the reverse – on panel – 16 x 12in. *(Sotheby's)*   **$495 £330**

JOHN WOOTTON – A Horse's Head – inscribed and dated 1745 – pen and brown ink – 8½ x 6¾in. *(Christie's)*   **$1,944 £1,296**

CHARLES JERVAS AND JOHN WOOTTON – Portrait Of Sir Robert Walpole With His Family And Friends, In An Extensive Landscape – 73 x 89in.
(Sotheby's) **$66,000 £44,000**

PHILIPS WOUVERMAN, Follower of – The Ambush – on canvas – 17¼ x 24½in.
(Sotheby's) **$803 £550**

ABRAHAM BRUININGH VAN WORRELL – The Giraffe, Accompanied. By His Keeper, William Mayor – signed and dated 1828 – 30 x 25in.
(Sotheby's) **$66,000 £44,000**

GEORGE WRIGHT – Waiting For The Coach – signed – 14 x 24in.
(Sotheby's) **$6,270 £4,180**

GEORGE WRIGHT – Playful Puppies –
signed and dated '88 – 13¾ x 17½in.
(Christie's) **$2,574 £1,728**

GEORGE HAND WRIGHT – Turning
Point – signed and dated 1894 – oil on
canvas – 19¼ x 29¼in.
(Christie's) **$6,050 £4,030**

GEORGE HAND WRIGHT – Near Noon
– signed and inscribed – pencil on paper
– 11 x 12¼in.
(Christie's) **$440 £318**

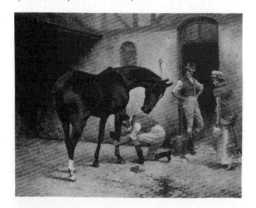

GILBERT S. WRIGHT – A Groom
Attending A Horse – signed – 12 x
15in.
(Sotheby's) **$2,475 £1,650**

JOHN MASSEY WRIGHT – At The Inn
– watercolour over pencil – 9 x 13½in.
(Sotheby's) **$363 £242**

JOHN MICHAEL WRIGHT – Portrait Of
Heneage Finch, 1st Earl Of Nottingham –
inscribed and dated 1675 – oil on canvas
– 49 x 39in.
(Sotheby's) **$19,800 £13,200**

S. WRIGHT – View Of Mr. Homer's
House At Moseley Near Birmingham –
signed and dated 1799, and inscribed on
the reverse – watercolour heightened with
white over pen with black ink – 9 x
12½in.
(Sotheby's) **$990 £660**

ROBERT W. WRIGHT – Geese In A Garden – signed and dated 1904 – on panel – 14 x 11in.
(Lawrence) **$858** **£572**

JOACHIM ANTONISZ. WTEWAEL – Mars And Venus Surprised By The Gods – signed – on copper – 8 x 6¼in.
(Sotheby's) **$379,500 £253,000**

JOACHIM WTEWAEL, Circle of – A Shepherd – on panel – 19½ x 19½in.
(Sotheby's) **$2,475** **£1,650**

PAUL WUNDERLICH – Das Weisse Laken – inscribed and dated 1972 on the reverse – 35 x 45¾in.
(Christie's) **$4,415** **£3,024**

THOMAS WYCK, Follower of – Portrait Of King William III After The Battle Of The Boyne – oil on canvas – 28¾ x 22¼in.
(Sotheby's) **$858** **£572**

WILLIAM WYLD – A View Of The Bay Of Monte Carlo With A Shepherdess Resting In The Foreground – signed and dated 1871 – 34½ x 54½in.
(Christie's) **$2,430** **£1,620**

WYLD

WILLIAM WYLD – A View Of Dresden
– signed – watercolour over pencil, with
scratching out – 6½ x 9½in.
(Sotheby's)   **$1,155**   **£770**

WILLIAM WYLD – The Market Square
At Darmstadt, Germany – signed –
watercolour heightened with white – 8
x 11½in.
(Sotheby's)   **$1,353**   **£902**

WILLIAM WYLD – Italian Peasants By
A Well – signed – oil on board – 7 x
9½in.
(Sotheby's)   **$1,284**   **£880**

WILLIAM WYLD – The Rialto Bridge,
Venice – signed – watercolour – 15 x
24¼in.
(Christie's)   **$2,916**   **£1,944**

CHARLES WILLIAM WYLLIE –
Young Fishers – signed and dated 1888
– 18 x 32in.
(Sotheby's)   **$6,424**   **£4,400**

CHARLES WILLIAM WYLLIE – The
Young Fishermen Unloading Their Catch
– signed – on canvas – 18 x 32in.
(Sotheby's)   **$1,122**   **£748**

**WILLIAM LIONEL WYLLIE, Attributed
to** – Shipping In The Bacino E Canele Di
San Marco, Venice – bears signature – on
canvas – 22 x 39in.
(Sotheby's)   **$1,320**   **£880**

WILLIAM LIONEL WYLLIE – An
Estuary Scene – signed and dated 1927
– watercolour – 8 x 16in.
(Sotheby's)   **$1,565**   **£1,045**

W. YATES – Haymaking By The Coast – signed – on canvas – 8 x 15¾in.
(Sotheby's) **$803 £550 Pair**

WILLIAM FREDERICK YEAMES – And
When Did You Last See Your Father?,
verso; and Playing With The Kitten, recto
– on panel – 21 x 17in.
(Sotheby's) **$825 £550**

JACK BUTLER YEATS – Calamity Jane
– signed – oil on panel – 14 x 9in.
(Christie's) **$4,860 £3,240**

ARTS REVIEW

JACK BUTLER YEATS – Playing Horses – oil on canvas – 14¼ x 18in.
(Christie's) $7,290 £4,860

JACK BUTLER YEATS – The Game Of 'Under Or Over' – signed – pen and ink – 22 x 18½in.
(Christie's) $3,676 £2,484

WILLIAM YELLOWLEES – Portrait Of James Mure Campbell, Fifth Earl Of Loudon – on panel – 7¼ x 5½in.
(Sotheby's) $742 £495

ALEXANDER YOUNG – Unloading The Catch – signed and dated 1890 – on canvas – 16 x 24in. *(Sotheby's)* **$674 £462**

F. YOUNG – County Scenes – indistinctly signed – 20 x 30in. *(Sotheby's)*
$1,485 £990 Pair

OSSIP ZADKINE – Couple – signed and dated '66 – pen and ink – 10 x 7¼in.
(Sotheby's)   **$660   £440**

OSSIP ZADKINE – Nu Assis – signed and dated '66 – pen and indian ink and wash – 11¾ x 7¾in.
(Sotheby's)   **$478 ,   £330**

G. ZAIS – An Italianate River Landscape With Peasants, A Tower Beyond; and A Wooded Italianate Landscape With Peasants On A Path, A Villa Beyond – 14¾ x 25in. *(Christie's)*   **$6,480   £4,320 Pair**

KIRIL ZDANEVICH – Abstract Compos-
itions – signed – collage on printed ground
– 8¾ x 6in.
(Sotheby's)   **$957**   **£660 Three**

JANUARIUS ZICK – The Sacrifice Of
Isaac – 13 x 16½in.
(Christie's)   **$2,916**   **£1,944**

RICHARD ZIMMERMANN – A Winter
River Landscape With Skaters On The
Ice By A House – signed and dated 1861
– 32 x 42¾in.
(Christie's)   **$12,787**   **£8,640**

ANNA ZINKEISEN – The Life Force –
signed -- oil and gold paint on canvas –
21½ x 29¾in.
(Christie's)   **$1,458**   **£972**

RICHARD ZOMMER – Nomads In The
Pass Of Kara Derbend – signed – 16½ x
25¼in.
(Sotheby's)   **$660**   **£440**

ANDERS ZORN – Opal – signed,
inscribed and dated 1891 – 20½ x 13in.
(Christie's)   **$27,172**   **£18,360**

FRANCESCO ZUCCARELLI – An Extensive River Landscape With Peasants And Their Animals In The Foreground – signed in monogram – pen and brown ink and gouache over traces of black chalk – 319 x 540mm. *(Sotheby's)*   **$9,900 £6,600**

FRANCESCO ZUCCARELLI – Elegant Riders Buying Fruit From A Peasant Woman – pen and brown ink and grey wash heightened with white – 310 x 450mm. *(Sotheby's)*   **$3,960 £2,640**

TADDEO ZUCCARO, After – The Concert Of The Muses On The Parnassus – 40½ x 29in.
(Sotheby's) **$1,320** **£880**

FRANCESCO ZUCCHI, Attributed to – The Courtyard Of The Doge's Palace, Venice – pen and brown ink and grey wash over red chalk – 149 x 201mm.
(Sotheby's) **$1,650** **£1,100**

FRANCESCO ZUCCHI, Attributed to – A View Of Gaeta – inscribed – pen and brown ink and grey wash – 97 x 152mm.
(Sotheby's) **$495** **£330**

ANTONIO ZUCCHI – Classical Scenes – canvas laid on board – 20½ x 14½in.
(Sotheby's) **$781** **£550 Pair**

JOHANN BAPTIST ZWECKER – The Old Man And The Roses – signed with initials and dated 1858 – 17½ x 21½in.
(Sotheby's) **$1,980** **£1,320**